I||| | ||| ||||||||| ||| ||||||||| |||
I0046131

RISC-V Architecture and Implementation Guide

Definitive Reference for Developers and Engineers

Richard Johnson

© 2025 by **NOBTREX** LLC. All rights reserved.

This publication may not be reproduced, distributed, or transmitted in
any form or by any means, electronic or mechanical, without written
permission from the publisher. Exceptions may apply for brief excerpts
in reviews or academic critique.

Contents

Introduction

The RISC-V architecture represents a significant advancement in the field of computer processor design and implementation. This guide provides an extensive overview of RISC-V, encompassing its architectural principles, instruction set design, implementation methodologies, and the broader software and hardware ecosystem.

At its core, RISC-V is founded on principles of simplicity, extensibility, and openness. These guiding tenets have fostered a modular instruction set architecture (ISA) designed to balance minimalism with the flexibility to adapt to evolving technological needs. The architecture's clean, well-defined base integer instruction sets serve as the foundation for a diverse range of extensions tailored to address specific application requirements, including compressed instructions for code density, floating-point support for scientific computation, and privileged modes for secure system operation.

This book delves deeply into the structural elements of the RISC-V ISA, providing detailed examinations of the base instruction set features and exploring the standard and experimental extensions that enhance functionality. Emphasis is placed on the architectural modularity that promotes compatibility and forward evolution, ensuring that RISC-V remains adaptable to future innovation while preserving ecosystem stability.

A comprehensive understanding of microarchitecture design

considerations is critical for implementing efficient and high-performance RISC-V cores. Consequently, this guide addresses pipeline architectures, hazard management, branch prediction, memory hierarchy integration, and performance monitoring. These topics are developed with attention to both theoretical frameworks and practical design strategies, equipping engineers with the knowledge necessary to optimize performance and resource utilization.

System-level features such as privilege architecture, memory translation, interrupt handling, and debugging support are foundational for building secure, robust computing platforms. This text explores these aspects within the RISC-V specification, highlighting their role in enabling trusted execution environments and seamless software-hardware integration.

Hardware implementation practices form another central focus, covering development methodologies, prototyping with FPGAs, SoC integration, and power management. Discussions extend to physical design, timing closure, and verification techniques, illustrating best practices for delivering reliable, manufacturable silicon designs that comply with stringent quality standards.

The software ecosystem supporting RISC-V is equally important. The book surveys the landscape of compilers, toolchains, debugging tools, and operating system support, capturing the interplay between hardware capabilities and software optimization. Cross-compilation and bootstrapping processes are analyzed to facilitate robust development workflows across diverse target environments.

Customized extensions and domain-specific accelerators epitomize RISC-V's potential for innovation. The text investigates mechanisms for defining and integrating custom instruction sets, including vector processing, cryptographic enhancements, and accelerators for artificial intelligence and machine learning workloads. It further discusses compiler adaptation and co-verification methods to validate custom implementations.

Security, reliability, and robustness are paramount concerns in modern system design. This guide addresses threat modeling, secure boot protocols, hardware security extensions, fault tolerance, formal verification, and supply chain integrity to ensure comprehensive coverage of defenses necessary for trustworthy systems.

Finally, the volume contemplates future directions for the RISC-V ecosystem, examining governance models, emerging research trajectories, and deployment across cloud, edge, and high-performance computing domains. It highlights challenges and proposed roadmaps, providing insight into the evolution of the architecture and its growing influence in industry and academia.

Through a rigorous and detailed treatment of the multifaceted aspects of RISC-V architecture and implementation, this book serves as an essential reference for professionals, researchers, and students engaged in the design, development, and deployment of RISC-V based systems. It consolidates foundational knowledge with cutting-edge developments, fostering a comprehensive understanding of this transformative technology.

Chapter 1

RISC-V Architectural Foundations

Trace the origins of RISC-V and uncover how its principles of simplicity, modularity, and openness have sparked a global movement in processor innovation. This chapter invites you to understand not just what RISC-V is, but why it matters—exploring the key ideas, philosophies, and ecosystem dynamics that distinguish it from decades of traditional architectures.

1.1. RISC-V Design Philosophy

The foundation of the RISC-V architecture is grounded in a triad of core values: radical simplicity, modular extensibility, and an unwavering commitment to an open, royalty-free model. These principles were deliberately chosen to foster an ecosystem that balances technical rigor with broad accessibility, shaping not only the architecture itself but also its usability, adaptability, and the ethos of its growing community.

5

At the heart of RISC-V lies radical simplicity, a philosophy that advocates for a reduced and clean instruction set architecture (ISA) rather than an extensive, complex one. This principle reflects a reaction against historically intricate and proprietary ISAs that complicated hardware design and inhibited innovation. Radical simplicity manifests in the minimal base integer ISA, which provides only the essential instructions necessary for computation, branching, and memory access. This lean foundation enables straightforward implementation, verification, and optimization of RISC-V cores. From a hardware designer's perspective, the simplicity results in reduced silicon area and power consumption, facilitating deployment across a spectrum of devices, from microcontrollers to high-performance processors.

At the same time, this minimalism does not equate to impoverishment; rather, it leaves deliberate space for extensibility. Extensibility in RISC-V is not an afterthought but a fundamental architectural attribute. The ISA is designed as a modular structure, with clearly defined standard extensions and provisions for custom extensions. Standard extensions, such as those for floating-point arithmetic, atomic operations, and vector processing, offer reusable building blocks tailored to various application domains. This modularity enables academic researchers to experiment with novel instruction sets and microarchitectural innovations without departing from a common architectural framework. The clear separation between a minimal core and optional extensions lowers barriers to entry for experimentation and eases the process of integrating innovations into standard implementations.

In industry, this extensible paradigm maps effectively to market demands for differentiation and specialization. Semiconductor companies can craft proprietary extensions that provide competitive advantages while retaining compatibility with the standard base ISA. Such interoperability ensures that software ecosystems can remain portable even when hardware implementations diverge partially. The clean modularization also accelerates time-to-market by enabling incremental development, reuse of verified components, and easier scalability across multiple product lines.

The third pillar of RISC-V's philosophy is its foundation as an open, royalty-free architecture. Traditional commercial ISAs have historically been tied to intellectual property and licensing fees, which impose substantial costs and limitations on adoption, particularly for startups, academia, and emerging markets. RISC-V's open model eliminates these barriers, promoting widespread diffusion across a diverse landscape of stakeholders. This openness is not merely legal but technical as well-the ISA specification is freely available, fostering transparency and enabling any developer, educator, or company to build, modify, and distribute compliant implementations.

This open model also underpins a collaborative and community-driven ethos that distinguishes RISC-V from proprietary counterparts. The RISC-V International organization and its global network of contributors facilitate shared governance, transparent decision-making, and consensus-driven evolution of the architecture. The community's adherence to open standards engenders trust, reduces vendor lock-in, and facilitates robust security audits-an increasing concern in modern processor design. The open ecosystem has also stimulated a vibrant tooling and software stack, with compilers, simulators, operating systems, and middleware being developed and shared freely, further lowering barriers to practical deployment.

The confluence of simplicity, extensibility, and openness affects several usability and adaptability dimensions. From a software perspective, the predictable and orthogonal instruction set simplifies compiler design and performance tuning. The modular extensions allow tailoring compiler support and runtime environments to match hardware capabilities closely. Hardware designers enjoy a scalable ISA that matches their implementation goals and market segmentation without compromising binary compatibility at

7

the base level. Moreover, the open model fosters a competitive landscape of implementations, driving innovation while reducing costs.

The RISC-V design philosophy also reflects a shift in ecosystem dynamics, privileging collaborative innovation over proprietary competition. By decoupling ISAs from vendor control, RISC-V promotes a more distributed and inclusive approach to processor architecture development. This democratization powerfully impacts research and education, enabling institutions worldwide to participate actively in hardware design and experimentation. Students gain hands-on experience with a real-world architecture without licensing constraints, and researchers can propose, test, and submit changes for consideration by the broader community.

In industrial contexts, the royalty-free nature removes historical barriers to entry and supports business models aligned with custom silicon design, system integration, and software services. The ability to produce RISC-V-based chips free from IP encumbrances has catalyzed a proliferation of startups and established companies alike, leveraging the architecture's adaptability to meet the exacting performance, power, and cost requirements of specialized markets such as embedded systems, edge computing, artificial intelligence accelerators, and more.

Significantly, RISC-V's design philosophy shapes future-proof adaptability. Its open and extensible nature allows the architecture to evolve organically and transparently in response to technological advances and market needs. New extensions can be added collaboratively to support emerging computational paradigms without disrupting existing software ecosystems. This contrasts with proprietary ISAs that often require trade-offs or complete redesigns to incorporate novel features, hindering rapid innovation.

The RISC-V design philosophy-anchored by radical simplicity, modular extensibility, and an open, royalty-free license-forms

8

the foundation of a dynamic and inclusive computing ecosystem. This philosophy not only influences the architecture's technical merits but also governs its usability, community engagement, and industry impact, fostering a resilient and adaptive platform for present and future computational challenges.

1.2. Overview of RISC-V ISA

The RISC-V instruction set architecture (ISA) epitomizes a streamlined and modular design philosophy that promotes clarity, extensibility, and efficient implementation. At its essence, RISC-V is a reduced instruction set computing (RISC) architecture tailored for modern software and hardware systems, emphasizing simplicity and scalability across a broad spectrum of computing platforms. The ISA delineates the behavior of instructions, registers, and memory interaction, forming the foundation upon which compilers, operating systems, and hardware are built.

Fundamental to the RISC-V design is the clear separation of the ISA into distinct components: a fixed base integer instruction set and optional extensions that enable additional functionalities. This modular structure enables implementations to be tailored precisely to target applications, from deeply embedded microcontrollers to high-performance servers, while preserving software compatibility through a standardized core. The base integer instruction set, denoted as RV32I for 32-bit, RV64I for 64-bit, and RV128I for 128-bit address spaces, encapsulates essential computation and control capabilities that serve as the building blocks of the architecture.

The core integer instructions are meticulously organized into logical categories that facilitate both hardware simplicity and compiler efficiency. These include arithmetic and logical operations, control flow instructions, load-store memory access, and system instructions. Arithmetic and logical instructions encompass addi-

9

tion, subtraction, bitwise AND, OR, XOR, and shifts, all operating primarily on registers within a uniform register file consisting of 32 general-purpose integer registers. This uniform and consistent register set reduces complexity in pipeline design and register renaming, simultaneously offering comprehensive capability to the compiler for register allocation and instruction scheduling.

Load and store instructions serve as the sole mechanisms to move data between registers and memory, embodying a clean load/store architecture. Such strict separation augments pipeline regularity and eases hazard tracking, abetting efficient out-of-order execution designs. The addressing modes in these instructions are confined to a base register plus a signed 12-bit immediate offset, avoiding complex or variable-length addressing schemes that typically complicate decode stages and increase power consumption. This constraint promotes straightforward hardware address computation while affording adequate flexibility for access patterns common in systems-level programming.

Control flow instructions in RISC-V are composed of unconditional jumps, conditional branches, and procedure calls and returns. Conditional branch instructions rely exclusively on comparisons between registers and support a small set of relational operators (equal, not equal, less than, and less than unsigned), fostering simplicity in branch prediction and speculation architectures. The use of the program counter relative addressing for branches and jumps generates compact encoded forms, facilitating dense instruction encoding and improving instruction cache utilization.

Levels of abstraction in RISC-V ISA design manifest distinctly between the user-level ISA and privileged ISA, the latter addressing system software demands such as memory protection, virtualization, and interrupt management. The base user-level instructions maintain independence from the privileged specification, ensuring that user programs can be efficiently implemented on a variety of privilege modes without modification. The privileged specification further divides into machine, supervisor, and user levels, each defining control registers, exception delegation, and memory management units, while preserving clear isolation from the user-level functional ISA. This layered approach simplifies the conceptual model for both hardware designers and system software developers, as each abstraction boundary is well-defined and minimally intertwined.

The RISC-V ISA employs fixed 32-bit instruction encoding for its base instructions, standardized as the "R-type," "I-type," "S-type," "B-type," "U-type," and "J-type" formats, each serving distinct roles in representing operations and operand specifications. This uniform instruction length eliminates complexities associated with variable-length instruction sets, such as alignment exceptions and unpredictable instruction boundaries, thereby streamlining fetch and decode stages. Furthermore, encoding fields are allocated to optimize clarity, such as explicit opcode, funct3 and funct7 subfields for operation decoding, and dedicated bits for register indices, immediate values, and conditional codes. The use of compressed 16-bit instructions (the C extension) further bolsters instruction density for embedded environments without sacrificing base instruction simplicity.

An important facet of RISC-V's clean design is its well-defined general-purpose register file paired with a simple calling convention, generating predictable and uniform behavior across diverse implementations. The register zero (x0) is hardwired to zero, enabling simplified instruction semantics and certain optimizations like conditional moves and address computations that avoid additional instructions. Conventionally, registers are assigned fixed roles-return addresses, stack pointers, frame pointers, and temporaries-facilitating ease in debugging, exception handling, and consistent ABI (Application Binary Interface) construction, all while preserving flexibility for compiler optimizations.

The minimalistic instruction set reduces hardware complexity by enabling shallow pipelines, rapid decode, and straightforward control logic. Since instructions are orthogonal and general-purpose, decoding logic and pipeline forwarding mechanisms become more trivial compared to complex or irregular ISAs. This results in lower design cost, shorter verification cycles, higher clock frequencies, and reduced power consumption. Moreover, the repeatable nature of the base instruction set encourages textbook compiler backends, lowering barriers for adopting RISC-V in academic and industrial settings.

On the software complexity dimension, the ISA's regularity benefits compiler and operating system development substantially. The fixed and small instruction set allows compilers to implement mature optimization strategies with fewer corner cases. Software-made assumptions about instruction atomicity, branch delay slots, or specialized instructions do not apply, preventing obscure bugs and simplifying debugging. The architecture's explicitly defined status and exception registers permit deterministic and manageable interrupt workflows. Furthermore, RISC-V's open and documented ISA specification fosters active community participation in toolchain and ISA extension development, broadening ecosystem support with consistent and well-understood semantics.

In sum, the RISC-V ISA's structured layering from a minimal, extensible base integer set to optional extensions, combined with orthogonal instruction formats and a uniform register model, epitomizes a clean and modern machine architecture. Its design philosophy prioritizes hardware simplicity and software friendliness simultaneously, achieving a balance that facilitates broad applicability-from constrained embedded environments to large-scale data center processors-while considerably lowering complexity across the entire hardware-software stack. This coherent framework enables rapid innovation and adoption within both academic research and commercial deployment contexts.

1.3. ISA Modularity and Standard Extensions

The RISC-V instruction set architecture (ISA) embodies a fundamentally modular design philosophy, which distinguishes it from many traditional ISAs by explicitly segmenting the core instruction set from a suite of optional, standardized extensions. This approach fosters a clear delineation between the minimal base ISA-providing essential computational functionality-and optional extensions that enhance capability, scalability, and applicability across a wide spectrum of computing domains. The underlying rationale for this modularity emphasizes flexibility, extensibility, ease of implementation, and long-term compatibility.

At the foundation lies a minimal baseline known as the *base integer ISA*, which is either 32-bit (RV32I), 64-bit (RV64I), or 128-bit (RV128I), depending on the addressing and register width requirements. The base integer instructions include arithmetic, logical, control-flow, and load-store operations sufficient to build a functioning machine. By isolating this base, RISC-V mandates only a minimal commitment from hardware implementations, thereby facilitating lightweight and embedded applications without sacrificing the clean and rigorous semantics of the ISA.

The modular additions to this base are manifested as *standard extensions*, categorized and named with uppercase letters, such as M for integer multiplication and division, F and D for single- and double-precision floating-point arithmetic, A for atomic operations, and C for compressed instructions. Each extension augments the base ISA by introducing new instructions, registers, or execution semantics that serve specific purposes or performance domains. Extensions are crafted with precision to avoid conflicts and to integrate seamlessly with the base set, ensuring orthogonality and minimal complexity.

A key compatibility consideration in this modular system is the preservation of the *base ISA semantics* across all implementations and extensions. The base ISA instructions maintain consistent opcodes, behavior, and effects regardless of which extensions are present. Extensions are designed to add functionality without modifying existing instructions or their encodings. This strict backward compatibility guarantees that software compiled for a given base ISA will run correctly on any conforming implementation that supports the base and potentially more extensions. In essence, upward compatibility is safeguarded: binaries targeting a minimal ISA subset execute as intended even if extended functionality is absent.

The standardized encoding space is partitioned carefully to assign instruction fields in ways that prevent overlap between base instructions and extension opcodes, as well as among mutually exclusive optional extensions. For example, the C (compressed) extension introduces a distinct 16-bit instruction format that is recognized and handled separately but expands code density without disrupting 32-bit instruction decoding. Similarly, the M extension adds multiply and divide instructions using reserved opcode spaces in the base ISA, preserving opcode alignment for future expansions.

This modularity extends beyond instructions to architectural register sets as well. Extensions may define additional registers, such as floating-point registers introduced by F/D or control and status registers (CSRs) for configuration and system management. However, all such registers and their access methods are carefully integrated so that in the absence of a given extension, the corresponding registers are either unimplemented or reserved, preventing unintended usage.

The design and ratification of RISC-V standard extensions undergo rigorous specification processes to ensure clarity, utility, and long-term stability. Extensions are organized into *standardized* and *custom* categories. Standardized extensions undergo community and industry vetting, promoting interoperability across diverse implementations and toolchains. Custom extensions allow implementers to tailor features for specialized applications, while typically preserving the base ISA semantics for compatibility purposes.

A prominent example of modular extension design lies in the A extension, which introduces atomic memory operations essential for multiprocessor synchronization. Since atomic operations demand specific hardware support and concurrency semantics, isolating these instructions into an optional extension allows implementations targeting simple microcontrollers or deeply embedded devices to omit complex atomic hardware without fragmenting the ISA.

Another illustrative case is the C extension, which reduces code size by compressing frequently used instructions into 16-bit forms. This extension does not alter the execution semantics but improves system performance by enhancing instruction cache efficiency and reducing memory footprint. Since the C extension only adds new compressed encodings without changing existing 32-bit opcodes, it maintains full compatibility with non-compressed implementations.

The implications of ISA modularity are pronounced in software toolchains and ecosystem development. Compilers, assemblers, simulators, and debuggers adapt to the presence or absence of extensions through well-defined configuration mechanisms. Compiler backends generate code targeted at specific ISA subsets, enabling fine-grained control over performance, code size, and power consumption. This configurability also aids in defining Application Binary Interfaces (ABIs) that predicate calling conventions and register usage based on the enabled extensions, thereby harmonizing across heterogeneous implementations.

From a hardware design perspective, modularity fosters incremental implementation strategies. Designers can implement the base ISA initially and gradually integrate extensions to enhance functionality, manage complexity, or meet evolving requirements. This incremental model aligns with both commercial product lifecycles and academic research prototypes, allowing early-stage designs to be validated and extended systematically.

The modular ISA structure also facilitates ecosystem scaling into emerging computing paradigms. For instance, vector processing capabilities are encapsulated in the V extension, which introduces vector registers and operations without disrupting scalar base instructions. Similarly, bit-manipulation features reside in the B extension, tailored for cryptographic and data-processing workloads. Each new extension enriches the ISA's capability set and enables specialization without forfeiting a common foundational base.

A critical outcome of this modularity is hardware and software portability. Software components compiled against a defined ISA profile can be deployed across diverse hardware platforms supporting the profile, facilitating code reuse and reducing fragmentation. Hardware designs can be validated against the base ISA before integrating optional features, reducing verification complexity. Conformance testing focuses on base and extension subsets independently, reducing certification overhead.

RISC-V's modular ISA architecture is a deliberate and foundational design choice that balances minimalism, extensibility, and compatibility. By decoupling the base integer instruction set from a suite of rigorously specified optional extensions, RISC-V establishes a scalable and sustainable standard applicable to constrained embedded microcontrollers, high-performance processors, and domain-specific accelerators alike. The structural clarity and extensibility of this modular approach empower hardware and software developers to negotiate the tradeoffs between simplicity, performance, and feature richness on a per-application basis, securing both immediate practicality and future evolvability.

1.4. RISC-V Specification Documents

The RISC-V architecture is distinguished not only by its open, modular design but also by the comprehensive suite of official specification documents that underpin the ecosystem. These documents define the ISA (Instruction Set Architecture) itself, including the standard base and optional extensions, as well as privileged architectures and compliance requirements. Mastery of these works is essential for architects, implementers, and toolchain developers who seek precise understanding and conformance.

At the core of the specification corpus are three hierarchical layers: the *User-Level ISA specification*, the *Privileged Architecture specification*, and a set of *Supplementary Specifications* including debug, vector, and bit-manipulation extensions. The User-Level ISA defines the architectural state visible to applications and defines fundamental instruction encodings, register sets, and behaviors for integer and floating-point operations. The Privileged Architecture document specifies operating modes, memory models, exception handling, and control and status registers (CSRs) necessary to implement operating systems and hypervisors. Supplementary documents extend functionality with optional features standardized through iterative community consensus.

Version management is a critical facet of the RISC-V specification set. The design embraces iterative evolution while maintaining backward compatibility where feasible. To this end, specification versions are strictly numbered and dated; each published revision receives a version identifier, for example, 2.2, 2.3, etc., accompanied by a date of issue. Revisions introduce new architectural features, correct ambiguities, and refine language clarity. Formal change logs accompany each release, enumerating errata, clarifications, and new instructions or CSRs. These logs are indispensable in tracking the historical evolution of architectural semantics and for aligning implementation targets.

A notable feature of the specification management process is its transparent, consensus-driven development model guided by the RISC-V Foundation's Technical Committee (TC). This committee governs contributions and modifications to the specifications, drafting proposals known as Requests for Comments (RFCs). Open governance invites participation from a broad global base of industry and academic stakeholders. The process mandates peer review, commentary periods, and community voting before RFCs are integrated into official releases. This openness ensures specification quality, neutrality, and relevance to diverse use cases. It also guarantees that documentation remains freely and publicly accessible, reflecting the open-source ethos foundational to RISC-V.

Navigating the official specifications requires a strategic approach due to their breadth and technical density. First, identifying the specific needs relative to one's project scope is vital: whether designing a core, developing toolchain support, or implementing system software, the applicable subset of documents varies. The three major categories-User-Level ISA, Privileged Architecture, and Extensions-serve as logical entry points. For baseline core designs, full comprehension of the latest stable User-Level ISA document is mandatory. Operating system developers must also integrate privileges and memory models detailed in the Privileged Architecture specification.

Each specification document is composed of a formalized structure to aid comprehension. Definitions of architectural state precede encoding tables and detailed semantics. The semantics sections use precise natural language augmented with pseudo-code and state transition descriptions to unambiguously define instruction behaviors. Additionally, a thorough enumeration of exceptions, memory ordering constraints, and side effects underscores the care taken to accommodate complex microarchitectural implementations while ensuring consistent software-visible behavior.

Reference implementations and validation suites are often released in conjunction with specification updates. These provide practical, executable models of architectural features and permit implementers to test conformance. The open provision of these tools fosters standardization and enables early detection of discrepancies between the specification and implementation. While the specifications themselves describe behavior at an architectural level, these runtimes and test suites validate correctness from microarchitectural and system perspectives.

To remain current, practitioners should regularly consult the official RISC-V International repository (commonly hosted at the RISC-V International website and associated GitHub repositories). This includes not only the formal specification PDFs but also accompanying documents such as errata summaries, RFC archives, and technical whitepapers. Active monitoring of mailing lists, TC meeting minutes, and issue trackers is also recommended to capture ongoing discussions and emerging proposals that may influence future versions. Engaging with the community through these channels can clarify subtle points and provide early insight into architectural roadmaps.

The ecosystem's open governance also maintains a systematic approach to backward compatibility and deprecation. When revisions retire or modify instructions, the specifications clearly annotate compatibility notes and migration guidelines. These practices mitigate fragmentation, enabling hardware and software ecosystems to co-evolve smoothly. Implementers targeting multiple specification versions can thus plan staged support strategies while preserving user-base stability.

In sum, the official RISC-V specification documents collectively embody rigorous engineering discipline layered with inclusive community governance. Leveraging well-defined versioning, a structured document hierarchy, and publicly accessible resources, these documents enable developers to design, implement, verify, and optimize RISC-V solutions with confidence. Navigating the ecosystem demands disciplined study and active engagement, but these investments yield reliability and interoperability within the rapidly expanding landscape of RISC-V technology.

1.5. Comparison with Legacy ISAs

Instruction Set Architectures (ISAs) constitute the foundational contract between software and hardware, defining the capabilities, complexities, and limitations imposed on system designers and programmers. A deep understanding of RISC-V's features necessitates contrasting its design philosophy and implementation with well-established architectures such as x86, ARM, and MIPS. This comparison elucidates the unique properties of RISC-V, particularly regarding instruction set simplicity, openness, extensibility, and the trade-offs typically encountered in commercial and academic domains.

The x86 architecture, originating from the Intel 8086 processor, embodies a Complex Instruction Set Computing (CISC) paradigm characterized by a rich and varied instruction repertoire. This design choice aims to reduce the number of instructions per program by enabling complex operations within fewer instructions. However, the inherent complexity introduces challenges in decoding, pipeline design, and power efficiency. Variable-length instruction encoding, multiple addressing modes, and a large number of specialized instructions contribute to a steep hardware implementation curve. These factors often result in substantial silicon area, increased power consumption, and design intricacies to maintain high-performance pipelining and out-of-order execution.

In contrast, RISC-V adheres strictly to the Reduced Instruction Set Computing (RISC) philosophy, emphasizing a small, fixed-length instruction encoding (32-bit base instructions) and a universally orthogonal register set. This simplicity enables streamlined decoding logic, efficient pipeline designs, and scalability across various implementations-from deeply embedded microcontrollers to high-performance processors. RISC-V's instruction set consists of a minimal base (RV32I or RV64I) complemented by optional standard extensions, which collectively cover arithmetic, control flow, atomic operations, and floating-point instructions, among others. Unlike x86, this modularity provides the invaluable flexibility to implement only the necessary subsets tailored to specific application requirements, thus optimizing silicon utilization and power consumption.

ARM architecture offers a middle ground, originally founded on RISC principles but evolving to include multiple instruction sets (ARM, Thumb, and ARMv8's AArch64) and varying instruction lengths to balance code density and performance. ARM's conditional execution and predicated instructions provide enhanced instruction-level parallelism without extensive branching, alongside extensive support for low-power modes and security extensions such as TrustZone. However, ARM's proprietary nature restricts unrestricted adoption and modification, requiring licensing fees and limiting customization opportunities. While ARM cores are prevalent in mobile and embedded markets due to their efficient power-performance trade-offs and mature ecosystem, the closed licensing model stands in contrast to RISC-V's open standard that invites innovation and broad collaboration.

MIPS, a pioneering RISC architecture, shares philosophical commonalities with RISC-V in emphasizing fixed-length instructions, load/store operations, and a relatively simple register file. Historically, MIPS played a significant role in academia and embedded systems, with a clean and orthogonal ISA facilitating compiler optimizations and hardware simplicity. Nonetheless, MIPS became constrained by limited extensibility, proprietary control, and diminished commercial momentum in the wake of ARM's growth and the rise of RISC-V's open ecosystem. MIPS instruction encodings primarily rely on three instruction formats (R-type, I-type,

J-type), promoting hardware simplicity but offering fewer extensions for modern workloads such as vector processing or compressed instructions, areas where RISC-V anticipates and incorporates explicit support.

Openness represents a critical differentiator for RISC-V. The ISA specification is fully open and royalty-free, inviting academic researchers, startups, and large corporations alike to develop processors and system designs without encumbrances. This contrasts sharply with x86, ARM, and MIPS, where proprietary rights constrain development, increase costs, and impair transparency. The result is a rapidly growing ecosystem with diverse implementations ranging from low-power microcontrollers to high-performance multicore processors and accelerators, achievable through community contributions and commercial ventures.

Extensibility further distinguishes RISC-V by design. The ISA defines a minimal base, with multiple standard and custom extensions designed to coexist cleanly and evolve over time. These extensions include: integer multiplication and division (M), atomic operations (A), single and double-precision floating-point (F and D), compressed instructions (C), and vector instructions (V). This modular approach allows implementations to balance complexity, performance, and area. For example, a deeply embedded system may implement only RV32I with compressed instructions, minimizing footprint and energy, while a data center processor may fully exploit vector extensions for parallelism. Legacy ISAs tend to struggle with extensibility in a clean manner due to entrenched backward compatibility requirements and monolithic instruction sets.

The trade-offs inherent to these architectural choices revolve around complexity, performance, compatibility, and ecosystem maturity. x86 achieves broad software compatibility with decades of legacy support and sophisticated microarchitectural optimizations, albeit at the cost of complex hardware and power efficiency challenges. ARM provides superior power efficiency and performance per watt, benefiting from a focused instruction set and broad commercial licensing, but restricts design freedom. MIPS, despite its simplicity, suffers from limited ecosystem growth and rejuvenation. RISC-V, by contrast, offers unparalleled flexibility and simplicity alongside rapidly expanding toolchain and application support but currently faces challenges related to software maturity, particularly in legacy x86-dominated environments.

Another noteworthy distinction lies in instruction encoding and code density. x86's variable-length instructions achieve high code density but complicate instruction fetch and decode stages, impacting pipeline complexity. ARM's Thumb mode and RISC-V's compressed extension (C) target similar goals for code size reduction without sacrificing the predictable behavior of fixed-length instructions. MIPS historically did not incorporate compressed instruction sets, which, for embedded applications, can be a significant disadvantage in instruction cache utilization and memory footprint.

The ecosystem and toolchain support are vital practical differentiators. x86 enjoys extensive optimization and debugging tools due to its prevalence in general-purpose computing. ARM benefits from a vibrant commercial toolchain and middleware ecosystem, supported by major chip vendors and software developers. RISC-V, despite its comparatively recent emergence, is rapidly maturing with open-source and commercial toolchains (such as GCC, LLVM, and proprietary offerings), simulators, verification frameworks, and operating system support expanding in tandem with hardware developments.

Considering performance, x86's complex instructions can deliver high single-instruction throughput but at the cost of increased execution latency for instruction decode and hardware manage-

23

ment. ARM and RISC-V achieve comparable or superior performance efficiency through simpler instructions that facilitate deep pipeline designs and aggressive out-of-order execution while reducing power consumption. MIPS's comparatively simpler approach can yield high clock frequencies but may lag in feature-richness and modern extension support.

The distinction among RISC-V and legacy ISAs is best understood within the interplay of design philosophy, openness, extensibility, and ecosystem. RISC-V's simplicity and modularity reduce hardware complexity and enable customization, its open specification fuels innovation and adoption, while legacy architectures provide entrenched software compatibility and mature tooling environments. Appreciating these contrasts equips designers and researchers with the mindset required to evaluate the suitability of ISAs in diverse computing applications and emerging technology landscapes.

1.6. Evolving RISC-V Ecosystem

The RISC-V instruction set architecture (ISA), introduced as an open standard in 2010, has undergone substantial maturation, transitioning from a primarily academic interest to a competitive alternative within commercial and industrial markets. Its modular, extensible design, coupled with license-free availability, has galvanized a diverse ecosystem encompassing academia, industry, and open-source communities.

RISC-V's ascendancy is marked by rapid proliferation in both research and commercial environments. Its adoption can be characterized by three principal domains: microcontroller units (MCUs), embedded systems, and general-purpose computing platforms.

In the domain of MCUs, RISC-V cores such as SiFive's E-series and the open-source CV32E40P have enabled cost-effective and customizable solutions for IoT endpoints and edge devices. Industrial consortiums such as RISC-V International facilitate collaborative specification development, fostering interoperability and toolchain advancement. This has led to the emergence of silicon vendors offering RISC-V IP integrated within heterogeneous SoCs, blending specialized accelerators with RISC-V compute cores.

Embedded systems, traditionally dominated by ARM and proprietary ISAs, are witnessing increased adoption of RISC-V-based designs, attributable to its royalty-free model and growing software ecosystem. Major semiconductor companies have begun contributing to and leveraging RISC-V: examples include Western Digital's decision to base its storage controllers on RISC-V cores, aiming for scalability and reduced dependencies on third-party ISAs. Additionally, automotive safety-critical systems are exploring RISC-V's potential to meet stringent certification requirements while ensuring architectural transparency.

In general-purpose processors, efforts by companies such as SiFive, Andes Technology, and Alibaba's T-Head division illustrate RISC-V's push toward higher performance domains. Implementations target applications ranging from data center acceleration to AI inference, with designs supporting extended instruction sets, vector processing, and custom extensions.

The early deployments of RISC-V act as a bellwether for its viability beyond academic prototypes. Notably, Western Digital, with a stated plan to ship billions of RISC-V cores in its storage products, represents one of the largest industrial commitments to date, anchoring the ISA's commercial credibility. Similarly, NVIDIA incorporated RISC-V cores for secure boot and management functions in its GPU architectures, underscoring confidence in RISC-V for complex system control.

Open-source hardware projects have substantially propelled RISC-V processor and toolchain development. The Rocket Chip Generator, developed at Berkeley, serves as a foundational platform that many derivative designs build upon. This has accelerated the innovation cycle by providing a generative approach to RISC-V core configuration, facilitating rapid prototyping.

The RISC-V Foundation, recently rebranded as RISC-V International, has played a pivotal role in ecosystem cohesion. Through working groups, the organization standardizes supplemental ISA extensions, security features, debugging infrastructure, and verification methodologies, ensuring broad hardware and software interoperability. Furthermore, the collective stewardship over open-source compilers such as GCC and LLVM ensures robust software support-the cornerstone of sustainable processor deployment.

Community participation is robust, encompassing developers, researchers, vendors, and end-users. Open hardware platforms such as HiFive boards, SiFive Freedom series, and others provide accessible entry points, fostering experimentation and education. Additionally, numerous open-source tooling projects, simulators, and verification suites contribute to lowering adoption barriers.

The RISC-V ecosystem's breadth of application spans multiple sectors, evidencing its adaptability and technical merit.

- **Semiconductors and Data Storage:** Western Digital's strategic pivot to RISC-V cores for its proprietary storage controllers exemplifies the quest for optimized silicon designs unconstrained by ISA royalties. This enhances customizability and cost efficiency. Similarly, other storage device manufacturers adopt RISC-V to implement secure and low-power controller units.

- **Consumer Electronics and IoT:** RISC-V based MCUs power a wide array of intelligent edge devices, benefiting from customizable clock and power domains and the absence of license fees. Vendors integrate RISC-V cores into wireless modules, smart sensors, and wearable technology, leveraging the ISA's flexibility for energy efficiency.

- **Automotive and Safety-Critical Systems:** The automotive sector values RISC-V for transparency and security, crucial for functional safety compliance and auditability. The availability of formal verification methods for RISC-V cores supports certification efforts. Moreover, RISC-V's extensibility facilitates the integration of domain-specific accelerators needed in advanced driver-assistance systems (ADAS).

- **Artificial Intelligence and Machine Learning:** RISC-V's vector and custom extension capabilities enable implementation of domain-tailored accelerators. This is exemplified by projects targeting AI inference engines and neural network accelerators, where the ISA extensibility permits optimized instructions for matrix computation and tensor operations.

- **Cloud Computing and Data Centers:** Although still emerging in this segment, efforts are underway to deploy RISC-V based general-purpose processors and accelerators for cloud workloads. The open nature of the ISA opens potential for custom high-throughput cores with specialized extensions conducive to parallel computations and security-enhanced cloud environments.

The evolution of the RISC-V ecosystem is a dynamic interplay between hardware innovation, software maturity, and community engagement. Key trends include:

- **Expansion of Standardized Extensions:** The core ISA continues to be augmented with standard extensions such as vector (RVV), bit manipulation, and privileged levels tailored for heterogeneous computing. Protocols for debug and trace are being expanded to improve development tooling and reliability.

- **Improved Software Support:** Compiler toolchains, operating system kernels, hypervisors, and debugging tools have reached significant maturity levels, enabling usage in complex production environments. Efforts to upstream RISC-V support in mainstream Linux distributions and real-time OS projects remain critical.

- **Security Enhancements:** Given growing cybersecurity concerns, RISC-V's transparent design facilitates advanced security primitives including secure enclaves, trusted execution environments, and hardware roots of trust. Emerging standards for cryptographic instructions and side-channel attack mitigations are under development.

- **Custom Extensions and Configurations:** The ISA's openness incentivizes development of application-specific extensions, which, while promising, necessitate rigorous ecosystem coordination to prevent fragmentation. Toolchain adaptability to custom instructions remains a developmental focus.

- **Academic and Industrial Collaboration:** Universities and industrial consortia collaborate intensively to explore architectural research, verification techniques, and novel applications leveraging RISC-V. This symbiosis accelerates innovation cycles and instills rigorous methodology into open-source hardware design.

- **Global Market Dynamics:** The geopolitical context surrounding intellectual property and supply chain security elevates RISC-V's relevance as a non-proprietary alternative to established ISAs. Countries and corporations seek to reduce dependency, fostering investment in RISC-V silicon and software infrastructure.

Despite the multifaceted strengths, RISC-V faces challenges including ecosystem fragmentation risks, the inertia of legacy architectures, and continued need for comprehensive commercial-grade tooling and verification frameworks. However, ongoing ini-

28

tiatives such as the Universal Verification Methodology (UVM) adoption for RISC-V cores and expanded ecosystem funding are mitigating these barriers.

The RISC-V ecosystem exemplifies a rapidly evolving confluence of open standard design, community-driven innovation, and industrial adoption. Its trajectory suggests a foundational role in future computing architectures, where flexibility, transparency, and collaborative development underpin sustained technological advancement.

Chapter 2

Instruction Sets and Extensions

Step beyond the fundamentals into the rich tapestry of RISC-V's instruction set architecture, where flexibility and innovation converge. This chapter demystifies the foundational instruction sets as well as the powerful extensions that enable RISC-V to serve applications from microcontrollers to supercomputers. Discover how strategic modularity empowers both compatibility and creative hardware advances.

2.1. Base Integer Instruction Sets (RV32I/64I/128I)

The foundational RISC-V integer instruction sets—RV32I, RV64I, and RV128I—serve as the essential backbone for all compliant processors. These base instruction sets define the core integer computational model, including arithmetic, logic, control flow, memory access, and system-level operations. Their design is guided by two primary principles: simplicity and compactness. This ensures ease of implementation, facilitates formal verification, and provides a consistent base upon which extensions and higher-order bitwidth capabilities can be constructed.

RISC-V base integer instructions utilize a small, well-defined set of instruction formats designed for both expressive power and streamlined decoding. Five principal formats cover all base instructions: R-type, I-type, S-type, B-type, and U/J-type. They accommodate general register operations, immediate arithmetic, memory access, branching, and control-transfer instructions. The 32-bit fixed-length encoding is uniformly employed across RV32I, RV64I, and RV128I.

The encoding scheme uses a 7-bit opcode field located in bits [6:0] to determine instruction class and operation. Adjacent fields such as funct3 (bits [14:12]) and funct7 (bits [31:25]) further refine the operation within the opcode group, enabling a concise yet flexible instruction set. Registers are specified through 5-bit fields, enabling up to 32 integer registers denoted x0 through x31, which remain constant across all base widths. Register x0 is hardwired to zero, a feature that enhances instruction compactness by eliminating special-case instructions for zero constants.

Immediate values are encoded differently depending on instruction type. For example, I-type instructions place a 12-bit immediate in bits [31:20], sign-extended as needed. Branch (B-type) and jump (J-type) instructions employ a distributed immediate encoding, optimized for relative addressing and providing a balance between offset range and instruction bit economy.

Format	Purpose and Encoding Highlights
R-type	Register-register operations: two source registers, one destination
I-type	Immediate operations, loads, and ecall/ebreak
S-type	Stores: address computed as base register plus immediate offset
B-type	Conditional branches: PC-relative offset as immediate
U-type	Upper immediate instructions (lui, auipc): 20-bit immediate shifted
J-type	Unconditional jumps (jal): PC-relative target with a 20-bit immediate

This uniform 32-bit instruction width across RV32I, RV64I, and RV128I greatly simplifies instruction fetching and decoding logic, while allowing future expansion via compressed instructions (not part of the base sets).

Simplicity stems from the need to support a diverse ecosystem ranging from deeply embedded microcontrollers to high-performance CPUs. A minimal and orthogonal base instruction set eases implementation complexity, verification effort, and extensibility. The base integer set foregoes complex addressing modes, variable-length instructions, or side effects that could complicate pipelining and speculative execution.

Compactness is achieved through a fixed 32-bit instruction length with careful bitfield allocation, optimizing simultaneous decodability and minimizing instruction cache pressure. The fixed instruction length eliminates decoding ambiguity and reduces hardware area devoted to instruction alignment and pre-decoding. The decision to fix register specifiers at 5 bits enforces a uniform register file size, enabling straightforward hardware implementations.

By restricting immediate sizes and instruction formats, RV32I/64I/128I instructions seamlessly blend control flow and arithmetic within a minimal instruction palette. This encourages compiler backend simplicity, reduces microarchitectural

33

overhead, and fosters higher code density compared to more complex instruction sets.

While the base instruction set semantics remain nearly identical across the three variants, the primary differentiation lies in the width of integer registers and the associated operations. RV32I uses 32-bit integer registers and operations; RV64I extends this to 64 bits, and RV128I to 128 bits. Crucially, instruction encodings are preserved, ensuring binary compatibility and code reuse within the ecosystem.

This design choice enables software portability and pipelined hardware implementations that share front-end decoding with the capacity to transparently handle wider integer operations. For example, arithmetic instructions operate identically, except that the operand and destination registers correspond to the wider bitwidth registers in RV64I or RV128I.

Extensions beyond the base integer set—for example, floating-point, SIMD/vector, and atomic instructions—build atop this uniform foundation. This ensures that the integer base remains a universal platform for all higher-level functionalities.

The consistent use of a 32-register architectural integer register file simplifies register renaming, hazard detection, and context switching in hardware. Each register maintains a full-width representation corresponding to the implementation variant (32/64/128 bits). Register x0 being hardwired to zero means instructions relying on zero operands (e.g., comparisons, conditional branches) do not require separate zero-immediate encodings.

Typical instructions include:

```
add rd, rs1, rs2        # rd = rs1 + rs2
addi rd, rs1, imm12     # rd = rs1 + sign-extended imm12
lw rd, offset(rs1)      # load 32-bit word with base+offset
    addressing
sw rs2, offset(rs1)     # store 32-bit word with base+offset
    addressing
beq rs1, rs2, label     # branch if equal
jal rd, offset          # jump and link for procedure calls
```

34

```
ecall                    # system call trigger
```

Despite their apparent simplicity, these instructions compose all essential programming constructs: arithmetic, data movement, control flow, and environment interaction. They ensure that starting from an RV32I core, designers can scale performance and register width without sacrificing decoding and instruction scheduler compatibility.

The base integer instruction sets adopt a load/store architecture, where only explicit load and store instructions access memory. This design eliminates memory access complexity from arithmetic and control instructions, streamlining pipeline design and simplifying hazard handling.

Address calculations are performed by integer register arithmetic with base plus offset addressing, enabling flexible pointer arithmetic with minimal instruction overhead. The immediate offsets are sign-extended 12-bit values, enabling fast access within a typical local stack frame or data structure.

Load and store instructions specify the size of memory accesses explicitly: lb, lh, lw, ld (for 8, 16, 32, and 64 bits respectively), with the latter used only in RV64I and RV128I (where ld becomes natural). RV128I generalizes these operations to 128-bit loads and stores, with explicit extension semantics supporting both signed and unsigned loads.

Control flow instructions include conditional branches and unconditional jumps, which use PC-relative addressing for efficient code locality and relocation independence. The jal instruction saves the return address in a register, facilitating standard procedure call conventions without implicit stack operations at the hardware level.

System-level interaction is supported by environment calls (ecall) and breakpoints (ebreak), enabling operating system services and

35

debugging through standardized traps and interrupts. Exception handling infrastructure depends on this foundation, as the base integer instruction sets contain all mechanisms required to trigger and return from exceptions.

The base integer instruction sets' fixed-width, minimal design yields compact instruction decoding hardware with predictable cycle timing in simple or pipelined microarchitectures. The uniformity between 32, 64, and 128-bit variants allows microarchitectural features such as decoding, scheduling, and forwarding to be reused with minor modifications for operand width.

From the software perspective, the base sets establish a stable ABI and machine interface. Compilers generate highly optimizable code due to predictable instruction latencies and encoding patterns. Debuggers and profilers benefit from the clean semantic model without architectural complexity or hidden side effects.

Moreover, the simplicity and orthogonality foster a modular ecosystem where extensions and custom instructions augment rather than alter the fundamental base. This modularity is essential for rapid innovation and adoption in diverse application domains.

The RV32I/64I/128I base integer instruction sets embody a disciplined balance between minimalism and expressiveness. Their instruction formats and encoding strategies enable a compact yet powerful architecture. By maintaining consistent semantics across bitwidths and focusing on a load/store, fixed-length instruction model, these base sets form the universal foundation underpinning all RISC-V compliant processors.

2.2. Compressed Instructions (C)

The compressed instruction set extension, commonly designated as the C extension within reduced instruction set architectures (RISCs), constitutes a pivotal mechanism for reducing code size and enhancing instruction-fetch efficiency in memory- and cost-constrained systems. This extension introduces an alternative 16-bit instruction encoding that coexists alongside the conventional 32-bit base instructions, thus achieving a more compact representation of frequently used instructions without sacrificing functional completeness.

Motivation and Design Principles

The impetus behind instruction compression arises from the fundamental trade-offs inherent in embedded and resource-limited environments: restricted memory capacity, limited bandwidth for instruction fetch, and the consequential power and cost constraints. Streamlining the bit-width of instructions facilitates denser code storage, which not only curtails memory footprint but also reduces average memory access latency and energy consumption by increasing the instruction fetch unit's effective throughput.

The C extension adheres to stringent design principles to preserve binary compatibility with the full 32-bit instruction set architecture (ISA). Its encoding scheme is backward-compatible-meaning legacy tools can safely ignore compressed instructions-and it retains the semantics of equivalent uncompressed instructions, enabling seamless interoperation and easing compiler and assembler design.

Instruction Encoding and Format

Compressed instructions are fixed at 16 bits, half the width of standard instructions. Their encoding incorporates implicit constraints and field redefinitions that allow essential operations to be represented succinctly. The immediate fields, register specifiers, and opcode elements are carefully reallocated to maximize expressivity within the 16-bit frame.

Each compressed instruction word is parsed by identifying specific prefix bit patterns that delineate the type of instruction or encoding variant. Generally, the least significant two bits of the 16-bit instruction, termed opcode[1:0], serve as the principal discriminator; common patterns are 00, 01, and 10.

Compressed instruction formats frequently leverage register subset encodings, for example, limiting register operands to the lower registers x0–x7 (called the "compressed register file"), which reduces the bit-width needed to encode register operands. Certain instructions that utilize 5-bit register fields in their 32-bit form instead use 3 bits in their compressed counterparts, resulting in shorter instruction length.

The encoding supports an assortment of instruction types including register-immediate arithmetic, load/store with small offset immediates, control flow instructions like jumps and branches with limited displacement ranges, and register-register operations. Control and data flow instructions are adapted with reduced immediate sizes and restricted branch ranges, reflecting the trade-offs necessary for dense encoding while preserving useful functionality.

Instruction Set Coverage and Equivalence

The compressed set covers a subset of the base integer ISA, concentrating on instructions that are prevalent in code and particularly beneficial to compress. These include load and store instructions with small positive immediates, ADDI with zero register equivalence, common branch and jump instructions with limited ranges tailored for code locality, and register-register operations constrained to the lower register set.

The semantics of compressed instructions are defined to be equivalent to specific 32-bit ISA instructions. This equivalence enables

38

software tools to expand compressed instructions transparently and guarantees that program behavior remains functionally identical when compiled or executed on implementations that support compression. For example, a 16-bit compressed load word instruction (c.lw) corresponds precisely to a 32-bit lw with a constrained offset and limited registers.

Code Size Reduction and Fetch Efficiency

Empirical studies demonstrate that the inclusion of compressed instructions can reduce code size by approximately 25% to 35% on average, with variance depending on the application domain and compiler optimization strategies. This reduction is particularly pronounced in code segments dense with simple arithmetic, control flow, and data movement operations, which are the prime targets for compression.

By shrinking the average instruction length, the C extension facilitates improved instruction fetch efficiency. Fetch units can retrieve a greater number of instructions per memory access cycle, effectively increasing the instruction bandwidth without increasing memory frequency or bus width. This reduction in fetch pressure contributes to lower power consumption and reduced memory subsystems cost in embedded microcontrollers, real-time systems, and application-specific integrated circuits (ASICs).

Moreover, the compressed instructions impact cache utilization positively, as the higher density of instruction storage improves cache line utilization and reduces cache miss rates, enhancing overall execution efficiency.

Implementation Considerations

Support for the compressed instruction extension requires modifications in the instruction decode stage of the processor pipeline. The decode unit must correctly identify and expand compressed instructions into internal micro-operations or microcode sequences compatible with the existing 32-bit datapath. This process may

39

involve register mapping, sign-extension of immediate fields, and control signal generation adjustments.

From a hardware complexity perspective, the instruction decoder grows moderately in complexity; however, the downstream execution units generally remain unchanged, as the compressed instructions map precisely to existing 32-bit operations. This design enables efficient reuse of existing pipeline stages and functional units while yielding tangible improvements in code density and fetch throughput.

Compilers and assemblers must be enhanced to generate and optimize compressed instructions appropriately. Heuristics for instruction selection and scheduling hinge on identifying candidate patterns amenable to compression, balancing code size reduction against potential performance costs associated with compressed instruction range limitations.

Limitations and Trade-offs

While the compressed instruction set extension offers substantial benefits, it imposes limitations dictated by the compact encoding's constraints. The reduced immediate width curtails the range of offsets and constants available in a single instruction, necessitating sequences of instructions or load-from-memory operations for larger immediate values.

The restriction to the low register subset in most compressed encodings constrains register allocation flexibility and may force additional register spills or reloads. Furthermore, branch and jump instructions are limited in their displacement ranges, potentially requiring trampolines or supplementary instructions for long-range branches and calls.

The C extension is primarily advantageous in scenarios with tight memory budgets or energy constraints. In high-performance settings with abundant memory and aggressive instruction-level parallelism, the benefits may be diminished or offset by decode overhead and pipeline complexity.

Interaction with Other ISA Extensions

The compressed instruction extension is designed to coexist with other RISC extensions, such as multiplication, atomic operations, or floating-point support. The interaction entails careful opcode space partitioning to avoid overlaps while maintaining functional orthogonality. Extensions that influence register usage or instruction semantics necessitate corresponding compressed encoding considerations or explicit forbidden encoding regions.

Notably, compressed floating-point instructions are typically excluded from the base C extension due to encoding density limitations, leading to the development of specialized compressed floating-point subsets in advanced ISA variants or vendor-specific extensions.

Integrating the C extension into processor designs yields compelling advantages, particularly for systems where cost, power, and memory footprint are pivotal design metrics. By effectively halving the storage requirement of common instructions, this extension directly translates to smaller non-volatile memory footprints, reduced instruction fetch bandwidth requirements, and increased cache efficiency.

Consequently, the compressed instruction set extension is frequently a core feature of microcontrollers, embedded SoCs, and low-power devices, forming an integral component of modern RISC designs. Its architecture and encoding strategies embody a pragmatic compromise between complexity, functionality, and resource efficiency, affirming its status as a foundational advancement in instruction set design.

2.3. Multiplication/Division and Atomic Operations (M/A)

The M and A extensions to the base RISC-V ISA provide critical enhancements addressing two fundamental aspects of modern processor design: efficient arithmetic and robust synchronization primitives. The M extension enriches the integer instruction set with multiplication and division operations, while the A extension introduces atomic memory operations essential for multithreaded and parallel programming environments. Together, these extensions enable high-performance computation and correct concurrent data sharing, indispensable in contemporary computing workloads.

The M extension: Multiplication and Division

Multiplication and division extend beyond simple addition and subtraction but are crucial for many computational tasks such as cryptography, digital signal processing, numerical methods, and general-purpose computing. While early minimal ISAs excluded these operations to simplify hardware, the M extension integrates them as architectural primitives to significantly accelerate performance.

Multiplication Instructions

The M extension includes several integer multiplication instructions supporting different operand sizes and signedness:

- MUL: Computes the lower 32 bits of the product of two 32-bit integers.

- MULH: Produces the higher 32 bits of a signed multiplication.

- MULHU: Produces the higher 32 bits of an unsigned multiplication.

- MULHSU: Produces the higher 32 bits of a mixed signed-unsigned multiplication.

These variants allow efficient extraction of either the full 64-bit product or its components depending on the application's precision and sign requirements. Inclusion of high-part multiplication instructions is particularly relevant in cryptographic algorithms and multi-precision arithmetic where partial product accumulation is necessary.

From an implementation standpoint, integrating multiplication raises considerations regarding latency and hardware complexity. Hardware multipliers often consume more silicon and increase cycle times compared to simpler arithmetic units. Designers commonly implement multiplication either as a multi-cycle microcoded operation or as a combinational circuit with potential pipelining. The RISC-V ISA specifies only the architectural contract, allowing flexibility for microarchitectural decisions aimed at balancing die area, power, and performance.

Division and Remainder Instructions

The division instructions provided by the M extension complement multiplication with integer division support, including:

- DIV and DIVU: Signed and unsigned integer division.

- REM and REMU: Signed and unsigned remainder operations.

Division instructions are essential for tasks like scaling, hashing, and algorithms involving modular arithmetic. Unlike multiplication, division is inherently more complex and typically incurs substantial latency, especially in hardware without specialized dividers. Architectures frequently implement integer division via iterative non-restoring or restoring algorithms, SRT dividers, or by microcoded software sequences if hardware dividers are omitted for cost reasons.

43

The ISA mandates the architectural semantics but permits implementations to yield varying latencies. The exact number of pipeline stages or cycles to execute a division might differ, influencing instruction throughput and pipeline design. Designers must weigh the performance benefits of hardware division against its impact on critical path and power consumption.

The A extension: Atomic Memory Operations

Atomic operations are the cornerstone of shared-memory concurrency by guaranteeing indivisible memory updates. The A extension supports a set of atomic read-modify-write (RMW) instructions indispensable for building synchronization primitives such as locks, semaphores, and lock-free data structures.

Fundamental Atomic Instructions

The A extension defines atomic instructions that operate on naturally aligned memory operands of standard word size (typically 32 or 64 bits depending on the ISA width):

- LR.W / LR.D: Load-reserved instructions for 32-bit and 64-bit words.

- SC.W / SC.D: Store-conditional instructions paired with LR, used to build atomic sequences.

- Atomic RMW instructions: AMOSWAP, AMOADD, AMOXOR, AMOAND, AMOOR, AMOMIN, AMOMAX, AMOMINU, AMOMAXU.

These allow atomic replacement, fetch-and-add, bitwise logical operations, and min/max updates on shared values. The Load-Reserved/Store-Conditional (LR/SC) mechanism enables flexible construction of atomic operations with conditional retries, providing powerful synchronization capabilities beyond fixed RMW operations.

Importance in Multithreaded Systems

44

Multithreaded and multiprocessor systems rely on atomic operations to ensure memory coherence and synchronization. Without
atomic instructions, coordinating changes to shared memory demands costly software constructs that degrade scalability and increase context-switch overhead. Atomic primitives facilitate implementation of mutexes, barriers, concurrent queues, and other
lock-free or wait-free algorithms that improve responsiveness and
throughput.

The A extension is critical for ensuring linearizability-the property
that concurrent operations appear atomic and sequentially consistent. This consistency is necessary to prevent elusive bugs such as
data races and stale reads. Modern operating systems, language
runtimes, and parallel libraries leverage atomic instructions to implement fundamental synchronization mechanisms.

Implementation Trade-offs

Implementing atomic operations introduces significant hardware
complexity. The processor's memory subsystem must guarantee
exclusive access and consistency semantics atomically and often
at high frequency under contention. The implementation involves
coupling the cache coherence protocol closely with reservation registers or store-conditional monitors.

Key trade-offs include:

- **Granularity and Alignment**: Atomic operations generally require naturally aligned memory operands of fixed size.
  Relaxing these constraints increases complexity or may require software emulation.

- **Performance under Contention**: Contention on atomic
  memory locations can serialize execution and stall pipeline
  stages. Optimizations such as backoff algorithms or specialized coherence enhancements (e.g., cache line locking) may
  be employed.

45

- **Power and Area**: Hardware to track reservations for LR/SC and to enforce atomicity for RMW instructions adds to chip area and power consumption, influencing processor design choices.

- **Memory Model Compliance**: Correct implementation must obey the RISC-V memory consistency model, especially ensuring proper ordering and visibility of atomic operations among threads to avoid subtle hazards.

Some implementations allow optional support for advanced atomic instructions or higher granularity atomics (e.g., 128-bit atomics) depending on target use cases and fabric constraints.

Interaction Between M and A Extensions

The M and A extensions collectively enhance the computational and concurrency capabilities of the processor. Notably, atomic RMW instructions often rely on internal integer arithmetic units to perform the relevant arithmetic or logical function atomically. Efficient integer multiplication facilitates implementing complex atomic operations or accelerating atomic counters and accumulators used in parallel algorithms.

Many parallel applications employ both heavy arithmetic and synchronization, requiring careful balancing of resource allocation within the processor pipeline. Designers may choose to pipeline multiplication/division units and atomic units independently to avoid resource contention. Since multiplication/division instructions may be relatively slow, prioritizing atomic instructions in pipeline design helps reduce synchronization latency and contention bottlenecks in multithreaded workloads.

Design decisions around M and A extensions influence the processor's overall throughput, latency, power profile, and support for parallel software environments. Compiler and runtime systems leverage these ISA features to generate efficient synchronization constructs and arithmetic kernels, amplifying their architectural impact.

Summary of Architectural and Microarchitectural Considerations

From the perspective of ISA design and microarchitecture, inclusion of M and A extensions embodies a balance of complexity and functionality:

- The M extension adds indispensable arithmetic instructions dramatically improving execution efficiency in numerically intensive applications. Their architectural inclusion standardizes behavior while leaving implementation choices open.

- The A extension provides atomic operations foundational for safe and efficient multithreaded programming, ensuring correctness and performance of concurrent data structures.

- Both extensions elevate hardware complexity, requiring increased logic resources and careful timing to avoid degradation of pipeline throughput and cycle time.

- The interaction of multiplication/division with atomic operations calls for judicious pipeline resource management and microarchitectural optimizations tailored to target workloads.

Together, M and A extend the base ISA into a more powerful and flexible platform capable of supporting a wide spectrum of high-performance and parallel applications, reflecting the intrinsic needs of advanced computing systems.

2.4. Floating-point Extensions (F/D/Q)

The IEEE 754 standard for floating-point arithmetic establishes the foundational framework for representing and manipulating

47

real numbers in modern computing systems. Floating-point extensions for single (F), double (D), and quad (Q) precision widen this framework by specifying formats and operations that meet distinct precision and range requirements across scientific computing and media-rich applications. These extensions augment the core architectures by enhancing numerical accuracy, dynamic range, and computational efficiency without sacrificing standard compliance or interoperability.

The fundamental difference among the three extensions lies in their bit-width and the resulting precision and exponent range. Single precision (F) is defined using 32 bits: 1 sign bit, 8 exponent bits, and 23 fraction (mantissa) bits. Double precision (D) expands this allocation to 64 bits: 1 sign bit, 11 exponent bits, and 52 fraction bits. Quad precision (Q), or quadruple precision, further extends the format typically to 128 bits, comprising 1 sign bit, 15 exponent bits, and 112 fraction bits. These bit allocations afford increasing precision-from roughly 7 decimal digits in single precision, to 15–17 digits in double precision, up to about 33–36 digits in quadruple precision-alongside significantly enlarged exponent ranges for representing extremely large or small values.

Compliance with IEEE 754 in these extensions ensures consistency in rounding modes, exceptional values (NaN, infinities), and special cases such as denormalized numbers and zeroes. The standardized rounding methods-round to nearest even, round toward zero, round toward positive infinity, and round toward negative infinity-are uniformly applied in the F/D/Q formats, preserving predictable results crucial in both iterative algorithms and reproducibility-sensitive computations. Signaling NaNs, quiet NaNs, positive and negative infinity encodings, and the handling of underflow and overflow conditions continue to conform strictly to the IEEE specification, supporting fault tolerance and exception diagnostics in floating-point-intensive workflows.

The hardware implementation implications of these extensions are non-trivial yet manageable due to the structured design of IEEE 754 formats. Single precision floating-point units are compact and optimized for throughput, primarily serving graphics processing, digital signal processing, and simpler scientific models. As precision demands escalate, double precision units often replace or augment single precision implementations, enabling simulations, financial modeling, cryptographic computations, and more accurate scientific calculations while maintaining acceptable latency and energy footprints. Quad precision, while less common in commodity processors, finds particular use in specialized high-performance computing environments demanding extreme precision-such as quantum physics simulations, numerical weather prediction, and robust iterative refinement in linear algebra solvers.

Algorithmically, the increased precision in double and quadruple extensions supports more stable numerical methods by reducing rounding errors and improving convergence behaviors. Many iterative algorithms, including multigrid solvers and optimization routines, benefit directly from the enhanced precision, which permits relaxed stopping criteria without compromising accuracy. Conversely, the computational overhead of quad precision necessitates judicious application, often accompanied by mixed-precision strategies where single or double precision is used in initial stages, elevating precision only at convergence-critical phases.

From a systems perspective, software and hardware support for F/D/Q floating-point extensions entails compatibility considerations. Compilers must generate appropriately sized load/store instructions alongside optimized vectorized floating point arithmetic operations respecting precision-specific instruction sets (e.g., SSE, AVX, ARM NEON, or IBM's PowerISA). Instruction-level parallelism and pipelining in floating-point units are tailored differently for each precision level to balance latency, throughput, and power consumption, with quad precision often implemented via software emulation or microcoded sequences due to its complexity.

Media-rich applications, such as real-time graphics rendering, augmented reality, and video processing, predominantly leverage single and double precision floating-point arithmetic due to their computational speed and sufficiently accurate representation of visual data. The relatively narrower dynamic range and precision are well-suited for the smooth shading calculations, texture blending, and matrix transformations ubiquitous in these domains. However, emerging demands for high dynamic range (HDR) imagery and physically accurate lighting models increasingly exploit double precision operations during computationally expensive precomputation phases or in offline rendering pipelines, particularly in film production and advanced visualization tasks.

In stark contrast, pure scientific computing disciplines adhere to rigorous precision requirements, compelling use of double and quad precision to circumvent pitfalls posed by catastrophic cancellation and accumulated floating-point errors in simulations driven by partial differential equations, stochastic processes, or large-scale matrix decompositions. For instance, quad precision formats facilitate trapezoidal and Gaussian quadrature schemes in numerical integration with extremely fine tolerances, as well as stable eigenvalue and singular value decompositions in the presence of ill-conditioned matrices-a recurring challenge in high-resolution climate modeling and computational fluid dynamics.

The IEEE 754-2008 revision, underpinning these extensions, introduced fused multiply-add (FMA) operations across precisions, which perform multiplication and addition in a single, non-intermediate-rounding step. FMAs significantly improve both performance and accuracy in floating-point multiply-add pipelines, reducing rounding errors and power consumption. FMA operations are ideally suited for polynomial evaluations, dot-product computations, and iterative algorithms common in linear algebra libraries, thus enhancing the practical utility of F/D/Q extensions in scientific workloads.

Typical encoding patterns for each precision maintain constant lead bits and exponent biasing to enable hardware detection of special values. For single precision, the exponent bias is 127; double precision uses 1023; and quadruple precision applies a bias of 16383. The exponent encoding determines the range of representable numbers; for example, single precision floating-point numbers span approximately from 1.4×10^{-45} to 3.4×10^{38}, double precision extends over 4.9×10^{-324} to 1.8×10^{308}, and quadruple precision supports an astronomical range from roughly 6.5×10^{-4966} to 1.2×10^{4932}. This progressive extension enables increasingly subtle numerical distinctions.

Conforming to these ranges, denormalized (subnormal) numbers accommodate gradual underflow, allowing the representation of numbers smaller than the smallest normalized value by sacrificing precision. Their presence ensures continuity in the floating-point number line, ameliorating abrupt transitions to zero and assisting algorithms sensitive to smooth numeric behavior near zero. The cost, however, lies in the additional hardware complexity and potential performance penalties when processing subnormals, an aspect carefully considered in processor design.

Floating-point extensions embody a scalable progression balancing precision, performance, and complexity. Single precision provides the computational efficiency demanded in high-throughput media pipelines, double precision enables reliable and repeatable results in robust scientific and engineering tasks, and quadruple precision offers the exceptional numerical fidelity required in extreme-accuracy contexts. IEEE 754 compliance across all extensions guarantees interoperability, uniform error handling, and support for a wide variety of software and hardware ecosystems. The practical implications of adopting each extension depend heavily on application-specific trade-offs involving accuracy requirements, computational resources, execution time, and power consumption, making these extensions indispensable across the spectrum of contemporary computational fields.

51

2.5. Privilege Modes and ISA Separation

Modern processor architectures employ privilege levels to establish distinct execution domains, ensuring controlled access to resources and protecting system integrity. RISC-V delineates its privilege architecture with a hierarchical model consisting primarily of three hardware-supported privilege modes: *User* mode (U), *Supervisor* mode (S), and *Machine* mode (M). Each mode is associated with a specific subset of the instruction set architecture (ISA), forming increasingly privileged layers that safeguard control, security, and isolation within the system.

The **Machine mode** represents the highest privilege level and acts as the root of trust for the system's operation. It has comprehensive access to all physical resources and can execute any instruction. It oversees low-level hardware control, including initialization, configuration of timers and interrupts, memory management unit (MMU) setup, and privileged control and status registers (CSRs) management. Typically, machine mode is reserved for firmware such as bootloaders or trusted monitor code responsible for establishing the initial system state.

Beneath machine mode is the **Supervisor mode**, which serves as the fundamental execution domain for operating system kernels and hypervisors. Supervisor mode accesses a subset of privileged instructions that include those to manage virtual memory translations, interrupt controllers, traps, and inter-processor interrupts (IPIs). Unlike machine mode, supervisor mode cannot execute instructions affecting machine-level configuration, preserving system stability by isolating low-level hardware configuration from OS-level code. The supervisor mode's ISA subset is designed to enable efficient control of user-space applications while imposing restrictions that prevent direct hardware manipulation or privilege escalation without explicit mediation.

The **User mode** sits at the base of the privilege hierarchy and corresponds to the least privileged execution environment. This mode supports unprivileged instructions encompassing arithmetic, logical operations, memory loads and stores, and control flow instructions. User mode does not have access to privileged CSRs or memory management control, ensuring applications, services, and user-space programs cannot alter the global system configuration. This isolation is fundamental to operating system security and stability because it prevents user code from compromising the system or interfering with other executing processes.

Privilege separation in RISC-V extends beyond simply defining operational boundaries; it also involves strict ISA partitioning. Instructions are categorized as either *privileged* or *unprivileged*. Unprivileged instructions form the base ISA, executable in user mode and upwards, providing functionalities common to all software tiers. Privileged instructions, restricted to supervisor and machine modes, control critical aspects, such as CSR access, exception and interrupt handling, timer management, and memory protection mechanisms. Attempting to execute privileged instructions in user mode triggers an exception, thereby preventing unauthorized system-level manipulations.

RISC-V implements traps as a mechanism to transition securely from less privileged modes to more privileged ones, primarily to handle exceptions (such as illegal instructions or page faults) and interrupts. When a trap occurs, the current program counter and cause are saved into privileged CSRs, and control is transferred to a trap handler executing in a higher privilege mode. This design preserves the principle of least privilege by enabling controlled intervention only when necessary and by trusted supervisory code. The trap return instructions leverage the saved states in CSRs to resume execution in the original privilege context after completing exception handling.

Memory protection and translation in RISC-V are integrally linked to privilege modes. Machine mode retains authority over the memory management hardware, including page table configuration and translation control registers, while supervisor mode operates virtual memory through privileged instructions to manage mappings in accordance with operating system policies. User mode accesses memory via virtual addresses translated and validated by the supervisor-mode-managed MMU, preventing direct physical memory access and enforcing process isolation. The architecture's modularity supports multi-level page tables and diverse schemes, depending on implementation and requirement.

Interrupt handling within RISC-V is similarly stratified by privilege. Machine mode has exclusive control over machine-level interrupts and their prioritization, including the delegation of selected interrupts to supervisor mode. Supervisor mode manages operating system interrupts and enables preemptive multitasking through timer interrupts and inter-processor notifications. User mode has no direct interrupt control but relies on the higher privilege levels for asynchronous event delivery, which in turn facilitates timely process switching, signal handling, and real-time responsiveness.

Control and Status Registers (CSRs) embody the state and configuration context necessary for privilege separation. RISC-V divides CSRs into *user-level, supervisor-level,* and *machine-level* categories, each accessible only within their defined privilege boundaries. Writing or reading privileged CSRs from unauthorized modes results in exceptions, further reinforcing the enforcement of privilege boundaries. For example, the mstatus register controls machine-level global interrupt enablement and mode-dependent flags, whereas the sstatus register pertains to supervisor mode context, reflecting the ISA's layered control dynamics.

RISC-V supports optional extension interfaces allowing implementers to disable or reduce privilege modes for specialized configurations, e.g., embedded systems where only machine and user modes might be present. Nevertheless, the full three-privilege model enhances system robustness by enabling layered software stacks, secure virtualization, and comprehensive access control.

The privilege mode transitions are orchestrated through well-defined instructions such as MRET, SRET, and URET (if implemented), which restore execution state and privilege level after traps. Transitioning down privilege levels for context switches or raising privilege via traps is tightly controlled and verified by hardware logic. This ensures that code running at lower privileges cannot arbitrarily elevate itself without executing a legitimate trap and handler sequence supervised by more privileged software.

```
uint64_t sstatus = csrr(SSTATUS);    // Read supervisor status
    register
sstatus |= STATUS_SIE;               // Enable supervisor
    interrupts
csrw(SSTATUS, sstatus);              // Write updated status
    back
```

Output: Supervisor mode interrupts enabled in sstatus CSR; no exception raise
d.

RISC-V's privilege modes and ISA separation construct a funda-mental foundation for secure and stable system operation. By clearly defining user, supervisor, and machine privilege levels with corresponding ISA accesses and control domains, RISC-V enables layered software execution, effective hardware resource protec-tion, and scalable support for complex system software such as op-erating systems, hypervisors, and security monitors. This architec-tural paradigm establishes essential safeguards against accidental or malicious interference among software components, solidifying RISC-V's position as a robust open ISA for diverse computing en-vironments.

2.6. Non-standard and Experimental Extensions

The RISC-V architecture distinguishes itself by its modular and extensible design, enabling the addition of instructions beyond its standardized base and extension sets. Beyond the well-established standard extensions such as the integer (I), multiplication (M), atomic (A), and floating-point (F and D) extensions, the ecosystem has seen significant innovation through custom, vector, and experimental instructions. These non-standard extensions serve a dual purpose: allowing domain-specific optimization not achievable by standard instructions, and providing a platform for ongoing architectural innovation within a flexible specification framework.

Custom instructions allow implementers to augment the ISA with application- or domain-specific operations tailored to particular workloads or hardware capabilities. Unlike fixed architectures, which force software to rely solely on a standardized instruction set, RISC-V's open specification permits designers to introduce bespoke instructions without breaking binary compatibility with standard software components, provided such instructions are managed carefully. Custom instructions typically reside in the opcode space reserved as "custom" by the specification, often under the 0x0B opcode range or the custom-0, custom-1, custom-2, and custom-3 opcode encodings.

The use cases for custom instructions vary widely: from accelerating cryptographic primitives, enabling specialized bit-field manipulations, to supporting fine-grain domain-specific accelerators such as digital signal processing (DSP) or machine learning (ML) kernels optimized for latency or power consumption. For example, custom bit-manipulation instructions such as CLZ (count leading zeros) or BSWAP (byte swap) often appear early as ad hoc custom instructions, later candidates for standardization due to their general utility.

56

Implementing custom instructions introduces challenges, particularly in software toolchain support. The assembler and compiler need symbolic support to encode these instructions correctly, while binary translators and debuggers require awareness to disassemble and interpret them meaningfully. Consequently, a common development pattern involves defining custom instructions with dedicated encodings and incorporating them into Instruction Set Simulators (ISS) and hardware description languages to prototype behavior before more extensive ecosystem integration.

The RISC-V Foundation and its community members maintain an experimental extension stage explicitly aimed at fostering architectural innovation without committing immediately to standardization. These extensions, often under active development by research institutions or companies, allow exploration of novel instruction semantics, encoding strategies, and execution models.

Experimental instructions frequently address domains or features where performance and efficiency gains remain elusive with existing extensions. For instance, investigations into compressed vector instructions, more granular privilege-level control, speculative execution hints, or transactional memory support have emerged as experimental mechanisms prior to standardization or abandonment.

The process used to propose experimental instructions is informal but community-driven. Researchers submit extension proposals often accompanied by a preliminary architectural specification, reference implementations in RTL and ISS, and benchmarks illustrating improvements. Discussions proceed through dedicated RISC-V Technical Forums and Special Interest Groups (SIGs). Community feedback informs iterative revisions emphasizing backward compatibility, security, and ease of implementation.

Unlike standard extensions, experimental instructions carry no guarantee of future support or ubiquity. As such, software relying on them must either isolate these instructions behind runtime feature detection or maintain alternate code paths. This approach ensures broad compatibility while enabling early adopters to leverage cutting-edge technology.

While RISC-V has ratified the standard vector extension (denoted V), ongoing enhancements and variant proposals extend beyond the initial specification. These vector instruction variants are often non-standard or experimental, either in the form of expanded data-types, improved masking schemes, or enhanced memory access patterns.

For example, proposals exist extending vector-length agnostic algorithms with support for predicated execution beyond masks, novel scatter/gather addressing modes, or augmented floating-point support including half-precision and bfloat16 tailored for machine learning workloads. These proposals demand substantial architectural and microarchitectural changes, such as scalable vector register files, flexible vector length control, and dynamic dispatch mechanisms, highlighting the trade-offs involved in vector processing customization.

Experimental vector extensions often assist hardware designers in assessing the feasibility of these techniques, providing feedback to the RISC-V Vector Working Group. The vector architecture's parameterization and the vector unit's configurability serve as a litmus test for scalable vectorization, reflecting a deliberate design choice that facilitates the co-existence of vector features at different maturity levels.

The process for experimentation in the RISC-V ecosystem balances openness with rigorous technical validation. Proposals for custom or experimental instructions typically undergo the following workflow:

1. *Specification Drafting:* Proposers author detailed extension documents covering motivation, encoding format, operand semantics, effects on pipeline stages, and interactions with

existing features.

2. *Reference Implementation:* Authors provide implementations in RTL simulators and integrate modifications into software simulators such as Spike or QEMU variants. This step
enables early functional validation and impact evaluation
across hardware and software stacks.

3. *Community Review:* Proposed extensions enter community discussion forums, where constructive critiques focus
on complexity, benefits, compatibility, and security implications.

4. *Toolchain Enablement:* Support materializes progressively
in assemblers, compilers, and debugging environments, ensuring developers can adopt new instructions with continuity.

5. *Benchmarking and Refinement:* Implementations undergo
performance and functional benchmarking. Feedback from
silicon prototypes or FPGA-based testbeds informs further
tuning.

The RISC-V Foundation encourages this process within a lifecycle
that permits temporary experimental and custom instructions to
mature into draft specifications and potentially standardized extensions once demonstrated stable and beneficial.

Several prominent examples elucidate the scope and impact of non-
standard and experimental extensions:

Bit-Manipulation Extensions

Prior to finalizing the B standard extension, bit manipulation instructions were available solely as custom or experimental opcodes.
These included instructions for parallel bit extraction, insertion,
rotate, and population count. Early adopters leveraged these instructions extensively in security and compression workloads, pro-

viding critical data to define the standardized bit-manipulation instruction set.

Cryptographic Accelerators

Cryptographic functions benefit significantly from dedicated instructions enabling constant-time execution and atomic complex operations. Various organizations have developed experimental extensions implementing instructions such as AES encryption rounds or SHA hashing primitives. These efforts emphasize integration with privilege and memory models to preserve confidentiality and integrity guarantees.

Prefetch and Memory Hints

Emerging experimental instructions allow finer control over prefetching latency and cache behavior. These furnish the processor pipeline with anticipatory information, thereby optimizing memory-level parallelism, especially for irregular or pointer-chasing workloads. These extensions explore encoding lightweight hints without inflating complexity or power consumption.

Custom, vector, and experimental extensions manifest significant influence across the RISC-V software and hardware stack. From a hardware perspective, the flexible instruction encoding and modular pipeline stages facilitate integration of new instructions with minimal disruption to core processors, enabling silicon designers to tailor chips precisely for targeted markets. They can evaluate trade-offs between architectural complexity, silicon area, performance gains, and power efficiency early in the design cycle.

On the software side, compilers are crucial in exploiting new instructions. Intrinsic functions and compiler built-ins abstract custom instructions for optimized library implementations. The LLVM and GCC backends for RISC-V routinely incorporate such intrinsics, permitting higher-level languages to seamlessly benefit from hardware extensions.

Operating systems and runtime environments implement query mechanisms such as the RISC-V standard Z extension discovery or hypervisor-level feature reporting, allowing adaptive software to detect and leverage available instructions dynamically. Such mechanisms enable software to maintain portability while exploiting the cutting edge.

The flourishing of custom and experimental extensions introduces challenges related to ecosystem fragmentation and verification complexity. Excessive proliferation of non-standard instructions risks undermining the promise of a simple, interoperable ISA. Consequently, coordinating efforts toward modular extension standards, clear documentation, and compatible toolchain evolution remains imperative.

Verification of experimental instructions, especially those with complex side effects or speculative execution implications, demands sophisticated formal methods and rigorous testing frameworks to preserve correctness and security. The RISC-V community actively explores formal verification techniques and conformance suites tailored to extensible architectures.

Looking forward, the combination of non-standard and experimental extensions with emerging trends such as heterogeneous computing, security-enforced enclaves, and domain-specific accelerators promises to drive further transformation within RISC-V. This continuous innovation cycle underscores the ISA's vitality and responsiveness to evolving application demands.

Non-standard and experimental extensions constitute a dynamic and vital aspect of the RISC-V ecosystem. Their design and adoption reflect the architecture's foundational principles of openness, modularity, and innovation, enabling a broad spectrum of hardware-software co-design possibilities beyond conventional ISA boundaries.

2.7. Instruction Set Compatibility and Forward Evolution

RISC-V's architecture uniquely balances the demands of backward compatibility with the imperative for forward evolution, enabling the platform to adapt to emerging computational needs without sacrificing the integrity of existing ecosystems. This balance is primarily achieved through a modular ISA design, strategic encoding choices, and disciplined versioning policies, which collectively allow for the integration of new instructions and extensions with minimal disruption to software and hardware.

The foundation of RISC-V's compatibility model lies in its fixed base instruction set, which defines a stable core upon which all extensions rest. This base serves as an unchanging anchor, ensuring that software developed for prior versions continues to function correctly on future implementations. Notably, the base set includes essential integer computational instructions and defines the conventions for registers, addressing modes, and exception handling mechanisms. The stable general-purpose register set and the mandatory 32-bit instruction length provide a predictable framework for both hardware implementers and compiler developers.

Key to maintaining compatibility is RISC-V's extensible encoding space. The instruction word format reserves specific opcode fields for standard and custom extensions, with a clear separation between user-defined and standardized extensions in the encoding map. This separation minimizes the risk of opcode conflicts when new extensions are introduced. In particular, RISC-V utilizes an opcode prefixing scheme and categorizes instructions into major opcode groups, each with their own sub-opcode fields. By constraining new instructions to unallocated opcode spaces and honoring alignment and length conventions, new extensions can coexist without invalidating existing binaries.

The use of variable-length instruction encoding, especially the introduction of compressed 16-bit instructions (RVC extension), exemplifies RISC-V's approach to evolution without disruption. The compiler and assembler can transparently select between 16-bit compressed and standard 32-bit instructions, optimizing for code density while preserving semantic consistency. Since decoders identify instruction size dynamically based on the first two bits of the instruction word, legacy programs remain unaffected by the presence or absence of compressed instruction support.

Forward evolution is also enabled by the versioning and standardization procedures governed by the RISC-V Foundation. Before ratification, new extensions undergo rigorous peer review focusing on backward compatibility and hardware feasibility. The architecture mandates that changes or additions do not redefine or repurpose existing encoding bits or behaviors in a manner that could alter the result of existing binaries. As a consequence, any new instruction or extension is additive and optional, allowing implementations to incorporate subsets of extensions as needed without forcing existing software to adapt.

Interoperability between different extension sets is maintained by careful definition of extension interaction rules, particularly in the context of atomic operations, floating-point units, and privileged instructions. For example, new atomic or vector operations introduced in an extension are designed to be orthogonal to the base ISA and established extensions, with explicit mechanisms to detect unsupported instructions and trigger well-defined exception handling. This approach enables software to query processor capabilities at runtime and adjust its behavior accordingly through feature detection mechanisms.

Hardware vendors benefit from this compatibility model by having the freedom to innovate with specialized extensions or accelerators, either standardized or proprietary, while still supporting legacy software. The modular design means that a baseline implementation can run a broad spectrum of software, with higher-end silicon adding optional extensions for enhanced performance or domain-specific optimization. This modularity extends to the privileged architecture as well, where changes related to system-level features such as virtual memory or interrupt handling are introduced via backward-compatible extensions or alternative modes.

The RISC-V specification's commitment to preserving the Application Binary Interface (ABI) across versions further reinforces forward compatibility. ABI stability ensures that compiled code maintains the same calling conventions, register usage, stack frame layout, and exception behavior, making it feasible to run legacy applications across different versions of the architecture without recompilation. When new extensions introduce additional registers or capabilities, they are integrated into the ABI via standardized extension-specific calling conventions, leaving the base ABI unaffected.

Implementation strategies at the microarchitectural level also reflect this emphasis on compatibility. Pipeline designs and decoders accommodate multiple instruction lengths and extension sets, often through microcode or configurable logic, allowing hardware to support diverse combinations of extensions without functional conflict. From a testing perspective, compliance suites verify that implementations correctly handle both legacy and newly introduced instructions, enforcing that deprecated or altered instruction forms do not appear or are properly trapped.

With respect to software ecosystems, compiler toolchains like GCC and LLVM maintain multiple target profiles that correspond to specific RISC-V extension combinations. These profiles guide the code generation process to emit instructions conforming to the target hardware capabilities while preserving backward compatibility. This layered approach enables cross-compilation and progressive adoption of new features; software developers can leverage extensions opportunistically without losing portability or breaking existing deployments.

The evolving vector and bit-manipulation extensions illustrate the forward evolution process in RISC-V. Introduced after the initial base ISA ratification, these extensions address emerging workload requirements such as high-performance computing and cryptography. Their design explicitly avoids overlap with existing instruction fields and incorporates mechanisms for compulsory feature negotiation, allowing software and hardware to evolve independently yet remain compatible.

RISC-V employs a combination of a stable base ISA, strategic encoding partitions, modular and optional extension inclusions, rigorous version control, and ABI preservation to achieve backward and forward compatibility simultaneously. This architectural philosophy not only safeguards existing investments in software and hardware but also fosters innovation through a flexible yet disciplined evolution path. As a result, RISC-V stands as a resilient platform capable of accommodating future computational paradigms without compromising the stability or consistency essential to long-term technological ecosystems.

Chapter 3

Microarchitecture Design Considerations

Peek beneath the surface of the instruction set to uncover the artistry and science required to build a high-performance RISC-V core. This chapter uncovers the subtle trade-offs, clever optimizations, and proven engineering patterns that shape the path from architectural intent to real silicon. Whether designing for power, speed, or efficiency, you'll gain the tools to architect RISC-V processors that excel in the modern landscape.

3.1. Pipeline Architectures

Pipcline architectures constitute a cornerstone in modern processor design, directly influencing performance metrics such as throughput, latency, and implementation complexity. The RISC-V instruction set architecture (ISA), characterized by its simplicity and extensibility, provides an ideal platform to explore a range of pipeline design methodologies. Here, the focus lies on three principal architectural models: single-cycle, multi-cycle, and deep pipelined designs-each presenting distinct trade-offs that shape the microarchitecture of RISC-V processors.

Single-Cycle Architecture

The single-cycle pipeline architecture executes an entire instruction in a single clock cycle. This design unifies the fetch, decode, execute, memory access, and write-back stages into one long combinational path. From a theoretical perspective, the cycle time (T_{cycle}) must accommodate the worst-case instruction with the longest delay, generally a load or complex arithmetic operation.

The primary advantage of the single-cycle model is its conceptual simplicity. Every instruction completes in one clock tick, resulting in straightforward control logic and easier verification. However, the necessity to accommodate the slowest instruction constrains the clock frequency, leading to lower overall throughput compared with more sophisticated pipeline designs.

For a RISC-V processor, single-cycle implementation typically limits the clock frequency due to the inclusion of multiple functional units and memory access within a single cycle. Instruction latency corresponds exactly to one cycle, but throughput, defined as the number of instructions completed per second, is limited by the inverse of this maximal cycle time.

- **Cycle time constraint:** $T_{\text{cycle}} \geq \max\{t_{\text{fetch}}, t_{\text{decode}}, t_{\text{execute}}, t_{\text{mem}}, t_{\text{writeback}}\}$
- **Instruction latency:** $L_{\text{instr}} = T_{\text{cycle}}$
- **Throughput:** $R \approx \frac{1}{T_{\text{cycle}}}$

Due to tightly coupled combinational paths, the single-cycle implementation faces challenges with dynamic power consumption and thermal dissipation in modern CMOS technologies, especially as the number of instruction types and supported extensions grows.

Multi-Cycle Architecture

68

The multi-cycle design decomposes the instruction execution into multiple clock cycles, with each clock cycle performing a distinct phase of the instruction pipeline. Such decomposition permits the reuse of functional units across multiple phases, optimizing hardware resource utilization and enabling a reduction in clock cycle time.

The cycle time in a multi-cycle design can be shortened to the duration of the longest single stage, significantly shorter than the longest instruction delay in the single-cycle approach. Latency increases because an instruction occupies multiple cycles (one cycle per stage), but throughput benefits from higher clock rates and improved resource sharing.

For RISC-V architectures, the canonical split into stages often includes:

- Instruction Fetch (IF)

- Instruction Decode/Register Fetch (ID)

- Execute (EX)

- Memory Access (MEM)

- Write-Back (WB)

Each instruction thus requires multiple cycles, but the cycle time is governed by the slowest single stage delay, such as instruction fetch memory access or ALU operation. This shorter cycle time directly translates into higher clock frequencies.

Control complexity is elevated compared to the single-cycle design since a finite state machine or microsequencer must govern the sequencing of stages per instruction type. Individual instructions may have differing numbers of clock cycles depending on the operation. This flexibility reduces hardware redundancy and eases critical path timing constraints.

69

Mathematically, assuming instruction I requires N_i stages, the latency and throughput in a multi-cycle processor become:

$$L_{\text{instr}}(I) = N_i \times T_{\text{cycle}}$$

$$R = \frac{1}{T_{\text{cycle}}}$$

where T_{cycle} is the duration of the longest stage within the processor.

From an implementation complexity perspective, multi-cycle designs are a middle ground-more complex than single-cycle due to additional state machine control and variable instruction lengths, yet fewer pipeline hazards and simpler forwarding compared to deep pipelines.

Deep Pipelined Architecture

Deep pipelining further subdivides instruction processing into multiple fine-grained stages, enabling a significant increase in clock frequency and thus throughput. This is achieved by breaking down combinational logic into smaller steps separated by pipeline registers, allowing concurrent execution of multiple instructions at different pipeline stages.

In the RISC-V context, deep pipelines may extend beyond five stages to ten or more, optimizing the critical path delay deeply but introducing new challenges. For example, a 7- or 10-stage pipeline may separate the instruction fetch into address generation and instruction memory access, divide execute into multiple stages (e.g., ALU setup, calculation, and result forwarding), and split memory access into address computation and data interaction phases.

This structural partitioning enables clock periods as low as the delay through a small combinational block plus register overhead, effectively maximizing throughput:

$$R \approx \frac{1}{T_{\text{stage}} + T_{\text{register}}}$$

where T_{stage} is the delay of the logic within one pipeline stage, and T_{register} accounts for pipeline register setup and hold times.

Latency and Throughput: Latency increases with pipeline depth, as an instruction requires progressing through all pipeline stages sequentially. For an n-stage pipeline:

$$L_{\text{instr}} = n \times T_{\text{clock}}$$

While latency may grow, throughput improves proportionally since one instruction completes per clock cycle once the pipeline is filled.

Hazard Management: Increased pipeline depth introduces multiple types of hazards-structural, data, and control hazards-due to overlapping instructions in separate stages. Structural hazards arise from resource contention, often resolved by replication or stalls. Data hazards occur when instructions depend on results of prior incomplete instructions, necessitating forwarding or pipeline stalls (bubbles). Control hazards from branches are aggravated in deep pipelines due to longer branch resolution times, often addressed with prediction schemes.

Design Complexity: Deep pipelines require sophisticated hazard detection and resolution units, complex forwarding paths, and branch prediction mechanisms to maintain throughput. With RISC-V's variable instruction lengths eliminated in its base ISA, pipeline control is simplified relative to architectures with complex instruction encoding, yet complexity remains considerably higher than in multi-cycle or single-cycle processors.

Trade-Offs: Although deep pipelines offer potentially higher throughput, they incur increased design and verification complexity, higher pipeline flush penalty upon misprediction, and increased power dissipation due to additional flip-flops and control logic. The deeper the pipeline, the more instructions are in flight, exacerbating the cost of pipeline stalls and hazards. Implementation must balance the marginal benefits in clock frequency and throughput against these costs.

Comparative Analysis

Comparison across the architectures illustrates distinct trade-offs in throughput, latency, and implementation complexity:

Architecture	Throughput	Latency	Implementation Complexity
Single-Cycle	Low (limited by longest instruction)	Low (1 cycle per instruction)	Low (minimal control complexity)
Multi-Cycle	Medium (higher clock frequency)	Medium (multiple cycles per instruction)	Medium (control FSM, variable cycles)
Deep Pipelined	High (max clock frequency)	High ($n \times T_{\text{clock}}$)	High (hazard detection, forwarding, prediction)

Table 3.1: *Comparison of pipeline architectures in RISC-V processors*

In a single-cycle design, the critical path limits the cycle time, making it less suitable for high-frequency designs but easier to implement and debug. Multi-cycle architectures achieve better throughput by splitting stages and reusing resources while maintaining moderate control complexity. Deep pipelines achieve the highest clock frequencies and throughput but require extensive hazard management and incur performance penalties from pipeline flushes typically induced by branch misprediction.

Implications on RISC-V Processor Design

The clean, load-store nature of RISC-V simplifies pipeline control by reducing instruction complexity and enabling more balanced pipeline stages compared to CISC counterparts. Consequently, multi-cycle and moderately deep pipelines are commonly favored in practice, offering a practical balance between performance and design complexity.

Deep pipelined designs are found in high-performance RISC-V cores targeting server-class and performance-driven environments, integrating branch prediction, speculative execution, and out-of-order mechanisms layered upon the pipeline framework. The fixed 32-bit instruction format of the RISC-V base ISA facilitates efficient instruction fetch and decode stages, reducing variability in pipeline stage timing.

Moreover, RISC-V's modularity allows pipeline depth tuning for various application domains-from deeply pipelined cores for compute-intensive tasks to shallow pipelines or multi-cycle architectures for embedded systems with stringent power and area constraints.

Summary of Pipeline Implementation Considerations

Key design considerations in choosing and implementing pipeline architectures for RISC-V processors include:

- **Clock frequency vs. cycle complexity:** Increased pipelining reduces combinational delay per cycle but increases control complexity.

- **Instruction set complexity:** The reduced and fixed-length RISC-V instructions simplify multi-cycle and pipelined designs.

- **Hazard handling:** Strategies such as forwarding, stall insertion, and branch prediction become increasingly essential with pipeline depth.

- **Resource sharing:** Multi-cycle architectures optimize chip area by reusing functional units, while single-cycle designs allocate dedicated units per function at the expense of area.

- **Power consumption:** Deeper pipelines may increase dynamic power due to more pipeline registers and control logic switching.

Understanding these architectural models establishes a foundational relationship between microarchitectural choices and their systemic impact on RISC-V processor performance and complexity. Each pipeline design represents a fundamental point on the spectrum of trade-offs where application requirements, design constraints, and target performance dictate the ultimate microarchitectural organization.

3.2. Hazards and Stall Management

The implementation of instruction pipelines in modern processors is essential for achieving higher instruction throughput and improved performance. However, pipelining inherently introduces several classes of hazards—conditions that prevent the next instruction in the pipeline from executing during its designated clock cycle. Understanding and managing these hazards is critical for the efficient design of pipelined cores. The primary categories of hazards are data hazards, control hazards, and structural hazards, each presenting unique challenges and necessitating specific resolution techniques.

Data Hazards

Data hazards occur when instructions depend on the results of previous instructions that have not yet completed their execution stages. These dependencies can manifest in three fundamental forms:

- **Read After Write (RAW):** Also known as true dependency, this arises when an instruction requires a register value written by a prior instruction that has yet to complete.

- **Write After Read (WAR):** Also called anti-dependency, this happens when an instruction writes to a register before a prior instruction has read it.

- **Write After Write (WAW):** Also known as output dependency, it occurs when two instructions write to the same register and must be ordered to preserve correctness.

In classic RISC pipelines with in-order issue and completion, the dominant data hazard is RAW. Contemporary pipelines typically avoid WAR and WAW hazards by employing techniques such as register renaming, which dynamically remaps architectural registers to a larger pool of physical registers, thereby eliminating false dependencies.

RAW hazards necessitate stalling or forwarding. The simplest solution to a RAW hazard is to stall the pipeline until the required data becomes available. This approach, however, degrades instruction throughput and increases latency. To mitigate this, *forwarding* (or *bypassing*) is employed.

Forwarding involves additional hardware paths that route the result of an instruction directly from the pipeline stage where it becomes available (e.g., the Execute or Memory stage) back to the earlier stages needing the data, circumventing the register file writeback delay. The canonical example is forwarding the ALU result from the Execute stage to the Decode stage of the subsequent instruction. Despite forwarding, there remain scenarios—such as load-use hazards—where forwarding alone is insufficient. For example, when an instruction depends on a loaded value from memory, the data is not available until after the Memory stage, so a stall is inevitable.

A formal hazard detection unit identifies these conflicts by comparing source registers of the instruction in the Decode stage with destination registers of instructions in later pipeline stages. Careful timing and control logic are employed to introduce stalls when forwarding cannot resolve conflicts, preventing hazards without compromising correctness.

The standard pipeline hazard detection condition for inserting a stall due to a load-use hazard can be expressed as follows:

$$\text{stall} = \left(I_{\text{Decode}}.\text{rs} = I_{\text{Execute}}.\text{rt}\right) \wedge \left(I_{\text{Execute}}.\text{opcode} = \text{LOAD}\right)$$

where I_{Decode} is the instruction currently in Decode with source register rs, and I_{Execute} is the instruction in Execute performing a load with target register rt.

Control Hazards

Control hazards arise from branches and other control flow instructions, which cause uncertainty about the next instruction to fetch. When a branch instruction is encountered, the pipeline must determine the branch outcome and target address to continue execution correctly. Given the pipeline stages, the branch condition is often resolved in the Execute stage, resulting in the fetching of potentially incorrect instructions after the branch instruction during the prior cycles—commonly referred to as *branch delay slots*.

Traditional pipeline designs address control hazards by stalling the pipeline until the branch outcome is known, flushing incorrect instructions when a misprediction occurs. This stall can incur significant performance penalties, especially in deep pipelines.

Classic methods to mitigate control hazards include:

- **Pipeline Stalling:** Halting instruction fetch until branch decision is finalized.

- **Branch Delay Slots:** Compiler scheduling forces useful instructions into slots immediately following a branch, which are executed regardless of the branch outcome.

More advanced techniques adopt *branch prediction* mechanisms, which predict the likely branch direction and fetch subsequent instructions along the predicted path to maintain pipeline utilization. When the prediction turns out incorrect, the pipeline discards speculatively fetched instructions (flushes the pipeline) and suffers a penalty proportional to the misprediction latency.

Popular branch prediction strategies include static prediction (e.g., always predict not taken), dynamic prediction with a saturating counter, and more sophisticated hybrid predictors combining local and global branch histories.

To formalize control hazard detection and resolution, consider a pipeline segment and branch instruction B at stage s_b, whose outcome is decided at stage s_d. The minimum branch penalty in cycles is $s_d - s_b$. During these cycles, subsequent instructions are fetched speculatively. The hazard resolution logic must:

- Confirm the branch target and outcome at stage s_d,

- Flush or commit instructions in fetched pipeline stages accordingly,

- Adjust the program counter or instruction fetch unit for correct instruction streams.

Structural Hazards

Structural hazards occur when hardware resources are insufficient to support all overlapping instructions simultaneously, leading to resource conflicts. For instance, if a processor pipeline has a single memory port used for both instruction fetch and data load/store, concurrent access requests may cause contention.

Effective pipeline design avoids structural hazards by replicating or partitioning resources where feasible. For example, instruction and data caches are separated (Harvard architecture), or multiport register files are deployed. When hardware replication is cost-

77

prohibitive, arbitration must enforce resource access serialization, introducing stalls.

Consider a pipeline where instruction fetch (IF) and data memory access (MEM) stages potentially contend for a common memory unit. The pipeline control logic must detect simultaneous requests and insert stalls accordingly:

$$\text{stall}_{\text{struct}} = (IF_{\text{req}} \wedge MEM_{\text{req}}) \wedge \neg \text{resource\_available}$$

where resource_available indicates memory port availability.

Hazard Detection and Management Infrastructure

The cornerstone for hazard management is a unit dedicated to monitoring register dependencies, resource usage, and control flow changes. This *hazard detection unit* acts as the central arbiter, equipped to:

- Compare instruction operands across pipeline stages to identify RAW dependencies,

- Track ongoing load-use scenarios where data is unavailable,

- Monitor control flow instruction outcomes and prediction correctness,

- Detect structural conflicts over hardware units.

Upon detection of unresolved hazards, the unit dispatches stall signals to the instruction fetch and decode stages and inserts *bubbles*—no-operation instructions—into the pipeline to avoid executing faulty or incomplete instructions.

Integration with forwarding units ensures dynamic hazard mitigation when data is timely available from functional units in intermediate pipeline stages.

78

Advanced Techniques

Increasingly complex pipelines leverage several advanced techniques to enhance hazard resolution:

Out-of-Order Execution: By dynamically analyzing instruction dependencies and employing register renaming, modern cores execute instructions non-sequentially and out-of-order while preserving program semantics, thus bypassing many data hazard stalls.

Speculative Execution: Combines branch prediction with out-of-order execution, enabling the pipeline to execute ahead of resolved branches. Incorrect paths are flushed upon misprediction.

Scoreboarding and Tomasulo's Algorithm: These techniques track operand availability and functional unit status to schedule instruction execution dynamically, resolving hazards without explicit stalling in simple pipelines.

Dual-Issue and Superscalar Pipelines: Parallel instruction issue increases hazard complexity, requiring enhanced dependency checking and stall strategies.

Load-Use Latency Reduction: Employ techniques such as *early load forwarding* where the pipeline attempts to forward data from memory or cache before typical timing or *load speculation*, predicting load data for speculative execution.

Example: Forwarding Path Implementation

The fundamental implementation of a forwarding unit hinges on multiplexers directing operand sources in the Decode or Execute stages. Consider the following logic example in a simplified 5-stage pipeline:

```
if (EX_MEM.RegWrite && (EX_MEM.RegisterRd != 0) &&
    (EX_MEM.RegisterRd == ID_EX.RegisterRs)) {
   ForwardA = 10; // Forward from EX MEM stage
} else if (MEM_WB.RegWrite && (MEM_WB.RegisterRd != 0) &&
          (MEM_WB.RegisterRd == ID_EX.RegisterRs)) {
   ForwardA = 01; // Forward from MEM WB stage
} else {
```

```
ForwardA = 00; // Use register file output
}
```

Analogous logic applies for ForwardB multiplexers controlling the second source operand. This logic dynamically selects operands from either register file or forwarding paths based on pending writes in pipeline registers.

Impact on Performance

The effective management of hazards directly influences pipeline throughput and efficiency. Stall insertion reduces instruction issue rates, forwarding pipelines minimize stalls at a modest hardware cost, and advanced speculation mechanisms offer substantial performance gains at the price of increased design and verification complexity.

A balanced design considers the trade-offs between added complexity, power consumption, and the achievable frequency of operation. Designers utilize quantitative metrics such as:

$$\text{CPI} = 1 + \text{Pipeline Stall Cycles per Instruction}$$

to evaluate the impact of hazard management strategies on processor performance.

Hazards in pipelined processors are inevitable due to instruction dependencies and resource sharing. Sophisticated detection, stall insertion, and forwarding techniques ensure correctness while minimizing performance degradation. Control hazards from branches add further complexity, often necessitating prediction and speculation mechanisms. Structural hazards demand judicious resource allocation and arbitration. The interplay of these hazard management strategies epitomizes the intricate balance in pipeline microarchitecture design, serving as a foundation for high-performance processor architectures.

3.3. Instruction Fetch and Decode Logic

Efficient design of the instruction fetch and decode stages is critical to maximizing instruction throughput and minimizing delays
within the processor's critical path. These stages form the front-
end of the pipeline, responsible for delivering the correct instructions and translating their encodings into control signals, especially in architectures like RISC-V, where modular instructions accommodate both compactness and extensibility.

Instruction Fetch Stage

The fetch stage's primary objective is to supply the pipeline with a
continuous stream of instructions at the highest possible rate without stalling, despite potential hazards such as branch mispredictions or cache misses. The program counter (PC) holds the address
of the instruction to be fetched, and its update logic must support
both sequential execution and control-flow changes.

Program Counter Management

To maintain high throughput, the PC update mechanism must be
tightly coupled with branch prediction logic, ensuring minimal delay in target resolution. Incrementing the PC is straightforward for
sequential execution and normally involves a fixed stride equivalent to the instruction length. RISC-V's variable-length encoding
scheme complicates this as instructions may be 16, 32, or 48 bits
wide, requiring the fetch unit to dynamically determine the instruction size for the PC increment.

Implementing a prefetch buffer or a small instruction queue helps
decouple the fetch unit from downstream stages and tolerates
cache access latencies. This buffer stores prefetched instructions,
allowing the fetch stage to continue while the decoding or execution stages resolve control dependencies. Fetch bandwidth may
be maximized by fetching multiple instructions per cycle in superscalar designs, but this amplifies alignment and instruction-size

81

decoding complexity.

Instruction Memory and Cache Considerations

Instruction fetch units heavily rely on effective instruction cache (I-Cache) design. To avoid pipeline stalls, I-Cache hit latency must be minimized, often by employing single-cycle hit times or splitting caches into multiple banks for parallel access. The fetch unit generates address requests, and the cache responds with instruction data aligned with the PC value.

Unaligned accesses due to variable-length instructions in RISC-V require special hardware support. The fetch unit must handle instructions crossing cache line boundaries, which can be implemented through prefetch buffers that span multiple cache lines or through dual-read ports. A branch prefetch mechanism can further reduce stall penalties on control-flow changes by speculatively loading target instructions.

Instruction Decode Stage

Decoding translates raw instruction bits into meaningful control signals governing the datapath. The RISC-V instruction set architecture (ISA) modularity introduces a well-defined encoding format, including fixed fields for opcode, source and destination registers, immediate values, and function codes. This regularity facilitates systematic decoder design but requires precise logic to handle various instruction formats efficiently and without increasing critical path delays.

Handling Modular Instruction Formats

RISC-V instructions are organized primarily into fixed 32-bit base instructions, with optional 16-bit compressed extensions and occasional longer instructions for specific extensions. The decoder hardware must first identify instruction length by examining the least significant bits of the first halfword, facilitating appropriate parsing strategy.

The decode stage logic is commonly partitioned into two components: length detection and field extraction. Length detection is aided by the instruction's format encoding bits; for example, a 16-bit compressed instruction occupies the least significant 16 bits, whereas a 32-bit instruction uses the full word. Once the length is ascertained, fields (opcode, rd, rs1, rs2, immediate, funct3, funct7) relevant to the instruction type (R, I, S, B, U, J) are extracted in parallel.

Parallel Decoding and Control Signal Generation

To maximize throughput, decoding is aggressively parallelized. Extracted fields feed simultaneously into control signal generators for register file read enables, ALU operation selectors, immediate value generators, and memory access controls. Using combinational logic trees with minimal depth ensures that signal propagation remains within one clock cycle under the target frequency.

The ISA's division of opcodes often allows grouping instructions into classes, with shared control logic derived from opcode and funct3 fields. For instance, all arithmetic immediate-type instructions share a similar decoder path but differ in ALU opcode parameters. This reduces the complexity of the decode logic by reusing functional blocks and employing multiplexers controlled by decoded signals.

Immediate and Offset Computation

Immediate values are critical not only as operands but also in branching and memory addressing instructions. Due to varied encoding across different instruction formats, immediate generation involves concatenating and sign-extending specific bit fields. Decoding hardware must implement immediate generators capable of efficiently reconstructing these values, typically via combinational logic that selects and concatenates bits according to fixed patterns.

Ensuring this logic resides within the decode stage's timing budget is nontrivial given the irregular distribution of bits in branching (B-type) and jump (J-type) instructions, where immediate fields are scattered and require careful reassembly. Optimizations often include pre-aligned concatenation and sign-extension units operating in parallel to opcode decoding.

Minimizing Critical Path Delays

The fetch and decode stages reside at the front-end of the pipeline; delays here limit the processor's clock frequency. To minimize critical path length, designers employ multiple strategies:

- **Pipelining Fetch and Decode**: Decoupling fetch and decode stages with pipeline registers breaks the timing path and reduces combinational depth.

- **Parallel Hierarchical Decoding**: Partitioning decoding logic into smaller, parallel units assigned to instruction fields reduces logic levels.

- **Pre-decoding and Caching**: Storing pre-decoded instructions or using trace caches to avoid repeated decoding of frequently executed instructions.

- **Speculative Fetch**: Integration with branch prediction hardware to hide branch resolution latency, allowing fetch to proceed along predicted paths.

- **Hardware Multiplexing**: Using optimized multiplexers and priority encoders in selecting instruction fields and control signals to reduce delay.

These techniques are often combined with aggressive gate-level optimizations and synthesis-directed floorplanning within the front-end logic to achieve timing closure at high clock rates.

RISC-V Extensions and Decode Scalability

84

RISC-V's design philosophy encourages clean extensibility with base instructions supplemented by standard or custom extensions. The fetch and decode logic must be designed with scalability in mind to accommodate future instruction formats or privileges without compromising existing performance.

Dynamic decoder configuration through programmable logic or microcode-assisted decoding is an option for complex or rarely used instructions, although this approach may introduce decoding latency and pipeline stalls. Alternatively, multiple parallel decoders, each specialized for a subset of extensions, can facilitate simultaneous recognition while keeping critical path delay low.

When dealing with compressed instructions, expansion units are integrated into decode logic to translate compact 16-bit instructions into full 32-bit equivalents before subsequent pipeline stages. This simplifies downstream datapath control at the expense of decode stage complexity and must be optimized carefully to avoid timing penalties.

Considerations for Superscalar and Out-of-Order Architectures

In superscalar implementations fetching multiple instructions per cycle, the instruction fetch unit must handle multi-instruction alignment, variable-length instruction boundaries, and concatenation of instruction bundles from the I-Cache. The complexity of instruction boundary detection grows exponentially with the number of instructions fetched simultaneously.

Decode logic, in turn, must service multiple decode ports and maintain synchronization with register renaming and instruction dispatch logic. Pipeline stalls due to decode hazards must be minimized by employing parallel decoders or allocating dedicated decode units per instruction slot.

For out-of-order processors, decode logic cooperates closely with front-end queues, reorder buffers, and branch target buffers to

85

maintain in-order instruction delivery while allowing speculative execution. Precise mapping between decoded instructions and fetched instruction addresses ensures correct exception handling and recovery.

Example: Immediate Generator Implementation in RISC-V Decode Logic

The immediate generator is an exemplar of decode complexity arising from RISC-V's modular instruction formats. Consider a simplified Verilog-like specification for generating the immediate field for B-type (branch) instructions:

```
wire [31:0] imm_b;
assign imm_b = {{20{instr[31]}}, instr[7], instr[30:25], instr
    [11:8], 1'b0};
```

This combines sign extension of the highest bit (`instr[31]`), and the scattered bits (7, 30:25, 11:8) shifted appropriately before concatenation and alignment by a least significant zero bit (branch addresses are always aligned). The combinational nature of this logic ensures immediate generation latency remains under the decode stage budget.

Achieving balanced performance in instruction fetch and decode stages requires careful trade-off analysis between logic complexity, pipeline depth, and clock frequency objectives. Modular instruction encodings in RISC-V provide a firm foundation for structured decode logic but increase complexity due to variable instruction lengths and formats. Fetch logic must be robust against misalignment and branching inefficiencies, frequently relying on multi-cycle buffering and prediction.

Holistic design of fetch and decode hardware, integrating carefully optimized combinational logic, configurable modular decoders, and sophisticated buffering and branch prediction strategies, drives high instruction throughput and low front-end latency essential for modern high-performance processors implementing the RISC-V ISA.

86

3.4. Register File and ALU Design

The design of register files and arithmetic logic units (ALUs) constitutes a cornerstone in the microarchitecture of RISC-V processors,
directly influencing performance, scalability, power consumption,
and ultimately, the efficiency of instruction execution. Intent focus on the architectural, timing, and energy trade-offs enables optimization tailored to diverse application and implementation targets, ranging from embedded systems with stringent area and energy constraints to high-performance computing requiring rapid
data throughput.

The register file is a critical state-holding element within the RISC-
V pipeline, typically composed of 32 general-purpose registers
(GPRs) each of 32, 64, or more bits depending on the ISA variant
(RV32I, RV64I). Key design parameters revolve around the num-
ber of read and write ports, register count, word width, and the
implications these have on datapath latency and area.

Multi-ported register files allow simultaneous access to multiple
registers, usually supporting two read ports and one write port
for the majority of RISC-V designs, aligned with the two-source
operand and single destination register model intrinsic to arithmetic and logic instructions. Scaling beyond this configuration,
such as adding extra read ports for speculative or out-of-order execution, leads to exponential growth in complexity and transistor
count owing to the quadratic increase in read wordlines and bitlines.

Physical implementations typically choose one of two architectural
paradigms: (1) monolithic multi-ported RAM arrays or (2) replicated register arrays with multiplexed output drivers. For small
register files (up to 32 registers), a monolithic array remains feasible, where high transistor densities and careful transistor sizing
address the increased pitch of multiport memories. The memory
cell design-commonly 6-transistor SRAM cells-must balance cell

87

stability, read access speed, and write performance. Differential read schemes, assisted by local sense amplifiers, mitigate the delay overhead associated with multiple read ports.

To scale register files for wide datapaths (e.g., RV64 or RV128), bit-slicing techniques are often deployed, whereby each bit-slice is designed as a replicated unit sharing global control signals but managing a single bit column. This allows fine-grained control over power gating and mitigates capacitive loading on wordlines and bitlines, which grows with word width.

Register file access contributes significantly to pipeline cycle time, particularly in low-latency pipelines where register-read occurs at the beginning of the instruction decode or execution stages. The access time, typically dominated by bitline and wordline propagation delays, sense amplifier activation, and output multiplexing, must be carefully minimized to avoid pipeline stalls.

Pre-decoding register addresses into one-hot signals reduces decoder complexity and enables faster wordline activation. Strong wordline drivers are balanced against increased power consumption and capacitive loading. Furthermore, transparent clocking or multi-phase clocking schemes can enable time borrowing and pipelining inside the register file access stage, improving frequency but introducing design complexity.

Energy-timing trade-offs manifest in the choice between static and dynamic read schemes. Static reads, while potentially faster due to the immediate availability of stable output voltages, consume continuous power. Dynamic reads precharge the bitlines and discharge based on stored data, reducing static power but incurring increased latency and sensitivity to noise.

Write operations typically occur at the end of the clock cycle, with write drivers and bitline precharge logic designed to reduce write disturb risks and maintain data integrity. The write bitline capacitance and driver strength must also be tuned to ensure timely write

88

completion without degrading cell stability.

Energy-efficient register file design is critical in embedded RISC-V processors and energy-constrained environments. Several techniques address static and dynamic power reduction:

- **Clock Gating and Power Gating:** Clock gating selectively disables clock signals to the register file write drivers and control logic during idle cycles, reducing dynamic power. Power gating switches off entire blocks when registers are not in use, trading off wakeup latency and state retention requirements.

- **Banking and Partitioning:** Dividing the register file into smaller banks or segments allows selective activation, minimizing switching activity and capacitance loading. Banks can be accessed independently to exploit operand locality, lowering active energy.

- **Operand Forwarding and Register Renaming:** Although more relevant to out-of-order designs, operand forwarding alleviates some register file pressure by short-circuiting the dependency chain, reducing frequent register access. Register renaming combined with scoreboarding reduces write conflicts, enabling clock gating opportunities.

- **Reducing Bitline Swing:** Employing differential or single-ended sensing techniques along with reduced swing voltages on bitlines minimizes dynamic energy during read and write operations.

Designers must carefully weigh these techniques against area overhead, access latency, and design complexity. For instance, excessive banking complicates timing closure and interconnect routing, while power gating requires retention strategies that may increase area and leakage.

The ALU executes integer arithmetic and logical operations essential to RISC-V ISA compliance. Key architectural considerations

89

include functional completeness, latency, throughput, and hardware complexity.

A conventional RISC-V ALU supports operations such as addition, subtraction, bitwise logical functions (AND, OR, XOR), shifts (logical/arithmetic), and comparison operations. Implementations vary from simple ripple-carry adders to more complex parallel-prefix designs, which reduce carry propagation delays significantly in wide datapaths. Popular parallel-prefix adder architectures include Kogge-Stone, Brent-Kung, and Sklansky trees, selected based on the trade-off between fan-out, wiring complexity, and logic depth.

Shifter units typically adopt barrel shifters executing multi-bit shifts in a single cycle. They are implemented using multiplexers arranged hierarchically, enabling shifts by varying amounts through controlled selection lines. Balancing multiplexing delay and layout area is essential, especially in 64-bit or wider implementations.

Logic operations are generally combinational and implemented through straightforward gate-level circuits integrated within the ALU datapath. Comparison is often realized by a subtraction followed by checking the sign bit, reusing the adder hardware to save area.

In high-frequency RISC-V cores, the ALU's critical paths-predominantly the adder and the shifter-define the cycle time. Partitioning the ALU into pipeline stages can alleviate timing constraints but introduces pipeline latency and complexity related to hazard detection and forwarding.

Optimizations include:

- **Speculative Precomputation:** Predicting operand-dependent branches inside the ALU, such as zero detection or sign evaluation, using early evaluation circuits reduces control hazards and improves throughput.

- **Operand Isolation and Gating:** Avoiding unnecessary switching activity when certain operations or operands are not used reduces dynamic power dissipation.

- **Customized Logic for Frequent Operations:** Dedicated hardware for common arithmetic functions like increment or decrement can be faster and more energy efficient than utilizing the full ALU datapath.

Moreover, emerging RISC-V extensions, such as the Multiply and Divide instructions (M-extension), impose further design challenges in integrating multiply-accumulate units or hardware dividers efficiently alongside the base ALU. Iterative or combinational multiplier designs offer trade-offs between area and latency, with partial-product accumulation strategies impacting the critical path.

Efficient integration between the register file and ALU critically shapes the overall processor datapath performance. Key considerations include:

- **Operand Delivery Latency:** Minimizing the delay in transfer of source operands from register file outputs to ALU inputs through careful pipeline and load balancing avoids stalls. This often requires matched wire lengths and balanced buffering stages.

- **Writeback Latency and Hazard Avoidance:** The ALU output must be written back into the register file within the same cycle or a controlled number of cycles to maintain data consistency. This necessitates careful timing coordination between ALU result readiness and register file write-enable timing.

- **Port Sharing and Multiplexing:** In power- or area-constrained designs, sharing ports between read and

91

write operations or using intermediate latches for operand staging may improve utilization but introduces latency and complicates timing closure.

- **Forwarding Paths and Bypassing Logic:** To mitigate hazards caused by operand dependencies, the design commonly incorporates forwarding paths that bypass the register file stages, feeding ALU inputs directly from execution or writeback stages. This reduces the load on the register file ports and lowers overall pipeline stalls.

Balancing these factors according to target frequency, power budget, and area constraints results in diverse RISC-V implementations, from minimalist in-order cores to aggressive superscalar or out-of-order designs.

The design of register files and ALUs in RISC-V processors involves intricate trade-offs:

- **Performance vs. Area:** Multi-ported register files and large, deeply pipelined ALUs improve throughput and reduce latency but increase silicon area and wiring complexity. Compact designs favor smaller port counts and simpler arithmetic units.

- **Power vs. Performance:** Aggressive clock gating, power gating, and operand banking reduce dynamic and static power but increase control logic and may impact latency. Wide datapaths and speculative execution demand more complex power management strategies.

- **Complexity vs. Scalability:** Scalable designs for varying datapath widths and architectural variants require modular register file and ALU designs that can be efficiently parameterized. This often necessitates systematic cell design and hierarchical implementation strategies.

Understanding these interactions enables architects and designers to optimize the register file and ALU subsystems to the unique requirements of the RISC-V processors, achieving a balance between speed, power, and chip area commensurate with the target application domain.

3.5. Branch Prediction and Control Flow

The efficacy of modern processor pipelines hinges critically on the ability to maintain a high instruction throughput by minimizing stalls and bubbles. Control flow instructions, especially conditional branches, present a fundamental obstacle to this goal because they introduce uncertainty about the next instruction address. Branch prediction is the hardware mechanism designed to alleviate such uncertainty, enabling speculative fetching and execution to keep the pipeline consistently busy.

Branch instructions, including conditional branches, indirect jumps, and function returns, occur frequently in typical code sequences. Without prediction, the processor must stall after fetching a branch instruction until its direction is resolved, resulting in pipeline flushes and significant performance degradation. For high-frequency and deeply pipelined architectures, such as RISC-V cores targeting a broad spectrum from embedded microcontrollers to high-performance computing, this latency can severely throttle instruction-level parallelism.

The impact of branch misprediction extends beyond wasted pipeline cycles; it affects power efficiency and complicates the control logic. Therefore, effective branch prediction is essential for achieving near-peak pipeline utilization. With larger pipelines and wider issue widths, the penalty for incorrect predictions grows, as the speculative window increases and more instructions must be discarded.

93

Branch predictors fundamentally comprise two key components: a mechanism to make a prediction prior to branch resolution and a means to update the prediction state based on actual outcomes. The design trade-offs revolve around prediction accuracy, latency, hardware complexity, and energy consumption.

Prediction accuracy is paramount. A high misprediction rate nullifies the benefit of speculative execution. To improve accuracy, designs exploit static heuristics, dynamic history-based methods, or combinations thereof. Latency constraints restrict predictor complexity since the prediction must be ready by the branch decode stage or earlier. High-complexity predictors potentially increase this timing delay.

Hardware complexity affects area and power budgets. Embedded RISC-V cores may prioritize lean, low-power predictors, whereas high-performance cores can afford larger, more intricate mechanisms. The update mechanism ensures the predictor adapts to changing branch behavior, often implemented via saturating counters or more elaborate finite-state machines.

Static branch prediction uses compile-time information or simple run-time heuristics. Examples include always-taken or always-not-taken assumptions, or predicting branch direction based on the sign of the branch condition. Although inexpensive, static methods suffer from low accuracy on complex branch behavior, rendering them insufficient for deeply pipelined RISC-V cores requiring high throughput.

Dynamic predictors leverage runtime branch history to forecast outcomes. The simplest dynamic predictor is a one-bit saturating counter per branch address that toggles prediction based on the last outcome. This model improves accuracy substantially but is prone to thrashing when behavior alternates rapidly (branch aliasing).

More robust dynamic predictors employ two-bit saturating coun-

94

ters, which only change prediction after two consecutive mispredictions, mitigating transient noise. These saturating counters are indexed by the lower bits of the program counter (PC) or branch instruction address, creating a Branch History Table (BHT).

Accuracy can be enhanced by considering the correlation between branch outcomes. Global history predictors maintain a record of recent branch results and use that vector as part of the indexing into the prediction table. This captures global path-dependent patterns that simple per-branch counters miss.

Local history predictors store the recent history specific to each branch, capturing patterns particular to it. Local predictors maintain a Pattern History Table (PHT) indexed by the local branch history, allowing detection of recurring patterns in branch direction sequences.

Hybrid predictors combine local and global histories with a meta-predictor that selects which component predictor to trust. This approach is common in higher-performance designs, improving accuracy by exploiting disparate branch behaviors.

Tournament predictors, exemplified by the Alpha 21264 architecture, arbitrate between local and global branch predictors. The meta-predictor uses a saturating counter to choose the better predictor for each branch dynamically. This mechanism increases prediction accuracy at the cost of additional hardware resources.

For RISC-V cores targeting high performance, the tournament predictor model can effectively address workload diversity. In contrast, embedded cores may implement simplified hybrid schemes focusing on local or global history alone to preserve area and power constraints.

To further enhance prediction accuracy, advanced techniques use longer histories and multiple indexing functions, such as perceptron-based predictors. The perceptron model applies a simple neural network to correlate history bits and predict the likelihood of a branch being taken. While more computationally intensive, perceptron predictors have shown significant accuracy improvements on difficult-to-predict branches. Their suitability in RISC-V implementations depends on pipeline timing and resource availability.

Return instructions pose a specific challenge for branch prediction because their target addresses are dynamic, dependent on the call stack rather than static fixed targets. A Return Address Stack (RAS) is a specialized predictor that maintains a hardware stack of the return addresses upon procedure calls. When a return instruction is encountered, the RAS provides the predicted return address, significantly reducing misprediction penalties for subroutine returns.

Indirect branches, such as jump tables or virtual function calls, typically have multiple potential targets, complicating prediction. Usually, an Indirect Branch Target Array (IBTA) or Branch Target Buffer (BTB) caches recent targets, indexed by branch PC and sometimes combined with history registers. Correct target prediction is essential to fetch the right instruction stream speculatively.

RISC-V processor cores vary widely in pipeline depth, issue width, and intended application domain. Branch predictor designs must carefully balance accuracy, cost, and latency according to the target complexity:

- **Simple RISC-V cores** (e.g., for microcontrollers): Typically adopt straightforward dynamic predictors, such as 2-bit saturating counters per branch with a small-sized BHT. These predictors, possibly combined with return address stacks, provide reasonable accuracy for embedded control flow patterns, maintaining low area and power consumption.

- **Mid-range cores** (e.g., general-purpose embedded or low-power processors): May implement local or global history-based predictors with moderate storage (several kilobytes),

96

enabling better capture of complex branch behavior with acceptable latency. Hybrid predictors or small tournament predictors are feasible, providing improved performance without excessive cost.

- **High-performance cores**: Deeply pipelined, wide-issue RISC-V CPUs benefit from advanced hybrid and tournament predictors with large history lengths, multiple interaction tables, perceptron predictors, and sophisticated meta-prediction logic. These designs integrate large BTBs, RAS, and complex indirect branch predictors to deliver near-optimal accuracy, preserving pipeline throughput in applications demanding high instruction-level parallelism.

Crucial to the practical deployment of branch prediction is the synchronized interaction with the pipeline's front end. A Branch Target Buffer (BTB) caches the target addresses of taken branches, allowing the instruction fetch stage to obtain the correct next PC without waiting for branch resolution.

The BTB is typically organized as a set-associative cache indexed by the PC bits of branch instructions, storing target addresses and prediction bits (or counters). Ensuring the BTB has sufficiently low latency to feed the fetch logic before instruction decode imposes tight timing constraints.

For conditional branches, the predictor determines the direction (taken/not taken), and if taken, the BTB provides the target. In the absence of a BTB hit, the next instruction address simply follows sequential execution. Efficient BTB design is essential for pipeline continuity and reducing bubbles.

Despite sophisticated branch prediction, mispredictions inevitably occur. Upon detection, the pipeline must be flushed of speculative instructions from the predicted (incorrect) path, and the fetch unit redirected to the correct address. This recovery process incurs a latency penalty proportional to the pipeline depth and impacts overall throughput.

Efficient recovery mechanisms prioritize rapid correction to minimize pipeline stalls. To facilitate this, modern processors implement precise exception architectures and mechanisms to track speculative state and reorder buffer contents until branch commitments are resolved.

Designers must carefully consider the following factors when implementing branch predictors in RISC-V processors:

- **Prediction Accuracy versus Complexity:** The marginal gain in accuracy from increasingly complex predictors must justify the area, power, and timing cost, tailored to the target domain.

- **Pipeline Latency Constraints:** Predictors must produce results in time for branch decode or fetch stages. Complex predictors may require multi-cycle computation or pipelined prediction.

- **Predictor Storage Size:** Larger history tables and saturation counters improve accuracy but consume silicon real estate.

- **Return and Indirect Branch Handling:** Specialized mechanisms like RAS and IBTA are essential for function calls and indirect branches.

- **Scalability Across RISC-V Core Profiles:** From embedded to high-performance implementations, predictor complexity and strategy must scale appropriately.

The continuous evolution of branch prediction techniques remains critical for unlocking the full performance potential of RISC-V pipeline architectures. Advances in prediction algorithms, hardware-friendly machine learning approaches, and co-design with compiler optimizations are promising avenues to further reduce branch penalties and enhance control flow speculation.

3.6. Memory Hierarchy Integration

Integration of the memory hierarchy components in RISC-V systems-comprising caches, memory controllers, and bus protocols-plays a pivotal role in balancing performance, complexity, and power consumption. Effective coordination among these components ensures high-bandwidth, low-latency access to data and instructions while preserving data consistency across multiple cores or threads. This section elucidates methods and architectural choices to achieve efficient memory integration, focusing on cache coherence protocols, prefetching strategies, and bus protocols tailored for RISC-V platforms.

Cache and Memory Controller Cohesion

A fundamental aspect of memory hierarchy integration is the symbiosis between on-chip cache hierarchies and external memory controllers. The memory controller interfaces with DRAM modules to manage the timing, scheduling, and command sequences necessary for efficient memory transactions. In RISC-V systems, scalable memory controller designs accommodate varying DRAM standards (e.g., DDR4, LPDDR) and emerging memory technologies (e.g., 3D-stacked DRAM, persistent memory), providing a configurable and extensible foundation.

Caches, arranged in multi-level hierarchies (L1, L2, and often L3 or last-level caches), rely on fast, predictable memory controller behavior to minimize stalls. Design choices include:

- **Cache Line Size and Alignment:** Proper alignment between cache line size and DRAM burst length optimizes bandwidth utilization. For instance, matching 64-byte cache lines with DRAM bursts reduces partial-line accesses, thereby enhancing data throughput.

- **Memory Controller Scheduling Algorithms:** Controllers often employ scheduling policies such as First Ready First Come First Served (FR-FCFS) to maximize row buffer hits. Optimizing scheduling reduces DRAM latency variability, benefitting cache refill times.

- **Write Buffer Management:** Write-back caches necessitate buffering and coalescing write data before committing to DRAM. Efficient write buffer algorithms in the memory controller reduce bus contention and improve write throughput.

Interfacing the cache controller with the memory controller requires well-defined protocols to manage cache misses, writebacks, and memory barrier operations, integral to coherent system operation.

Cache Coherence Techniques

In multicore RISC-V systems, maintaining data consistency among private and shared caches is critical. The integration of cache coherence protocols ensures that a read or write to a data item reflects the most up-to-date value, preventing stale or inconsistent views.

Two principal coherence protocol families are employed:

- **Directory-Based Protocols:** Scalable to large core counts, directory protocols maintain metadata that tracks sharing states and ownership of cache blocks. The directory resides in a centralized or distributed memory structure, storing per-block presence vectors and states such as Modified, Shared, or Invalid (MSI) or the enhanced MESI (Modified, Exclusive, Shared, Invalid) states.

- **Snooping Protocols:** Utilized mostly in small-scale or

tightly coupled multiprocessors, snooping protocols rely on broadcasting coherence transactions over a shared bus or ring interconnect to detect and react to cache line state changes.

For RISC-V systems, the TileLink protocol, an open-source coherence and interconnect specification designed for RISC-V, exemplifies a modern directory-based approach. TileLink supports various coherence operations-Acquire, Probe, Grant-allowing flexible and modular coherence enforcement.

The following algorithm outlines a simplified directory coherence mechanism employing MESI states:

Algorithm 1 Directory-Based MESI Coherence Handling

1: **On Read Miss (Core C_i):**
2: **if** block not in directory **then**
3:     Allocate directory entry with state Exclusive
4:     Issue read to memory controller
5:     Send data to C_i
6: **else**
7:     **if** block in Modified or Exclusive in another core **then**
8:         Send invalidation or downgrade request to owning core
9:         Owner writes back if modified
10:     **end if**
11:     Update directory sharing list to include C_i
12:     Send data to C_i, state Shared
13: **end if**
14: **On Write Miss (Core C_i):**
15: **if** block shared or owned by others **then**
16:     Send invalidations to sharers
17:     Directory marks C_i as exclusive owner
18:     Issue write request to memory controller if necessary
19: **else**
20:     Update directory state to Modified owned by C_i
21: **end if**

This model fosters minimal coherence traffic by invalidating or downgrading only when necessary, avoiding unnecessary stalls and optimizing system throughput.

Prefetching Mechanisms to Minimize Latency

Prefetching in memory hierarchies anticipates future data accesses by speculatively loading cache lines before explicit processor requests occur. This mechanism exploits access locality and predictable control flow in RISC-V applications to hide DRAM latency and reduce memory stall cycles.

Prefetching techniques can be broadly classified as:

- **Spatial Prefetching:** Based on the observation of spatial locality, this technique fetches subsequent cache lines adjacent to recently accessed ones. For instance, sequential and stride prefetchers predict linear or strided access patterns typical in loops.

- **Temporal or Context-Based Prefetching:** Using recorded access patterns and program counter history, more sophisticated algorithms (e.g., Markov-based or machine-learning enhanced prefetchers) predict the next set of addresses.

- **Load-Hint Prefetch Instructions:** RISC-V extensions provide PREFETCH* instructions allowing software-directed prefetching. Software or compiler can issue prefetch hints to preload data into L1 or L2 caches proactively.

Effective integration of prefetching requires coalescing with cache policies and memory controller scheduling. Prefetchers must balance aggressiveness and overhead: excessive prefetching can evict useful data and increase memory bus traffic, while conservative prefetching might underutilize available bandwidth.

Efficient Memory Access in RISC-V Bus Protocols

Bus protocols orchestrate communication among cores, caches, memory controllers, and peripheral devices. In RISC-V systems, the choice of bus architecture and protocol significantly impacts latency, scalability, and power.

Key characteristics and techniques include:

- **Non-Blocking Bus Systems:** Methods such as split-transaction buses allow overlapping of requests and responses, improving bus utilization in high-contention scenarios.

- **Hierarchical and Network-on-Chip (NoC) Intercon-nects:** As core counts increase, flat buses become bottle-necks. Hierarchical bus topologies and mesh or ring-based NoCs distribute traffic and support concurrent transactions with lower latency.

- **Transaction Ordering and Memory Consistency:** Protocols enforce ordering rules to comply with RISC-V memory consistency models (e.g., Release Consistency). Fence instructions synchronize memory operations, and bus protocol designs ensure correct serialization of reads, writes, and coherence messages.

Bus transaction formats in protocols like TileLink incorporate fields supporting atomic operations, cache state transitions, and QoS prioritization, enabling tightly coupled integration of cache and memory subsystems.

Example: Cache Refill and Coherence Interaction

When a cache miss occurs in a core's private L1 cache, integration among cache, memory controller, and coherence mechanisms pro-ceeds as follows:

- The cache controller issues a request to the coherence direc-tory via the bus protocol, specifying the miss address and de-sired state (e.g., shared for read, exclusive for write).

- The directory checks and updates the state of the requested cache line. If another core holds a conflicting copy in the modified state, it is requested to write back or invalidate its copy.

- Once coherence acknowledgments are received, the memory controller is engaged to fetch the block from DRAM if not cached elsewhere.

- The data block is transferred over the bus and inserted into the requesting cache with the proper coherence state.

This coordinated activity ensures consistency while optimizing latency and bandwidth. Notably, memory controllers capable of handling multiple outstanding requests concurrently reduce stalls and improve throughput. The bus protocol's support for out-of-order transaction completions further enhances pipeline utilization.

Summary of Design Considerations

The integration of memory hierarchy components in RISC-V systems demands careful consideration of multiple trade-offs:

- **Scalability vs Complexity:** Directory protocols scale better than snooping with core count but add overhead in directory storage and latency.

- **Prefetching Aggressiveness:** Overly aggressive prefetching can degrade effective cache capacity, while insufficient prefetching fails to hide long DRAM latencies.

- **Protocol Flexibility:** Open, modular protocols like TileLink allow evolutionary extensions in cache coherence and memory access semantics, supporting a broad class of RISC-V implementations.

- **Power Efficiency:** Bus protocols and memory controllers include low-power modes, dynamic clock gating, and reduced voltage operation to minimize power consumption in large-scale systems.

The evolving ecosystem of RISC-V encourages coherent integration frameworks that harmonize the open ISA philosophy with robust, high-performance memory subsystem designs.

Code Example: RISC-V Prefetch Hint Instruction

The RISC-V privileged architecture includes prefetch instructions to provide explicit hints to the hardware. An example assembly snippet illustrating sequential prefetching is shown below:

```
    la t0, array_start      # Load base address
    li t1, 8                # Number of cache lines to prefetch
prefetch_loop:
    prefetch.t0 (t0)        # Prefetch instruction to L1 cache
    addi t0, t0, 64         # Advance to next line (assuming 64
    bytes)
    addi t1, t1, -1
    bnez t1, prefetch_loop
```

This loop prefetches eight sequential cache lines starting at array_start. The compiler or software can insert such hints based on profiling or static analysis to improve data access latency.

```
Output:
(No direct output; prefetch instruction serves as a hint to hardware)
```

Prefetch instructions neither raise exceptions nor affect program correctness if ignored, allowing flexible hardware implementation. Their effective use requires coordinated timing relative to actual memory access patterns.

Overall, the integration of caches, memory controllers, and bus protocols within RISC-V systems forms a complex and nuanced domain, balancing performance gains with hardware complexity and energy considerations. Methodical design leveraging coherent protocols, intelligent prefetching, and efficient bus architectures builds a foundation for high-performance, scalable RISC-V memory subsystems.

3.7. Performance Monitoring and Microarchitectural Profiling

Performance monitoring and microarchitectural profiling constitute indispensable methodologies for observing, analyzing, and

106

optimizing the behavior of modern processors. These techniques leverage in-core hardware mechanisms designed to capture detailed run-time events at various granularities, providing critical insights that drive architectural refinement and software optimization. By harnessing such feedback, designers and developers can uncover performance bottlenecks, fine-tune resource utilization, and ultimately achieve higher efficiency and throughput in microarchitectural execution.

At the heart of performance monitoring lie hardware Performance Monitoring Units (PMUs) integrated within the processor core. PMUs facilitate event counting and sampling through a collection of programmable counters that track diverse microarchitectural signals. These signals range from basic instruction counts or clock cycles to elaborate events such as cache misses, branch mispredictions, pipeline stalls, instruction dispatch rates, and memory-level parallelism metrics. The availability of these counters is critical for both transient and sustained performance assessment, as they reveal how underlying architectural components behave under varying workloads.

Event counting provides aggregate statistics over specific intervals, often sufficient for coarse-grained analysis. However, sampling-based profiling extends this capability by periodically capturing program counter (PC) samples during event occurrences, enabling attribution of performance losses to specific instructions, code regions, or system components. This fine-grained correlation between hardware events and software execution paths facilitates the identification of instruction-level bottlenecks, such as inefficient branch prediction, frequent cache line evictions, resource contention, or pipeline hazards.

Microarchitectural profiling is not limited to counting or sampling; it also encompasses trace mechanisms that record the sequence of instruction retirements or micro-operations, accompanied by timing and dependency information. These traces enable reconstruction of execution dynamics, including instruction latencies, reorder buffer utilization, and pipeline occupancy. Capturing such detailed temporal information permits precise modeling of out-of-order execution behavior and memory subsystem interactions, instrumental for deep performance debugging and simulator validation.

A prevalent approach employs hierarchical event sets, grouped to reflect execution pipeline stages or functional units. For example, one group might track front-end events such as instruction fetches, decode rates, and branch prediction accuracy, while another monitors back-end execution parameters including execution port utilization, reorder buffer stalls, and load-store queue metrics. This structural grouping guides the analysis by segmenting the processor into logical regions, enabling targeted optimization efforts.

To interact with these monitoring features, architecture-specific programming interfaces expose control registers to configure event selection, sample frequency, and filtering criteria. For instance, Intel's Architectural Performance Monitoring provides Model Specific Registers (MSRs) which control up to several dozen event counters. Setting these MSRs involves specifying event identifiers (event codes), unit masks to refine event subtleties, and flags for edge detection or threshold triggering. The careful programming of these registers allows selective monitoring of high-value events, avoiding overwhelming volumes of data.

An illustrative command sequence for configuring and initiating an event counter on a typical architecture might include the following steps:

```
uint64_t event_select = 0x2E;   // Event code for Last-Level
    Cache (LLC) misses
uint64_t umask = 0x41;          // Unit mask for specific LLC
    miss types

// Configure Performance Event Select Register (PERF_EVT_SEL)
write_msr(PERF_EVT_SEL0, (umask << 8) | event_select | (1ULL <<
    16)); // enable counter
```

```
// Reset and start the performance counter
write_msr(PERF_CTR0, 0);
write_msr(PERF_GLOBAL_CTRL, 1);
```

Once enabled, counters accumulate data that can be read periodically or at program termination. Aggregated counts can identify, for example, whether cache miss rates exceed anticipated thresholds-indicative of spatial or temporal locality issues in code or architecture.

To manage the large volume of potential data and improve statistical relevance, sampling strategies employ event-based or time-based triggers. Event-based sampling activates a snapshot when a specified number of occurrences of a given event transpire, whereas time-based sampling collects data at fixed temporal intervals regardless of event counts. Event-based sampling is particularly effective for profiling rare but costly events, such as pipeline flushes, which might be diluted in uniform time sampling.

Advanced PMUs support filtering based on address ranges, privilege levels, or thread contexts, enabling selective profiling within complex heterogeneous environments. For multicore and simultaneous multithreading designs, such granularity enables isolating performance issues related to particular cores or logical processors, supporting fine-grained concurrency analysis.

Profiling data can be further enriched through hardware performance counters integrating with software profiling tools and runtime analysis frameworks. These tools decode sampled program counters into symbolic information, correlate hardware events with source code, and present visualizations such as heat maps or flame graphs. This tight hardware-software synergy accelerates the iterative process of diagnosing inefficiencies and validating optimization hypotheses.

The utility of in-core monitoring mechanisms extends to the evaluation of microarchitectural features such as speculative execution units, branch predictors, and execution ports. For example, counters that track branch target buffer hits or misprediction penalties elucidate the efficacy of branch prediction algorithms, while those measuring execution port conflicts reveal contention that reduces instruction-level parallelism. Feedback drawn from these monitoring events guides microarchitectural tuning-adjusting predictor sizes, cache associativity, or dispatcher widths-to balance complexity, power budgets, and performance gains.

Memory subsystem profiling benefits similarly from in-core mechanisms. Monitoring the interactions among cache hierarchies, translation lookaside buffers (TLBs), and memory controllers uncovers latency sources and bottlenecks. For instance, counters recording TLB misses or page walk cycles permit understanding of virtual memory translation impacts on pipeline throughput. Identifying memory stalls attributable to insufficient prefetching or bandwidth saturation inspires architectural or software prefetching strategies and memory system reconfiguration.

Moreover, microarchitectural profiling plays a vital role in validating and calibrating performance models and simulators. By comparing measured hardware event statistics against simulated predictions, discrepancies are highlighted that prompt revision of the architectural model or verification of underlying assumptions. This feedback loop is critical for designing next-generation processors and ensuring that simulation environments faithfully represent actual silicon behavior.

Energy and power considerations are increasingly incorporated into performance monitoring. On-chip energy counters alongside event counters enable correlation of power consumption metrics with specific microarchitectural activities. Profiling power-performance trade-offs informs power-aware scheduling and dynamic voltage/frequency scaling (DVFS) policies, vital for mobile and data center environments where energy efficiency is paramount.

In summary, in-core performance monitoring and microarchitectural profiling mechanisms provide a multifaceted view into processor behavior during runtime. Through event counting, sampling, tracing, and integration with software profiling tools, these mechanisms deliver granular and actionable feedback. This feedback forms the foundation for optimizing microarchitecture design, tuning software performance, enhancing power efficiency, and ultimately pushing the boundaries of computational throughput.

Chapter 4

Privilege Architecture and System Level Features

Dive into the bedrock of robust and secure system design: RISC-V's privilege architecture. This chapter reveals how carefully layered privileges and system-level mechanisms enforce trust and resource separation, establishing the platform for everything from secure multitenancy to responsive interrupt handling. With these concepts, you gain both control and insight into how RISC-V systems deliver resilience and flexibility across diverse deployment scenarios.

4.1. Privilege Levels and Protection Domains

The RISC-V architecture defines a rigorous privilege and protection model designed to support secure, efficient, and flexible system software. The core abstraction centers around

113

distinct privilege levels—Machine (M), Supervisor (S), User (U), and an optional Hypervisor (H) mode—which delineate execution contexts and enforce hierarchical access control over system resources. These privilege levels form the foundation for isolating resources, managing access rights, and maintaining security boundaries within RISC-V-based systems.

Machine Mode (M-mode)

Machine mode represents the highest privilege level in the RISC-V privilege architecture, having unrestricted access to all hardware and all privileged resources. At power-on, processors start execution in M-mode, making it the initial system context for firmware such as boot loaders or low-level supervisors. In this role, M-mode manages critical system initialization tasks, including configuring hardware units, enabling memory management units (MMUs), and setting up interrupt controllers.

The immutability and supremacy of M-mode enforce a strict security boundary; any misconfiguration or vulnerability here can compromise the entire system. Consequently, access to M-mode instructions and CSRs (Control and Status Registers) is strictly controlled, and transitions out of M-mode are designed to be deliberate and carefully managed by firmware or trusted execution environments.

Supervisor Mode (S-mode)

Supervisor mode is intended for operating system kernels and privileged system software. It provides a controlled environment with access to privileged resources but restricts certain operations that remain the exclusive domain of M-mode. S-mode supports a rich set of mechanisms for isolation, notably facilitating virtual memory with address translation and protection.

Central to S-mode is the management of protection domains

through page tables and permission bits, whereby user-space processes operate in a restricted environment enforced by the virtual memory system. The supervisor can configure address translation and memory protection policies, allocate hardware contexts, and handle exceptions raised by user-level programs. This separation enables reliable multitasking and resource sharing among multiple user applications.

From the perspective of the RISC-V privilege hierarchy, S-mode forms an intermediary trust level: it is trusted more than user-level applications but less than machine mode. The privilege architecture specifies instructions such as SRET (Supervisor Return) that allow safe transitions between S-mode and less privileged modes under controlled circumstances.

User Mode (U-mode)

User mode executes application-level code with the least privileges. Its capabilities are confined exclusively to a subset of instructions and registers, with no direct access to privileged resources or CSRs. The design intention is to protect the operating system and hardware from potentially malicious or faulty user programs by restricting memory access and disabling privileged instructions.

User mode relies on supervisor services, usually exposed through system calls and traps, to perform operations that affect system resources or require elevated privileges. The execution environment in U-mode is sandboxed by the protection domain constructed by S-mode, typically managed through virtual memory address spaces and hardware-enforced permissions. Exception delegation mechanisms forward certain faults or interrupts from U-mode to S-mode, enabling an operating system to mediate and respond securely.

Hypervisor Mode (H-mode, Optional)

An optional Hypervisor mode extends the privilege model to support virtualization. It mediates multiple supervisor-mode instances (guest operating systems) on a single hardware platform. H-mode can multiplex machine resources such as physical memory, I/O devices, and interrupt controllers, enabling each guest supervisor domain to operate in a virtualized environment with isolated and controlled access.

The hypervisor defines its own set of CSRs and controls otherwise privileged operations to enforce strong temporal and spatial isolation between guests. Techniques such as nested page tables (also known as second-level address translation) allow the hypervisor to implement fine-grained memory protection and management. H-mode interacts with both M-mode and S-mode in a controlled manner, often trapping and emulating privileged instructions issued by guest operating systems to maintain system integrity.

Transitioning Between Privilege Levels

Transitions between these privilege levels are orchestrated by explicit instructions and well-defined exception-handling mechanisms. The RISC-V architecture provides the MRET, SRET, and URET instructions to return from traps, each restoring the appropriate privilege level and program counter. Traps can be synchronous exceptions (e.g., illegal instructions, page faults) or asynchronous interrupts (e.g., timer-based, external devices), and their delegation is configurable to allow flexibility in system design.

Privilege-level transitions are carefully modeled to avoid privilege escalations. For example, attempts by U-mode code to perform privileged instructions generate exceptions and are intercepted by S-mode, which then validates and mediates the requested service. Similarly, the hypervisor, if present, manages trapping and emulation to prevent guest supervisors from performing unauthorized actions directly on hardware.

Protection Domains and Resource Isolation

Each privilege level corresponds to a protection domain, a conceptual boundary within which code operates with a defined set of access rights and capabilities. These domains are not merely hierarchical privilege tiers but comprehensive isolation mechanisms ensuring that faults or attacks in one domain cannot propagate unchecked to others.

Resource isolation is primarily enforced through hardware-enforced memory protection using the MMU and page-based virtual memory systems. S-mode configures page tables with permission bits (read, write, execute), user and supervisor access bits, and address translation mechanisms that rigorously restrict memory access in U-mode. M-mode maintains ultimate control but typically delegates memory management to S-mode during runtime.

Interrupt and exception handling also embody protection domain management. The delegation registers enable lower privilege modes to handle appropriate traps, with critical traps reserved for M-mode. Additionally, per-privilege-mode interrupt priority and masking mechanisms help contain interrupt handling within appropriate domains.

Security Implications of Privilege Levels

The RISC-V privilege architecture lays a foundation for robust system security by establishing clear boundaries and rigorous enforcement mechanisms. The strict separation between M-, S-, U-, and optional H-modes effectively isolates trusted system software from untrusted applications, mitigating attack surfaces.

Access control extends beyond memory protection to encompass control and status registers, I/O devices, and system configuration registers. The privilege levels define not only operational capabilities but also accountability, as fault and exception handling provide system software the means to detect and recover from erroneous or malicious behavior originating in lower privilege domains.

By leveraging the privilege modes, system designers can implement layered security models, such as trusted execution environments running in M-mode or H-mode, hardened OS kernels in S-mode, and sandboxed user applications in U-mode. The optional Hypervisor mode further enhances isolation in cloud and virtualization contexts, ensuring guest separation and hardware resource protection.

Privilege Level	Description and Capabilities
Machine (M)	Highest privilege level; full access to all hardware and CSRs. Responsible for system initialization, boot, and low-level control.
Supervisor (S)	Intermediate privilege, runs OS kernels or hypervisors; manages virtual memory, handles exceptions from lower levels, controls system resources.
User (U)	Lowest privilege; runs application code with limited access. Relies on traps and system calls for privileged operations.
Hypervisor (H)	Optional level between M and S, managing multiple supervisor instances; controls virtualization and enforces guest isolation.

The privilege and protection domain separation in RISC-V is intrinsic to its scalable, secure design. It enables the architecture to support everything from deeply embedded systems with a single privilege mode to complex virtualized environments with multiple nested privilege modes. The clarity and explicitness of privilege definitions in RISC-V reduce complexity and improve trustworthiness in system implementations.

118

4.2. Memory Translation and Protection Mechanisms

Memory management units (MMUs) employ translation and protection mechanisms to provide secure, efficient, and flexible utilization of system memory. At the core of these mechanisms lie paging systems, which facilitate virtual-to-physical address translation and enforce access permissions through hardware-assisted page table walks and protection schemes such as Physical Memory Protection (PMP). These elements work in tandem to ensure isolated execution environments, prevent unauthorized memory accesses, and enable dynamic memory allocation in multitasking systems.

Paging systems employ a hierarchy of page tables to translate virtual addresses (VAs) used by programs into physical addresses (PAs) required by memory hardware. The virtual address space is divided into fixed-size pages, typically 4 KiB or larger, while physical memory is similarly partitioned into page frames. This abstracted mapping enables processes to access isolated and contiguous virtual address regions without requiring contiguous physical memory, enhancing memory utilization and security.

A virtual address can be conceptually divided into two components: the *virtual page number* (VPN) and the *page offset*. The VPN indexes the page tables, whereas the offset identifies the specific byte within the page frame. Paging employs a multi-level page table structure to manage sparse address spaces effectively while minimizing the memory overhead of page tables themselves. Each level of the hierarchy contains entries pointing either to the next-level page table or directly to a physical page frame for leaf entries.

For example, a three-level page table system may partition the virtual address into three VPNs plus a page offset. The top-level page table (often called the page directory) references second-level page tables, which in turn reference third-level page tables or leaf page table entries (PTEs). This recursive pointer structure allows dynamic allocation and reclamation of page tables as processes allocate or deallocate memory.

Translation lookaside buffers (TLBs) serve as small, fast caches of recent virtual-to-physical translations to accelerate address translation operations. On a TLB miss, the hardware initiates a *page table walk* to resolve the virtual address. This process involves reading successive page tables from memory using the VPN components of the virtual address as indexes. The hardware performs these memory accesses automatically, without software intervention, to yield the physical address and access permissions from the leaf PTE.

The page table walk algorithm proceeds through each level as follows: starting from a base address held in a control register (e.g., satp in RISC-V systems), the hardware calculates the address of the relevant page table entry by combining the base with the VPN index and loads the PTE from memory. It verifies the validity of the entry by checking flag bits such as present, readable, writable, and executable permissions. If the entry is valid and points to a leaf page, the physical page frame number (PPN) is extracted, combined with the page offset from the original virtual address, and returned as the translated physical address.

At each level, the PTE must indicate a valid transition to the next level or to the leaf page. If an illegal or invalid PTE is encountered, a page fault exception is generated to transfer control to the operating system's page fault handler. This mechanism enables demand paging and swap-in operations, allowing programs to execute larger address spaces than physically available memory.

The hardware page table walker is typically pipelined and uses caching to reduce walk latency. Some processors support software-managed TLBs where the operating system handles page faults and updates TLBs explicitly; others incorporate hardware-managed TLBs for automatic page table walking.

Each page table entry encodes access rights and flags that enable fine-grained control over memory access. Typical flags include:

- Valid bit to indicate if the entry references a legitimate page or a subsequent page table.

- Readable, Writable, and Executable bits to specify permitted operations.

- User bit to distinguish user-mode and supervisor-mode access levels.

- Accessed and Dirty bits used by operating systems for page replacement decisions.

On each memory access, the MMU hardware checks these permissions against the current processor mode and access type (read, write, or execute). Violation of these constraints triggers protection faults to prevent illegal memory operations. For example, an execute-only page will fault on a read attempt, preserving instruction confidentiality. Similarly, kernel-mode-only pages prevent user-space programs from modifying kernel code or data.

This hardware-based access control mechanism provides a strong foundation for system security and process isolation. It ensures that malicious or errant programs cannot corrupt memory belonging to other processes or the operating system, forming the basis for enforcing privilege separation in multi-user or real-time systems.

Physical Memory Protection (PMP) complements virtual memory paging by providing hardware-enforced access control over physical memory regions. PMP is especially valuable in architectures and systems that operate without fully virtualized memory management units, such as embedded or real-time environments.

PMP divides physical memory into multiple regions, each described by a base address, size, and a set of access permissions-read, write, and execute. These regions are configured via dedicated machine-mode CSRs (Control and Status Registers) that allow defining protection domains. The hardware checks memory accesses against PMP rules before they reach the actual memory.

Each PMP entry specifies:

- The physical address range it covers; ranges are typically power-of-two sized and aligned.

- Permissions indicating allowed access types.

- Lock bits that prevent further modification once the PMP protections are set.

Upon access, the PMP logic sequentially checks the requested physical address against the PMP entries. If an address matches a PMP region, the access is authorized only if it satisfies the permission bits. Otherwise, an access fault exception is raised.

PMP supports several matching modes such as top-of-range (TOR), naturally aligned power-of-two (NAPOT), and exact matching, providing flexibility in defining memory protection boundaries. The fine granularity and direct mapping to physical addresses make PMP effective at sandboxing memory regions, protecting memory-mapped I/O, firmware sections, or sensitive data even in the absence of advanced virtual memory schemes.

Combining paging and PMP mechanisms results in a multi-layered memory protection framework. Paging abstracts memory organization and facilitates process isolation through virtual addressing, while PMP enforces hard limits on physical memory accessibility, preventing rogue or compromised privileged software from accessing or manipulating protected physical memory areas.

For example, in a system employing both, the page tables define access controls at the virtual address granularity, dictating what pages user or kernel-mode code can access. Meanwhile, PMP restricts the physical address ranges visible to those page frames, preventing the page tables from mapping physical memory outside permitted areas. This ensures even lower privilege layers cannot bypass protections by manipulating page tables or performing physical address indexing.

In virtualization or secure execution environments, PMP can isolate hypervisor or secure monitor memory from guest virtual machines, whose memory is managed through paging. Hardware-enforced PMP regions reduce the trusted computing base by restricting physical access explicitly, aiding in containment of faults and attacks.

Paging and PMP mechanisms introduce complexity and potential performance overheads due to multiple translation lookups and access permission checks. To mitigate these overheads, various optimizations are employed:

- **Translation Caches:** TLBs and page walker caches reduce page table walk frequency.

- **Large Pages:** Using larger page sizes minimizes page table levels and increases TLB coverage.

- **Software-Hardware Cooperation:** Operating systems and hypervisors manage page tables and configure PMP regions to minimize faults.

- **Speculative and Pipelined Page Walks:** Hardware accelerates page table walks through parallelism and prefetching.

- **Region Permissions Alignment:** Aligning PMP regions and page tables simplifies permission checks and reduces faults.

Careful design and tuning of paging and PMP configurations are essential in real-time and high-performance systems to balance protection guarantees with the lowest possible memory access latency.

A representative 64-bit page table entry (PTE) in a typical three-level paging system encodes physical page numbers, access permissions, and control bits. The format may be expressed as follows:

```
struct PTE {
    uint64_t valid      : 1;    // Entry is valid
    uint64_t readable   : 1;    // Read permission
    uint64_t writable   : 1;    // Write permission
    uint64_t executable : 1;    // Execute permission
    uint64_t user       : 1;    // User mode access allowed
    uint64_t accessed   : 1;    // Page accessed flag
    uint64_t dirty      : 1;    // Page written to
    uint64_t reserved   : 2;    // Reserved bits
    uint64_t ppn        : 44;   // Physical page number
    uint64_t reserved2  : 12;   // Reserved for software use
};
```

During a page walk, the CPU reads each PTE, validates permissions, and extracts the ppn to form the physical address by concatenating it with the page offset from the virtual address. The accessed and dirty bits are updated by the hardware on page use, assisting operating system page replacement policies.

The hardware enforces memory protection through a sequence of coordinated steps on every memory access:

1. The virtual address provided by the CPU is examined by the MMU.

2. The TLB is checked for a cached translation. On a miss, a page table walk initiates.

3. Each page table entry at successive levels is fetched and validated for correctness and permission.

4. On resolving the physical page frame address, PMP logic verifies that the physical access is permitted given the configured PMP entries.

5. If any validation or permission check fails, a page fault or access fault exception is triggered.

6. If all checks pass, the final physical address is computed, and the memory operation proceeds.

This tightly integrated mechanism provides strong isolation and controlled memory sharing, key properties for secure modern computing architectures.

4.3. Interrupt Handling and Exception Processing

The RISC-V privileged architecture defines a comprehensive mechanism for handling traps, which encompass interrupts and exceptions, ensuring system reliability and responsiveness. Trap handling requires precise management of privileged state transitions, efficient vectoring to appropriate service routines, and careful preservation of execution context. These mechanisms underpin the foundation of responsive, low-latency system control in the RISC-V architecture.

A *trap* is a synchronous or asynchronous event that diverts the processor from normal instruction flow to dedicated trap handler code. Traps include:

- **Exceptions**, which are synchronous events caused by instruction execution (e.g., illegal instruction, page fault).

- **Interrupts**, asynchronous events originating from external or internal sources (e.g., timer interrupts, I/O device requests).

Each trap is precisely identified by a *cause code*, which software examines in the mcause, scause, or ucause registers, depending on the current privilege mode. The cause code enables the operating system or runtime environment to distinguish among trap types and invoke appropriate handlers.

Trap handling induces transitions between privilege levels and modes in a strict protocol defined in the RISC-V privileged architecture specification. The usual privilege levels are:

- `M-mode` (Machine mode): highest privilege, mandatory on all RISC-V implementations.

- `S-mode` (Supervisor mode): privileges suitable for operating systems.

- `U-mode` (User mode): least privileged, for application code.

When a trap occurs, the processor transitions from the current execution mode to a designated *trap handler mode* (typically `M-mode` or `S-mode`):

- The `mstatus` (or `sstatus`) register records the privilege mode before the trap.

- The `mepc` (or `sepc`) register stores the program counter value at which the trap occurred.

- The `mcause` (or `scause`) register identifies the cause.

Restoration after trap handling involves returning to the saved execution point and privilege mode, via the `mret` or `sret` instructions.

The trap vector base address register (`mtvec` or `stvec`) controls the entry point for trap handlers. It can be configured in two modes:

- **Direct mode** — the processor jumps directly to the base address for all traps.

126

- **Vectored mode** — the processor jumps to an offset from the base address, indexed by cause code, supporting a trap vector table.

The privilege mode and state control registers enable fine-grained management of trap entry and exit, supporting nested traps and multi-level privilege models.

Vector tables provide structured and efficient redirection to trap handlers corresponding to specific trap causes. When mtvec (or stvec) is set to vectored mode, the effective handler address for a given trap is computed as

$$\text{HandlerAddress} = \text{BASE} + 4 \times \text{cause}$$

where BASE is the mtvec or stvec base address, and cause is the interrupt or exception cause number. The factor 4 corresponds to the 32-bit instruction word size, assuming each vector entry is a jump instruction or equivalent. This layout supports up to 256 distinct cause vectors, depending on the implementation.

Trap vector tables facilitate:

- Rapid dispatching to handlers without extensive cause decoding code.

- Leverage of position-independent handler code addresses.

- Low software overhead in identifying and responding to interrupts.

If multiple causes share a common handler, or if vectored mode is unsupported, direct mode can be used to dispatch all traps to a single entry point, which must then decode mcause explicitly.

Responsiveness and system stability critically rely on the preservation of CPU state across trap handling. The RISC-V privileged

127

architecture formalizes a minimal hardware-saved context, including the program counter, cause register, and status register snapshots. Additional context saving (such as general-purpose registers) is the responsibility of software trap handlers.

The recommended procedure involves:

1. On trap entry, the hardware saves pc to mepc and the cause to mcause.

2. The trap handler saves caller-save registers to a software-managed stack.

3. Handler-specific registers or state may be saved as needed.

4. Trap processing occurs.

5. Restore saved registers and state.

6. Execution resumes with mret or sret, restoring the saved pc and privilege mode.

Designing trap handlers with minimal latency requires efficient stack management and avoidance of unnecessary register spills.

RISC-V provides mechanisms to configure interrupt enable, pending, and priority via control and status registers (CSRs). The mie (machine interrupt enable), mip (machine interrupt pending), sie (supervisor interrupt enable), and sip (supervisor interrupt pending) registers enable software to selectively mask and acknowledge interrupts.

Interrupt prioritization is implementation-defined, leaving flexibility for platform-specific interrupt controllers (e.g., PLIC for RISC-V) to manage complex prioritization schemes externally. Delegation registers allow lower privilege levels to selectively receive certain interrupts, offloading handling from machine mode and supporting flexible privilege-based separation.

Achieving low-latency system reactions requires architectural and software approaches aligned with RISC-V's trap handling design:

- **Vectored interrupt handling** minimizes dispatch overhead by providing direct entry into cause-specific routines, absent explicit cause decoding.

- **Minimal software context saving** optimizes handler prologue and epilogue code, especially by leveraging register windows or selective saving based on interrupt source.

- **Prioritized interrupt masking** allows high-priority interrupts to preempt lower priority handlers, provided by external interrupt controllers working in conjunction with hardware CSRs.

- **Hardware-assisted tail-chaining** (platform-specific) permits consecutive interrupt servicing without full context restore-reload cycles.

- **Use of Fast Interrupt Requests (FIQ)** in vendor extensions may provide dedicated vectors and registers for critical interrupts.

Architects and OS designers can exploit the flexibility in `mtvec/stvec` configuration, CSR delegation, and interrupt controller integration to tailor interrupt responsiveness to system requirements.

Exceptions are synchronous events raised by the instruction execution pipeline due to illegal operations, memory access faults, or environment calls. The processor completes the current instruction sequence to a well-defined point, triggers trap handling, and precisely indicates the cause.

Key exception examples include:

- `Instruction address misaligned    or    Instruction access fault.`

- Illegal instruction.

- Breakpoint requests from debugging facilities.

- Load/store address misaligned or access fault.

- Environment call from U/S/M-mode, used to implement system calls and hypervisor calls.

Handling exceptions involves carefully unwinding pipeline state, saving the faulting PC, and preparing software to diagnose and recover or abort execution depending on the exception type.

The core CSRs relevant to trap management include:

- mtvec/stvec: trap vector base address and mode.

- mepc/sepc: program counter at trap.

- mcause/scause: trap cause code.

- mstatus/sstatus: privilege and interrupt enable bits.

- mip/mie/sip/sie: interrupt pending/enable bits.

- medeleg/mideleg: delegation of exceptions/interrupts to supervisor mode.

These CSRs provide the hardware-software interface controlling trap detection, prioritization, and handler dispatch, enabling flexible privilege separation and efficient trap processing.

The sequence of events when processing a trap in RISC-V is:

1. Trap occurs due to an exception or interrupt.

2. Hardware saves the faulting instruction's address to the epc register and trap cause to cause register.

130

3. Interrupt enable bits are cleared or set appropriately to disable further interrupts (based on mstatus or sstatus settings).

4. The program counter is set to the trap handler address, computed from the vector base and cause.

5. Trap handling software saves extended context as needed.

6. After service, the mret/sret instruction restores execution to the saved privilege mode and instruction address.

The design emphasizes precise control and scalability for multiple privilege levels, ensuring system security and responsiveness.

```
.section .text
.globl _start
_start:
    # Set mtvec to vectored mode, base address at trap_vector
    la t0, trap_vector
    li t1, 1                # MODE=1 for vectored mode, LS bits =
    1
    slli t1, t1, 0          # MODE occupies [1:0], shift to
    position (no shift here)
    or t0, t0, t1
    csrw mtvec, t0

    # Enable machine-level interrupts
    csrs mie, 0x888         # Enable timer, software, external
    interrupts
    csrs mstatus, 0x8       # Enable global interrupt enable (MIE)

    # Main loop
1:
    wfi                     # Wait for interrupt
    j 1b

    # Trap vector table (256 entries, here only first few)
    .align 2
trap_vector:
    j timer_interrupt       # Cause 7: Machine timer interrupt
    j external_interrupt    # Cause 11: Machine external interrupt
    j software_interrupt    # Cause 3: Machine software interrupt
    j default_handler       # Default handler for others

timer_interrupt:
    # Handle timer interrupt here ...
    mret
```

131

```
external_interrupt:
    # Handle external interrupt here ...
    mret

software_interrupt:
    # Handle software interrupt here ...
    mret

default_handler:
    # Handle unexpected traps
    mret
```

```
# Sample output during trap handling might include:
# Timer interrupt triggered at address 0x80400100
# External interrupt acknowledged from device 5
# Software interrupt for inter-processor communication
```

This structured approach exemplifies how low-level firmware or OS kernels leverage RISC-V privileged features for efficient, flexible, and responsive interrupt and exception management, forming the backbone of modern system control frameworks.

4.4. Supervisor Binary Interface (SBI) and Platform Software

The Supervisor Binary Interface (SBI) constitutes a fundamental abstraction layer within the RISC-V privileged architecture, providing a standardized interface that facilitates interaction between supervisor-level software, predominantly operating systems and hypervisors, and low-level platform firmware. The SBI's introduction addresses the critical challenge of platform heterogeneity and the consequent complexity in supervisor software portability by decoupling supervisor-mode software from platform-specific details. This separation simplifies operating system development and significantly accelerates ecosystem expansion.

At its core, the SBI offers a well-defined set of function calls, or service routines, that abstract hardware-specific operations such as inter-processor interrupts (IPI) management, timer configuration, console input/output, and power management. It resides below the supervisor mode and above the machine mode firmware, which is typically responsible for platform initialization and bringing the system into a state in which the supervisor environment can run. Unlike monolithic platform firmware implementations, the SBI encapsulates platform-dependent mechanisms behind a consistent Application Binary Interface (ABI), thus creating a contract upon which operating systems can rely.

The SBI interface defines two principal elements: a specification that formalizes the available supervisor calls and the application binary interface that ensures consistency in how these calls are invoked and their responses are returned. The specification itself is hardware-agnostic, enabling broad adoption across diverse RISC-V implementations, whereas the ABI dictates the register conventions, calling mechanisms, and error code semantics to ensure binary compatibility. For instance, supervisor software issues SBI calls via a special environment call (ecall) instruction in machine mode, with specific registers designated for passing function identifiers and parameters, and receiving return status and result values.

Among the primary SBI services mandated by the specification are:

- **Console I/O:** Providing mechanisms for character-based input and output via functions such as `sbi_console_putchar` and `sbi_console_getchar`, the SBI decouples console access logic from supervisor software, permitting uniform console drivers at the firmware level.

- **Inter-Processor Interrupts (IPI):** Functions like `sbi_send_ipi` enable one hardware thread (hart) to send interrupts to others. This facility is essential for synchronization and message passing in multi-core or multi-hart systems.

133

- **Timer Management:** Routines such as `sbi_set_timer` allow the supervisor environment to program timer interrupts with millisecond or nanosecond granularity, crucial for pre-emptive scheduling and timekeeping.

- **System Reset:** The `sbi_shutdown` function allows a controlled machine reset or shutdown, enabling supervisor software to initiate clean system halts or restarts.

The SBI's design adheres to extensibility principles by supporting additional platform custom extensions beyond the base services. These extensions enable specific implementations to expose vendor- or architecture-specific features while maintaining compatibility with supervisor software designed for the base SBI specification.

From an ecosystem perspective, the SBI significantly enhances portability. Operating systems and hypervisors need only target the SBI ABI rather than a multiplicity of platform-specific firmware interfaces. This uniform interface reduces fragmentation and development overhead, accelerates the adoption of RISC-V platforms, and fosters a more vibrant software community.

Tenant systems like Linux, FreeBSD, and other open-source operating systems leverage SBI for essential services. The SBI's abstraction allows these systems to run unmodified on a wide range of RISC-V platforms, with the guarantee that service invocations to platform firmware will function consistently. This decoupling mirrors the architectural philosophy observed in other well-established ISAs, such as ARM's Secure Monitor Call (SMC) interface, but with the open specification and modular design tailored for RISC-V's open-source ethos.

From an implementation standpoint, SBI firmware can be realized in several forms: as stand-alone machine-mode firmware, integrated within bootloaders, or embedded in system on chip (SoC) ROMs. Examples include OpenSBI, a widely adopted open-source

SBI implementation, which provides a rich set of platform drivers and extensible SBI services to support various RISC-V hardware families. OpenSBI also offers a reference framework for platform bring-up and debugging, further aiding platform vendors and OS developers.

The division between platform firmware and supervisor software facilitated by the SBI also permits innovation and evolution at either layer independently. Firmware can evolve to support new hardware features or optimizations without necessitating changes to the installed supervisor software, provided the SBI ABI is maintained. Conversely, operating systems can adopt enhancements rapidly, knowing that the underlying firmware services they utilize conform to the contractual interface.

The SBI's role in security and system integrity, while not directly encompassing security enforcement mechanisms, indirectly contributes by structuring the privilege separation and reducing attack surfaces. By constraining platform-specific operations behind a controlled interface, it minimizes error-prone direct hardware manipulations in higher software layers, thereby enabling more reliable and maintainable security models.

The Supervisor Binary Interface establishes a critical infrastructure component in the RISC-V ecosystem that promotes software portability, platform interoperability, and simplifies the complexity inherent in heterogeneous hardware environments. Its ascendancy reflects a strategic design decision to harmonize the diverse hardware implementations emerging within the RISC-V landscape and to support the sustainable growth of its system software ecosystem.

4.5. Debug Support and Hardware Trace

RISC-V architecture incorporates a comprehensive and extensible debug infrastructure designed to facilitate hardware bring-up, enable detailed software debugging, and support long-term maintainability of systems. Central to this capability is the RISC-V Debug Specification, which defines a standardized debug module interface encompassing mechanisms for controlling execution, inspecting registers, and accessing memory. This debug module integrates seamlessly with popular debug transport protocols such as JTAG, allowing interoperability with existing debugging tools and workflows.

The RISC-V Debug Module acts as a dedicated hardware block within a RISC-V implementation, typically residing between the system bus and the core's execution pipeline. It manages interaction with an external debug host, facilitating activities such as halting and resuming processor cores, single-stepping through instructions, and reading or writing core registers, including both general-purpose and control/status registers (CSRs). This access is achieved without disrupting normal system operation more than necessary, enabling hardware engineers and software developers to impose fine-grained control over the processor's execution state.

JTAG (Joint Test Action Group) serves as the conventional boundary-scan and debug transport interface, widely adopted across diverse processor architectures, and is fully supported within the RISC-V debug ecosystem. The debug module provides a JTAG TAP (Test Access Port) state machine that complies with the IEEE 1149.1 standard, enabling debug host communication via defined instructions and data registers. This standardization allows the reuse of mature, off-the-shelf JTAG host controllers and debuggers, thus lowering the barrier for entering the RISC-V debug environment.

Key registers within the debug module include the Abstract Commands registers, Debug Control and Status Register (DCSR), and Debug Halt Cause (DHCSR) registers. Abstract Commands provide a mechanism to issue high-level requests to the core, such as register read/write or memory access, abstracting away from the core pipeline's internal details. The DCSR holds the current debug status flags-halted state, stepping mode, and breakpoint hit indicators-which are critical for managing debug sessions and verifying breakpoint functionality.

One crucial feature is support for multiple hardware breakpoints and watchpoints. The debug specification delineates registers for configuring these breakpoints with flexible filtering capabilities, such as matching instruction addresses or data access addresses, and selectively triggering on load, store, or execute events. This hardware-assisted breakpoint support minimizes the need for intrusive software instrumentation, improving debugging accuracy and reducing performance impact during trace or analysis sessions.

The debug module also enables runtime visibility of the processor's internal state through a register file interface. This feature allows debuggers to extract and modify the values of integer registers, floating-point registers, and CSRs directly. Such transparent access is invaluable during both development and post-silicon validation, where observing core state changes without halting or with minimal intervention is often required.

In addition to basic debug control, RISC-V debug capabilities encompass hardware trace support, which is essential for post-mortem analysis, performance profiling, and real-time system observability in deeply embedded or safety-critical applications. Hardware trace records program flow and exception events with minimal processor overhead by streaming trace data off-chip or into on-chip buffers. While the specific trace implementation details may be vendor-dependent, the RISC-V debug architecture defines extensible interfaces to accommodate trace data outputs, such as configurable tracing buffers and triggers.

Hardware trace mechanisms are highly relevant during bring-up phases where intermittent faults or timing issues may not be reproducible via traditional debugging. Trace outputs can capture instruction sequences leading up to faults, providing insight into system behavior under complex real-world conditions. This is particularly critical for multi-core and multi-threaded processors, where concurrent execution can obscure bugs that surface only under specific timing or interaction constraints.

The integration of debug and trace components supports scalable monitoring schemes. For instance, in multicore systems, separate debug modules and trace generators may be employed per core, with an integrated aggregator facilitating centralized analysis. Furthermore, trigger logic can be programmed to initiate trace capture upon detecting specified conditions-such as entering a particular address range or observing designated CSR events-allowing for precise control over the volume and relevance of collected trace data.

From a maintainability perspective, the uniformity of the RISC-V debug module and its adherence to open standards are instrumental. The standardized debug interface ensures compatibility across different implementations and toolchains, simplifying the transition between silicon platforms and reducing the learning curve for new hardware designs. The openness of the specification encourages ecosystem development, promoting advanced debug and trace capabilities through vendor extensions and third-party tools that remain interoperable with the baseline specification.

Moreover, RISC-V's modular debug architecture supports future-proofing by permitting the addition of vendor-specific enhancements without breaking compatibility with standard debug operations. Debug modules can support extended commands or proprietary trace formats, enabling differentiation while preserving essential debug features accessible under the standard interface.

This flexibility fosters innovation in debug and trace solutions tailored to emerging use cases without fragmenting the debugging ecosystem.

The hardware debug support also interacts closely with software debugging tools and runtime environments. For example, debug-aware compilers and operating systems can leverage hardware breakpoints and watchpoints for improved performance monitoring, exception handling, and fault isolation. On the firmware level, lightweight exception vector instrumentation combined with hardware trace data empowers thorough post-fault diagnostics, facilitating root cause identification and shortening time-to-resolution in hardware validation and production testing.

To illustrate typical debug command usage, an external debug host might issue a sequence of abstract commands through the debug module to halt a core, read its integer register file to inspect variable states, and then step through instructions one at a time, all while monitoring the Debug Halt Cause register to detect breakpoint hits or exceptions. This process is encapsulated in the following conceptual command dialogue:

```
// Halt the processor core
write_debug_register(DCSR, HALT_BIT_SET);

// Read general-purpose register x10
write_abstract_cmd(READ_REG_CMD, REG_X10);
int reg_x10_value = read_abstract_data();

// Step one instruction
write_debug_register(DCSR, STEP_BIT_SET);

// Check halt cause
int halt_cause = read_debug_register(DHCSR);
```

Outputs from these interactions enable developers to correlate core state transitions with source code execution and verify hardware correctness under controlled execution conditions.

The RISC-V debug support and hardware trace capabilities are integral to efficient hardware bring-up and sustained maintain-

139

ability. They provide a standardized, extensible, and powerful interface for real-time inspection, control, and trace of processor operation. This infrastructure underpins robust development workflows, enabling detailed fault isolation, performance analysis, and system-level observability crucial to modern processor deployment.

4.6. Boot and Initialization Routines

The boot and initialization routines constitute the foundational procedures that bring a processor from a reset state to a fully operational environment, ready for complex software execution. At the core of these routines lies the imperative to ensure a secure and predictable environment, transitioning the machine through defined privilege levels while configuring critical architectural and platform-specific elements. These mechanisms emphasize a well-orchestrated startup protocol in machine mode, the highest privilege level, guaranteeing that the system's initial state supports robust operational security and consistency.

The initialization flow commences immediately following a power-on reset or system reset, where the processor enters machine mode (M-mode) at a defined reset vector address. This address is typically fixed in hardware but may be configurable via platform-dependent registers or settings. The instruction at this reset vector is the first to execute, and it is tasked with executing essential platform bring-up procedures. The firmware located at the reset vector is entrusted with establishing a minimalistic, stable execution context.

Critical registers such as the machine status register (mstatus), machine exception program counter (mepc), and machine cause register (mcause) are initially set by the hardware into a known default state to signify post-reset conditions. The mstatus register's fields related to interrupt enables and privilege modes are cleared

140

or set appropriately to prevent unforeseen exception handling or privilege escalation during the earliest cycles. This baseline configuration enables the firmware to incrementally elevate readiness without premature interruptions.

The boot firmware's first major task is the configuration of the physical memory protection (PMP) regions. PMP is crucial for protecting memory regions by defining access permissions for various privilege modes. Configuring PMP early ensures that subsequent privilege level transitions and executable code loads cannot inadvertently or maliciously access or alter sensitive memory regions. Typically, a boot routine programs PMP entries with granularity favoring aligned physically contiguous regions, restricting writable access to firmware code and critical data sections, locking these regions early to prevent post-configuration tampering.

Following PMP setup, the initialization code configures system timers and external interrupts. Timer registers control the system tick and other periodic interrupts essential for operating system schedulers or real-time task managers. External interrupts must be masked or configured to a known state, deferring handling until the software environment is prepared, thereby preserving deterministic startup behavior.

Privilege level transitions form an indispensable part of the boot process. While execution begins in machine mode, much of the system's software stack operates at lower privilege levels, such as supervisor (S-mode) or user (U-mode). Entering these modes securely mandates precise manipulation of the machine status and control registers. The control and status register mstatus contains delegation bits that determine which exceptions and interrupts are delegated from machine mode to supervisor mode. At startup, these delegation bits are typically cleared to maintain strict control within machine mode until the firmware has explicitly established trustworthy policies.

To facilitate transitions, the machine exception program counter

141

(mepc) register is set to the supervisor mode boot address once machine mode initialization is complete, and the instruction mret (machine-mode return from trap) is executed to effect the privilege environment change. This instruction restores the next program counter from mepc and updates the privilege mode from the mstatus register, allowing the processor to continue execution at the supervisor privilege level seamlessly.

The delegation mechanism ensures that exceptions and interrupts such as supervisor software interrupts, supervisor timer interrupts, and supervisor external interrupts are routed to the supervisor mode once delegation bits are set appropriately. This arrangement allows the runtime environment-typically a supervisor-level operating system kernel-to assume responsibility for system management, including memory protection via page tables and multitasking, without requiring continuous intervention from machine mode firmware.

Initialization of the memory management unit (MMU) also figures prominently within these routines. Given that many architectures support virtual memory, establishing the root page table and enabling address translation are essential steps. The root page table pointer is loaded into a control register (e.g., satp in RISC-V), and the translation mechanism is enabled by setting the appropriate bits in satp. This action modifies address translation behavior, mapping virtual addresses used by supervisor and user-level software to physical memory addresses.

Cache and bus coherence initialization is equally critical during the power-up phase. Hardware platforms often embed coherent caches and bus arbitration mechanisms. The firmware must issue cache flush or invalidate operations to ensure the caches start in a consistent state, avoiding stale or erroneous data visibility. Additionally, bus interfaces may require specific sequences to enable coherency protocols or synchronize clocks to the system fabric.

The secure transition to user mode (U-mode) ideally follows

142

after supervisor mode initialization, enabling reduced privilege software-for example, applications or user-space processes-to execute with minimal rights. This transition mirrors the approach from machine to supervisor mode but relies on the supervisor's control and status registers to manage privilege inversion securely. Supervisor mode software sets up the mstatus or equivalent register fields to specify user mode entry and places the program counter (sepc) to the user-level application entry point. Execution then resumes via the sret (supervisor return) instruction tracing a similar privilege demotion pattern.

Throughout all these transitions, the firmware maintains rigorous attention to exception handling and interrupt masking. Early in the boot sequence, all interrupts are usually masked to prevent asynchronous disruption. As each stage stabilizes, interrupts are selectively enabled and delegated following strict ordering protocols ensuring predictable system states. For example:

```
# Pseudocode for privilege delegation and interrupt enablement
clear all delegation bits in mideleg and sideleg registers
configure PMP to lock critical memory regions
enable supervisor interrupts in mie register
set mepc to supervisor entry address
execute mret to enter supervisor mode
```

These instructions symbolize the hardware control flow conditioning the transition from machine mode bootstrap routines to supervisor mode, embodying the principle of progressive privilege delegation guarded by precise hardware registers.

The deterministic nature of these sequences is paramount to secure systems. Improper or incomplete initialization can leave the system vulnerable to privilege escalation, memory corruption, or race conditions. Thus, many platforms utilize a combination of hardware-enforced security states, immutable read-only memory segments for initial firmware, and hardware timers that reset or halt the machine upon exceptional conditions during boot.

The boot and initialization routines underpin a carefully chore-

143

ographed sequence of activities starting from machine mode reset vector execution, through comprehensive configuration of memory protections, exception delegation, and system peripherals, culminating in well-defined and secure privilege level transitions. The result is a system state primed for predictable and secure operation under a layered software environment.

Chapter 5

Hardware Implementation Practices

From concept to silicon, this chapter unveils the practical steps and engineering wisdom that transform RISC-V designs into robust, manufacturable, and efficient hardware. Explore the best practices spanning RTL development, rapid prototyping, and SoC integration while mastering the art of balancing speed, power, and scalability. Whether building with FPGAs or for mass production, these insights are your gateway to state-of-the-art hardware realization.

5.1. RTL Development Methodologies

The design of digital hardware at the Register Transfer Level (RTL) entails the precise definition of data paths, control logic, and timing relations. This level of abstraction enables the synthesis of hardware from algorithmic descriptions, serving as a critical bridge between high-level architectural specifications and gate-level implementations. Proficiency in RTL development methodologies is indispensable for constructing intricate hardware systems such as RISC-V processors, where modularity, reuse, and verification rigor are paramount. Prominent languages and design approaches, namely Verilog, VHDL, and Chisel, offer distinct linguistic and methodological paradigms that profoundly influence design productivity, maintainability, and correctness guarantees.

Verilog: A Hardware Description Language Grounded in Procedural Abstraction

Verilog emerged in the mid-1980s as a hardware description language (HDL) emphasizing a syntax reminiscent of the C programming language, promoting a procedural style of hardware description. Its widespread adoption is largely attributable to its simplicity, extensive tooling ecosystem, and fine-grained control over hardware behavior. Verilog describes hardware components using constructs such as modules, with inputs, outputs, and internal registers defining the signal interface and state elements.

Modular design in Verilog is accomplished by hierarchical composition of modules, enabling encapsulation of functional blocks. Interface definitions rely on port declarations, and parameterization offers design flexibility through generics. However, earlier versions of Verilog lacked native support for certain abstraction mechanisms such as strong typing and concurrency safety, leading to increased reliance on coding discipline to ensure maintainability.

Code reuse in Verilog is facilitated through the use of parameterized modules and generate blocks, enabling replication of regular structures and configurable datapaths:

```
// Parameterized adder module
module adder #(parameter WIDTH = 32) (
    input  wire [WIDTH-1:0] a,
    input  wire [WIDTH-1:0] b,
```

```
    output wire [WIDTH-1:0] sum
);
    assign sum = a + b;
endmodule
```

Verification-first design practices hinge on the availability of simulation and testbench constructs. Verilog supports behavioral modeling and procedural testbenches using `initial` blocks and event-driven simulation semantics. Assertions and coverage metrics can be introduced using SystemVerilog extensions, broadening the verification capabilities. However, because verification was originally a secondary concern, adherence to robust verification methodologies such as constrained random testing and formal verification requires supplementary frameworks.

VHDL: Strong Typing and Rigorous Abstraction for High-Integrity Designs

VHDL, standardized by IEEE in the late 1980s, presents a strongly typed language influenced heavily by Ada. Its elaborate type system and concurrent execution semantics promote precision and rigor in hardware description. VHDL's verbosity nurtures clarity and fosters explicit intent, instrumental in safety-critical and high-reliability domains.

Entity-architecture pairs define the modular structure, with entities describing external interfaces and architectures encapsulating behavior and structure details. Generics provide parameterization mechanisms comparable to Verilog parameters but with stronger type constraints:

```
entity Adder is
    generic (WIDTH : integer := 32);
    port (
        a   : in  std_logic_vector(WIDTH-1 downto 0);
        b   : in  std_logic_vector(WIDTH-1 downto 0);
        sum : out std_logic_vector(WIDTH-1 downto 0)
    );
end entity Adder;

architecture Behavioral of Adder is
begin
```

147

```
    sum <= std_logic_vector(unsigned(a) + unsigned(b));
end Behavioral;
```

The strong typing system reduces common errors such as unintended width mismatches or signal misinterpretations. Furthermore, VHDL's support for package libraries encourages modular development and code reuse, supplying reusable data types, utility functions, and component declarations.

Verification methodologies in VHDL benefit from extensive assertion capabilities and the use of testbenches structured as separate design entities or processes executing in parallel. Design-for-Test (DfT) and formal verification strategies integrate tightly with VHDL, particularly in aerospace and defense sectors where proof of correctness is non-negotiable. Coverage-driven verification and constrained random stimulus generation are commonly facilitated by vendor-specific tools augmenting VHDL's base capabilities.

Chisel: Embedded Domain-Specific Language for Advanced Modular RTL Generation

Chisel (Constructing Hardware in a Scala Embedded Language) represents a paradigm shift from traditional HDLs by leveraging the expressive power of Scala as an embedded domain-specific language (DSL) for constructing RTL designs. Rooted in modern software engineering practices, Chisel facilitates the description of parameterizable hardware generators using object-oriented and functional programming abstractions.

Designs in Chisel are composed as hierarchical classes extending Module, encapsulating IO definitions and hardware construction logic within Scala methods. The use of generics, higher-order functions, and metaprogramming enables concise expression of complex parameterized hardware structures:

```
// Chisel 3 Adder module example
import chisel3._

class Adder(width: Int) extends Module {
  val io = IO(new Bundle {
```

148

```
val a   = Input(UInt(width.W))
val b   = Input(UInt(width.W))
val sum = Output(UInt(width.W))
})
io.sum := io.a + io.b
}
```

Modularity is deeply integrated into Chisel's construction philosophy. Reusable hardware generators can be composed flexibly, facilitating engineering of scalable data paths, complex control units, and parameter hierarchies. This composability is augmented by the full power of a high-level language, including advanced data structures, compile-time elaboration, and seamless integration of hardware and software co-design.

Code reuse extends beyond simple parameterization, enabling development of hardware libraries with rich APIs, supporting variant instantiation, and integration with external IP cores. Moreover, Chisel's output is synthesizable Verilog, harmonizing with established industry flows.

Verification is a primary concern in Chisel methodology. The inherent synergy with Scala allows the use of mature software testing frameworks such as ScalaTest and property-based testing libraries, facilitating the generation of comprehensive test vectors and coverage metrics. Chisel's ecosystem includes `chiseltest`, which enables cycle-accurate simulation and assertion-based verification within the Scala environment, fostering a verification-first workflow:

```
import chisel3._
import chiseltest._
import org.scalatest.flatspec.AnyFlatSpec

class AdderTest extends AnyFlatSpec with ChiselScalatestTester {
  "Adder" should "correctly add inputs" in {
    test(new Adder(8)) { c =>
      c.io.a.poke(10.U)
      c.io.b.poke(20.U)
      c.clock.step()
      c.io.sum.expect(30.U)
    }
  }
}
```

```
}
```

This integrated approach enables tight feedback loops between design and verification, reducing error-prone manual testbench coding and improving confidence in functional correctness.

Comparative Perspectives and Suitability for RISC-V RTL Development

RISC-V, as a flexible open instruction set architecture (ISA), demands RTL implementations that are modular, extensible, and verified to high standards. Each of the surveyed methodologies offers unique advantages:

- **Verilog** remains a foundational choice due to its ubiquity and straightforward mapping to hardware synthesis tools. Its procedural style supports fine control over timing and logic, yet it poses challenges regarding maintainability and complex reuse unless disciplined by coding guidelines and augmented with SystemVerilog features.

- **VHDL** is well suited for high-integrity designs that require formal validation processes and strict typing. Its verbosity and rigor promote safer, highly maintainable codebases, making it often preferred in environments where verification completeness is critical. However, its verbosity can increase development time.

- **Chisel** introduces a modern approach that marries hardware design with software engineering paradigms. Its advanced abstraction mechanisms and embedded DSL nature accelerate scalable, reusable design creation. The seamless integration with software testing frameworks elevates verification-first workflows and continuous integration practices, vital for evolving RISC-V cores that may undergo frequent extensions.

The choice among these methodologies depends on project scope, verification objectives, integration with tooling infrastructure, and team expertise. Contemporary best practices for RISC-V hardware increasingly favor verification-centric methodologies emphasizing modularity and automated validation. Chisel's ecosystem and functional style align strongly with these objectives, particularly in academic and open source communities. Conversely, mature industrial projects often continue to leverage the stability and predictability of Verilog/SystemVerilog or VHDL augmented with rigorous testbench frameworks.

Essential Methodological Themes Across RTL Languages

Despite linguistic differences, several methodological themes are prevalent across RTL development:

- **Modular Design:** Separation of concerns is realized by hierarchically decomposing the hardware into logically coherent modules or entities, facilitating independent development, debugging, and later reuse. Clear interface definitions and encapsulation prevent unintended signal dependencies and improve code clarity.

- **Code Reuse:** Parameterization, generation constructs, and libraries enable scalable design reuse. Repurposing well-verified modules and generators accelerates time-to-market while reducing defect rates. This approach supports the exploration of various design points with minimal code duplication.

- **Verification-First Development:** Embedding verification considerations from the outset-through assertion constructs, testbenches, and formal properties-ensures that design intent is continually validated against specification. Automated testing frameworks and coverage-driven verification illuminate corner cases and promote design robustness.

- **Toolchain Compatibility:** Effective RTL methodologies

recognize the imperative to integrate cleanly with synthesis, place-and-route, and verification tools. Standardized language subsets and adherence to coding conventions maximize portability and exploit vendor-specific optimizations.

- **Documentation and Maintainability:** Clear code structuring, comprehensive comments, and adherence to coding standards underpin maintainable RTL codebases that can accommodate future architectural enhancements, a common necessity for RISC-V cores and extensions.

Mastery of Verilog, VHDL, and Chisel requires more than syntactic fluency; it demands rigorous application of modularity, systematic reuse, and verification principles to produce RISC-V RTL implementations of the highest quality. Careful attention to these dimensions underpins the design of flexible, reliable, and scalable microarchitectures that fulfill the promise of the open RISC-V ecosystem.

5.2. FPGA-based Prototyping

Field-Programmable Gate Arrays (FPGAs) have emerged as a pivotal technology for prototyping RISC-V designs, offering a unique blend of hardware flexibility and rapid iteration capability. By leveraging FPGA platforms, designers can bridge the gap between architectural exploration and silicon realization, enabling early hardware/software co-verification and functional validation under real operational conditions.

The prototyping workflow for RISC-V cores on FPGAs generally unfolds across several core phases: design translation, synthesis and implementation, hardware/software integration, and validation. Initially, the Register-Transfer Level (RTL) description of the RISC-V core, often developed in hardware description languages such as Verilog or VHDL, undergoes transformation targeted to the FPGA fabric. This process incorporates technology mapping, placement, routing, and timing closure, all orchestrated by vendor-specific FPGA toolchains. Unlike final ASIC implementation flows, FPGA synthesis optimizes for reprogrammability and timing within the constraints of on-chip resources rather than transistor-level optimizations.

A key advantage of FPGA-based prototyping lies in its facilitation of iterative development cycles. The short feedback loop afforded by FPGA reconfiguration allows designers to incorporate architectural changes rapidly, exercising corner cases and exploring microarchitectural trade-offs without the overhead or expense of tape-outs. Modern FPGA toolflows support partial reconfiguration and incremental synthesis, further expediting these iterations by limiting recompilation to modified design regions. Consequently, performance bottlenecks and functional anomalies can be identified and mitigated early in the design life cycle.

Integration of software with the RISC-V hardware prototype is fundamental to validating architectural correctness and performance characteristics. Early software porting, including boot loaders, operating systems, and application code, can be executed directly on the FPGA-implemented core. This real hardware/software interaction exposes subtle issues related to timing, interrupts, bus architectures, memory systems, and peripheral interfaces that are often challenging to detect in simulation-only environments. To facilitate this integration, comprehensive FPGA prototyping platforms typically provide FPGA shells embedding memory controllers, debug logic, and interfaces for JTAG or UART connections, enabling seamless deployment and monitoring of executable software binaries.

Debugging and verification during FPGA prototyping encompass both functional correctness and performance metrics. Embedded logic analyzers and IP cores, such as Integrated Logic Analyzers (ILAs), enable the capture of internal signals and state transi-

153

tions at runtime with minimal intrusion. These hardware-based probes are crucial for capturing transient behaviors and concurrency issues that escape conventional simulation. Coupling hardware probes with software debug features—for example, on-chip breakpoints, performance counters, and trace buffers—provides a comprehensive visibility matrix for complex system validation.

Toolchains tailored for RISC-V FPGA prototyping have evolved to cover a full ecosystem, from RTL generation with parameterized hardware generators to software development and profiling environments. Popular open-source frameworks like Rocket Chip and BOOM provide parameterizable RISC-V cores designed for FPGA implementation, accompanied by robust Makefile-driven build systems and integration with FPGA vendor tools. Commercial toolchains augment these with high-level synthesis capabilities and automated testbench generation, thereby reducing manual intervention and minimizing iteration time further.

Beyond pure hardware/software verification, FPGA prototypes act as platforms for system-level performance characterization and architectural exploration. Designers can evaluate the impact of cache hierarchies, branch predictors, pipeline depths, and custom instruction extensions on overall system throughput and latency in scenarios that closely mimic target deployment conditions. As the RISC-V ecosystem embraces customizability, FPGA prototyping serves as an ideal medium to test application-specific extensions and accelerators, refining the instruction set and microarchitecture before committing to silicon.

Furthermore, FPGA prototyping supports validation of peripheral integration and system-on-chip (SoC) interfaces. Complex SoC designs incorporating RISC-V cores often integrate diverse IP blocks such as memory controllers, DMA engines, communication peripherals, and custom accelerators. The FPGA platform accommodates these heterogeneous components, enabling designers to test interconnect protocols (AXI, TileLink), interrupt handling, and power management schemes in a cohesive environment. Functional verification of these interactions on FPGA hardware substantially reduces risks of integration failures and shortens overall time-to-market.

Reliability assessment and fault injection experiments form another dimension of FPGA-based prototyping. By introducing controlled transient errors or simulating hardware faults at the FPGA logic level, designers can observe system resilience and validate error detection and correction mechanisms embedded within the RISC-V core or attached subsystems. These fault injection capabilities are integral to developing robust designs intended for safety-critical or mission-critical applications, where functional correctness under error conditions is paramount.

The physical constraints and architecture of FPGAs impose certain limitations on RISC-V prototyping, which must be managed carefully. FPGA fabric resources such as lookup tables (LUTs), block RAMs, and digital signal processing (DSP) slices define the upper bounds on design complexity and clock frequency. Designers often face a trade-off between the granularity of architectural details (e.g., number of pipeline stages, cache sizes) and achievable clock rates. Timing closure in FPGAs can be challenging, especially for deeply pipelined designs, necessitating careful floorplanning and retiming optimizations. Consequently, prototyping results must be interpreted with awareness of these factors, especially when extrapolating performance characteristics towards final ASIC implementations.

To streamline and scale FPGA prototyping efforts, automation has become an essential component of workflows. Scripted build systems integrate RTL compilation, constraint generation, and FPGA bitstream creation, enabling continuous integration pipelines that automatically synthesize updated designs, deploy them on development boards, and execute regression tests. When combined with hardware-in-the-loop testing setups, these automated flows accelerate verification cycles and improve confidence in design robustness.

Recent advancements in FPGA hardware platforms have additionally expanded prototyping capabilities. High-bandwidth memory (HBM)-enabled FPGAs, hard processor cores embedded within FPGA fabrics, and advanced high-speed I/O interfaces enhance the fidelity and performance of RISC-V prototypes. For instance, using HBM provides realistic memory subsystem testing, while embedded hard cores offer a reference platform for co-simulation of software stacks. These technological developments further narrow the fidelity gap between FPGA prototypes and final silicon, improving the effectiveness of early system evaluations.

FPGA-based prototyping constitutes an indispensable methodology for the development and verification of RISC-V designs. By providing a platform for iterative refinement, early hardware/software integration, and functional validation in realistic environments, it facilitates rapid innovation and mitigates downstream risks. The interplay of comprehensive workflows, advanced toolchains, hardware debug infrastructure, and emerging FPGA architectures continues to push the envelope in prototyping fidelity, thereby accelerating the journey from architectural concept to silicon implementation.

5.3. SoC Integration

Integrating RISC-V cores into complete Systems-on-Chip (SoCs) entails reconciling diverse elements—cores, interconnects, peripherals, and memory subsystems—into a cohesive, high-performance architecture. The modular and extensible nature of RISC-V defines unique opportunities and challenges at each stage, requiring careful design of the interconnect fabric, memory mapping schemes, and system-level architectural patterns that accommodate scalability and versatility.

Interconnect Architectures

At the heart of SoC integration lies the on-chip interconnect, an essential substrate that bridges processor cores with memories, peripherals, accelerators, and input/output interfaces. Selecting an appropriate interconnect topology and protocol is pivotal for balancing latency, throughput, scalability, and implementation complexity. Common interconnect structures suitable for RISC-V SoCs range from simple bus-based topologies to sophisticated network-on-chip (NoC) solutions.

Bus-based interconnects, such as AMBA AHB or APB, provide straightforward integration with well-established verification flows but typically exhibit limited scalability and result in contention under high concurrency. Conversely, advanced crossbar switches increase parallelism by allowing multiple simultaneous transactions but consume greater area and power. To overcome these constraints in larger SoCs, mesh-based or hierarchical NoCs are increasingly employed, offering scalable bandwidth distribution, localized traffic routing, and enhanced fault tolerance.

For RISC-V systems, open and configurable interconnect standards have emerged. The TileLink protocol, developed within the RISC-V ecosystem, is a modular coherent interconnect designed to support cache-coherent shared memory systems. TileLink permits decoupled request/response channels, supports multiple outstanding transactions, and enables diverse memory models, which are critical in multi-core and heterogeneous SoCs. Its integration facilitates streamlined interoperability between RISC-V cores, cache subsystems, and accelerators, fostering both performance optimization and system programmability.

Peripheral Integration and Adaptation

Integrating peripherals into a RISC-V SoC environment necessitates careful consideration of their interfaces, addressability, and

157

synchronization with the processor cores. Legacy and third-party IP blocks often arrive with disparate bus protocols and timing requirements. The SoC designer must employ bridging components that translate between these protocols—e.g., from TileLink to AXI or APB—effectively adapting varied peripherals without performance bottlenecks.

Moreover, clock domain crossing is a frequent challenge since peripherals typically operate at different frequencies than cores or memory subsystems. Clock domain crossing FIFOs and synchronous boundary wrappers must be inserted judiciously to maintain data integrity and avoid metastability. Power domain considerations also arise in integration, especially in power-sensitive embedded implementations, requiring integrated power management units (PMUs) that orchestrate clock gating, voltage scaling, and dynamic reconfiguration of peripherals.

The modular register-mapped I/O paradigm is prevalent for peripheral integration with RISC-V cores, facilitating standardization through Control and Status Registers (CSRs) exposed in predictable memory address spaces. This approach supports uniform software drivers and simplifies interrupt aggregation—critical when multiple heterogeneous peripherals coexist.

Memory Mapping and Address Translation

Memory organization within integrated RISC-V SoCs follows fundamental principles of address mapping and protection, but must contend with diverse memory types and the increasing complexity of heterogeneous components. Physical memory segments typically include on-chip SRAM, non-volatile memory, external DRAM, and memory-mapped peripherals. The manner in which these regions are mapped into the processor's address space directly influences performance and security.

A flat addressing scheme affords simplicity, but it becomes impractical as SoC complexity grows. Partitioning the physical address space into multiple regions with defined base addresses and size allocations improves modularity. Interconnect protocols like TileLink efficiently route requests based on address decoding, enabling scalable system growth without intrusive core modifications.

In multi-processor or accelerator-inclusive SoCs, memory management units (MMUs) or memory protection units (MPUs) play a crucial role by translating virtual addresses to physical addresses and enforcing access permissions. RISC-V's architecture supports configurable MMUs compliant with the Sv32, Sv39, and Sv48 virtual memory schemes, facilitating sophisticated operating system support and memory protection. The design of Translation Lookaside Buffers (TLBs) and page walkers must be optimized for latency and area, given the diverse workloads in heterogeneous systems.

Peripheral address spaces are commonly mapped to one or multiple distinct regions, sometimes resulting in sparse memory maps. To alleviate software complexity, Peripheral Component Interconnects (PCI) or System Address Translation Units (SATU) can translate addresses or implement windowing mechanisms, easing integration of external buses or dynamically reconfigurable components.

Architectural Patterns for Scalability and Versatility

Designing scalable and versatile platforms with RISC-V cores requires adopting architectural patterns that enable modularity, reuse, and incremental system expansion. The tile based architectural pattern is exemplary in this context, where each tile consists of a processor core, local memory, and peripheral interfaces, connected via a parameterizable interconnect mesh. Such an approach endorses extensibility by replicating and customizing tiles to meet varying performance and functionality requirements.

159

Hierarchical interconnects complement tile architectures by grouping cores and accelerators into clusters or subsystems, each with localized coherence domains. This hierarchy reduces global communication overhead and simplifies memory consistency management. Moreover, hierarchical clock and power domains in conjunction with subsystem-level reset controllers permit fine-grained control over power-performance tradeoffs.

To support heterogeneous integration, RISC-V SoCs increasingly incorporate accelerators tailored for workloads such as machine learning, cryptographic functions, or signal processing. Architectural patterns that promote accelerator sharing and seamless interfacing with cores employ dedicated interconnect endpoints and standard hardware interfaces, often implemented as AXI4-Stream or TileLink accelerator ports. Synchronization primitives such as doorbell registers or interrupt lines enable efficient host-accelerator coordination.

Firmware and bootloader architectures leverage the memory map and architectural patterns to initialize system components systematically, stage runtime reconfiguration, and support debug infrastructure. Debug subsystems incorporate JTAG or RISC-V Debug Module interfaces connected through the interconnect, enabling breakpoints, core halting, and trace capture without intrusive modifications.

Synchronization, Coherence, and Consistency

In multi-core RISC-V SoCs, maintaining coherence and synchronization among caches and shared resources is indispensable. TileLink supports cache coherence protocols such as MESI or MOESI variants, ensuring data consistency across private L1 caches and shared L2 caches or memory. The interconnect fabric enforces ordering constraints and atomic operations, essential for enabling multi-threaded software and operating systems.

Atomic memory operations extend from core ISA support to interconnect transactions, facilitating critical section management and lock-free data structures at runtime. The coherence protocol's complexity scales with the number of cores and cache hierarchy depth, necessitating rigorous verification techniques to avoid deadlocks, livelocks, and performance bottlenecks.

Consistent global memory views are ensured through memory fences and ordering semantics embedded in the RISC-V ISA, which the interconnect must preserve. Configurable memory consistency models permit system designers to tailor trade-offs between performance and programmability, especially when integrating accelerators that may not enforce strict ordering.

Verification and Validation Considerations

Given the increasing architectural complexity of RISC-V SoCs, verifying the correctness of core integration mechanisms, interconnect protocols, and peripheral functionality is paramount. Employing transaction-level modeling and assertion-based verification techniques enables early detection of protocol violations. Formal methods applied to coherence and memory ordering properties provide strong guarantees of system stability.

Integration validation often utilizes scalable verification frameworks with testbench modularity, supporting scenarios ranging from basic memory read/write operations to stress testing concurrent access patterns and peripheral interrupt handling. Observability features embedded in the SoC, such as trace buffers and performance counters, provide valuable feedback during silicon bring-up and software development.

Summary of Best Practices for RISC-V SoC Integration

The successful integration of RISC-V cores into SoCs depends on adopting open, extensible protocols like TileLink for coherent interconnects, employing modular peripheral interfaces with well-defined memory mapping, and applying hierarchical architectural

161

patterns to balance scalability and complexity. Attention to synchronization, memory consistency, and power management augments system versatility. Systems that implement these principles create robust platforms capable of evolving with emerging workloads and heterogeneous computing demands.

5.4. Clocking, Reset, and Power Domains

The complexity of modern digital designs necessitates a meticulous approach to managing timing, power, and system initialization to ensure reliable and efficient operation. Robust handling of clocking, reset, and power domains is fundamental for maintaining signal integrity, meeting timing requirements, and minimizing power consumption across diverse operational conditions. This section delves into key strategies for addressing clock domain crossing, reset synchronization, and power domain partitioning, which collectively establish a framework for dependable system behavior.

Clock Domain Crossing Strategies

Multiple clock domains arise in complex systems to accommodate varying performance, power, or interface requirements. Signals transferred between these domains must traverse clock domain crossings (CDCs), where source and destination clocks may differ in frequency, phase, or jitter. To prevent metastability, data corruption, and timing violations, careful synchronization techniques are indispensable.

Two primary classes of CDC problems exist: asynchronous CDC, where source and destination clocks are asynchronous and unrelated, and synchronous CDC, where clocks share a defined relationship (e.g., multiples or known phase shifts). The selection of crossing techniques hinges on this characterization.

A fundamental approach to minimize metastability involves synchronizer flip-flops at the receiving domain. For single-bit control signals, a standard two-stage synchronizer chain suffices:

```
reg sync_stage1, sync_stage2;
always @(posedge dst_clk or posedge reset) begin
    if (reset) begin
        sync_stage1 <= 1'b0;
        sync_stage2 <= 1'b0;
    end else begin
        sync_stage1 <= async_signal;
        sync_stage2 <= sync_stage1;
    end
end
synchronized_signal = sync_stage2;
```

This double-register pipeline reduces the probability of metastability to negligible levels within practical mean-time-between-failure (MTBF) metrics by allowing the first flip-flop output to settle before driving downstream logic.

For data buses crossing between asynchronous domains, handshake or FIFO-based methods are preferred. FIFO buffers operate across dual-clock ports, decoupling timing constraints and safely buffering multi-bit data. Control signals such as read and write pointers must be carefully gray-coded or encoded to avoid metastability in pointer comparisons. For instance, a dual-clock FIFO commonly employs gray-coded pointers with synchronizers on pointer signals crossing clock domains:

$$\mathrm{Gray}(n) = n \oplus \left\lfloor \frac{n}{2} \right\rfloor$$

where $\oplus$ denotes bitwise XOR.

Handshake protocols, such as request-acknowledge signals, provide controlled data transfer but often incur latency and complexity. Nonetheless, they can be beneficial for sporadic transfers or when strict ordering and acknowledgement are required.

For synchronous CDCs, data transfer often exploits the clock relationship. For example, in clock frequencies related by integer ratios, multi-cycle paths or clock gating can facilitate safe transfers

163

with designed timing margins.

Timing analysis must verify metastability escape times and ensure setup and hold times across synchronized boundaries. Formal CDC verification tools and static timing analysis techniques are valuable in identifying improper crossings or missing synchronizers, which are common sources of functional bugs.

Reset Synchronization and Distribution

Reset signals initialize system state machines, register contents, and ensure predictable start-up behavior. Despite appearing trivial, reset management across multiple clock and power domains is a complex task essential to guarantee design correctness.

Resets can be classified as asynchronous or synchronous. Asynchronous resets assert immediately, independent of the clock, forcing registers to predefined states. While ensuring fast and reliable initialization, asynchronous resets require careful deassertion synchronization to prevent metastability upon release. Conversely, synchronous resets deassert in synchrony with the clock, inherently avoiding release metastability but potentially complicating reset assertion timing and limiting scope in certain error recovery scenarios.

When asynchronous resets are employed, each clock domain must synchronize the reset deassertion using synchronizers akin to those described for CDC signals. Unsynchronized release can induce partial or inconsistent initialization, risking undefined system states.

Consider the following reset synchronizer example for reset deassertion in a given clock domain:

```
reg reset_sync_1, reset_sync_2;
always @(posedge clk or posedge async_reset) begin
    if (async_reset) begin
        reset_sync_1 <= 1'b1;
        reset_sync_2 <= 1'b1;
    end else begin
        reset_sync_1 <= 1'b0;
```

```
          reset_sync_2 <= reset_sync_1;
     end
end
synchronized_reset = reset_sync_2;
```

Here, the asynchronous reset is forced high on assertion and synchronized for a clean deassertion aligned to the clock.

Proper reset distribution must ensure minimal skew and balanced loading. In highly pipelined or complex clock trees, reset trees are designed analogous to clock trees, sometimes employing dedicated reset buffers or logic with controlled slew rates to mitigate simultaneous switching noise (SSN).

Complex systems often have multiple reset domains, distinct from clock domains, necessitating gating and hierarchical reset strategies. For instance, peripheral modules may have local resets for partial system re-initialization without disturbing global operation.

Reset sequencing plays a critical role when multiple resets interact. Reset controllers with programmable state machines orchestrate assert and release order along with delays, ensuring dependent blocks become operational in the correct sequence. This approach is vital in scenarios involving calibration sequences, memory initialization, or power domain bring-up.

Power Domain Partitioning and Management

Power domain partitioning addresses the imperative of reducing power consumption in complex devices and facilitating power-aware design. By dividing the chip into independently powered blocks, designers can selectively enable or disable sections depending on operational requirements.

A power domain is defined as a section of the chip sharing a common power supply and ground reference. Different domains may operate at different supply voltages or be completely powered down to save static and dynamic power. Domains may include

165

cores, I/O subsystems, memories, or analog blocks.

Key challenges in power domain partitioning include signal integrity across domain boundaries, level shifter insertion, and state retention management.

Power Domain Crossing and Level Shifters

Signals crossing from a powered domain operating at voltage V_A to another operating at voltage V_B (where $V_A \neq V_B$) require level shifting to translate voltage levels safely and reliably.

Level shifters are carefully designed circuits that translate signal voltage swing levels while preserving timing and noise margins. They must be placed on the domain boundaries and designed to handle both directionality and signal integrity.

For example, an up-shifter transfers signals from low-voltage to higher-voltage domains, while down-shifters perform the inverse. The directionality often mandates unidirectional level shifters, with bidirectional signals needing additional control circuitry.

Power Gating and Isolation Cells

Power gating disables power to inactive domains to reduce leakage power. This technique employs sleep transistors that cut off the domain from supply voltage or ground rails.

Before powering down a domain, all outputs that drive signals into other domains must be properly managed to prevent floating nodes and signal corruption. Isolation cells enforce deterministic output states during power-down phases by forcing signals to known values such as zero or one.

Isolation cells assert enable signals derived from domain power states to conditionally block or pass signals. Upon power-up, isolation cells maintain isolation until the domain stabilizes and resume normal operation.

State Retention and Retention Flops

Some flip-flops support retention modes, where their state is preserved during power gating. Retention flops, or state-retentive elements, rely on a secondary low-leakage power supply to maintain content across power-down cycles.

The design of retention registers involves dual supply pins and power gating aware clock/reset controls. Retention strategy enables fast wake-up times by preserving critical state such as configuration registers or control flags, obviating the need for lengthy re-initialization sequences.

Power Domain Integration and Verification

Effective partitioning requires a global power management strategy that harmonizes clock, reset, and power domain interactions, considering dependencies and wake-up sequences.

Power-aware timing analysis verifies signal integrity across level shifters and isolation cells, ensures timing closure with power gating transistors in the path, and validates that no data loss or glitches occur during power mode transitions.

Simulation environments incorporate power domain state transitions, modeling power-up, power-down, and wake-up scenarios. Static verification tools analyze isolation and retention cell placement and consistency of power domain crossings with established design rules.

Co-Design Considerations for Clock, Reset, and Power Domains

The interplay between clock domains, reset distribution, and power domain partitioning is intricate, demanding co-designed strategies to guarantee deterministic functionality.

Clock gating, a common power reduction technique, intertwines clock and power management by selectively stopping clock trees to reduce switching activity. Clock gating domains frequently align with power domains to avoid glitches when domains lose or regain power.

Reset signals must be qualified against power domain status to avoid releasing registers in unpowered domains, which could manifest as undefined behavior or increased leakage. Reset controllers often integrate power domain status inputs to mask resets and coordinate domain bring-up effectively.

Moreover, asynchronous resets crossing multiple clock and power domains typically require additional synchronization and gating logic to prevent metastability and spurious resets during power transitions.

Achieving reliable operation within contemporary high-complexity integrated circuits mandates a robust, integrated approach to clocking, reset, and power domain management. The confluence of clock domain crossing synchronization, reset control techniques, and power domain partitioning with isolation, retention, and level shifting forms the cornerstone of modern digital system design, ensuring functional correctness, power efficiency, and scalability.

5.5. Physical Design and Timing Closure

The backend design flow critically determines the ultimate performance, power, and area (PPA) characteristics of an integrated circuit (IC). Within this flow, the processes of placement and routing establish the physical topology of the design, directly influencing signal delays, clock distribution, and power integrity. Concurrently, static timing analysis (STA) systematically assesses timing characteristics against design constraints, iterating toward a converged solution known as timing closure. The interplay among these stages, governed by physical constraints such as cell density, metal layers, and design rules, profoundly shapes silicon cost and performance.

Placement assigns standard cells and macros to precise chip locations, establishing the groundwork for routing and timing optimization. The placement engine balances objectives including
minimization of wirelength, avoidance of congestion, and adherence to timing-driven heuristics. Timing-driven placement incorporates critical path delays and slack metrics to orient cells favorably, reducing net delays by shortening interconnect lengths on
critical paths. Congestion estimations are integrated at this stage
to guide cell distribution, preventing routing resource bottlenecks
that may compel detours and elongate signal paths. The placement
outcome dictates the initial push-and-pull forces between timing
and routability. Dense packing that aggressively minimizes area
may force complex routing topologies, increasing parasitic capac-
itances and resistance, thereby degrading timing margins. Conversely, a more relaxed placement reduces congestion and potentially improves timing but at the expense of chip area and cost.

Routing subdivides into global and detailed phases, each incrementally refining the interconnection fabric. Global routing develops
approximate paths for nets, allocating routing resources on various metal layers to balance congestion and delay. Detailed routing
finalizes wire geometries within these allocated regions, ensuring
compliance with design rules such as spacing, width, and via constraints. During routing, parasitic extraction is performed to create accurate timing models reflecting resistance, capacitance, and
coupling interferences. These parasitic elements significantly affect signal integrity and timing; accurate modeling is essential for
precise static timing analysis.

Static timing analysis evaluates the timing of all signal paths without requiring dynamic simulation. It constructs a timing graph
representing gates as nodes and interconnect or gate delays as
edges. STA computes arrival times and required times at each
node, assessing slack to reveal whether timing constraints are met.
Both setup and hold checks are performed to guarantee correct circuit operation across process-voltage-temperature (PVT) corners.

Setup slack determines if signals arrive early enough before the clock edge, while hold slack ensures signals do not arrive too soon. Violations necessitate iterative modifications in placement, routing, or logic synthesis. STA tools incorporate advanced modeling of on-chip variation, crosstalk noise, and clock uncertainty to provide conservative, accurate timing margins.

Achieving timing closure is a multidisciplinary convergence of design adjustments driven by the STA feedback loop. It demands iterative enhancements at multiple layers: the logical netlist, physical placement, and routing configurations. Common techniques include buffer insertion and gate resizing to modify delay characteristics on critical paths; net shielding or layer reassignment to mitigate crosstalk; and clock tree synthesis adjustments for balanced clock latency and skew reduction. Physical constraints impact the freedom of timing optimization. The number of available metal layers, pitch and spacing rules, and process-design rule limitations constrain the routing solutions, often forcing tradeoffs between performance and manufacturability.

Physical constraints also govern silicon cost. Larger die area increases wafer usage, die-to-wafer ratio, and mask complexity, elevating manufacturing expenses. Thus, aggressive compaction and layer minimization strategies reduce cost but may restrict timing closure. Conversely, increasing metal layers improves routing resources and timing results but escalates process complexity and fabrication cost. Early assessment of these constraints enables designers to select an optimal balance, trading silicon area against performance goals.

A significant challenge during timing closure is managing variability and uncertainty. Process variations introduce deviations in transistor threshold voltage, channel length, and interconnect dimensions, affecting delay distributions. To counteract variability, timing margins are enforced conservatively, impacting the performance ceiling. Physical design must incorporate variability-aware placement to spatially balance critical cells and routing to reduce systematic variations. Advanced methodologies leverage statistical STA (SSTA), integrating probabilistic models to guide design adjustments more effectively.

Timing closure frequently integrates power and signal integrity optimization to avoid localized IR drop and electromigration issues that could cause timing failures. Voltage drops throughout the power grid affect transistor speeds, influencing cell delays and clock timing. Thus, physical design tools analyze power delivery networks alongside timing to ensure robust operation under worst-case conditions.

The clock network is a specialized domain significantly impacting timing closure. Clock tree synthesis produces a low-skew, balanced network that delivers synchronous clock signals to sequential elements with minimal insertion delay variance. The physical design must accommodate clock buffers, clock gating cells, and shielding to protect clock nets from interference and latency uncertainty. Clock uncertainty is accounted for in STA through jitter and skew models, influencing required timing margins.

The backend flow's physical design stages operate as an iterative optimization framework driven by static timing analysis. Placement and routing must respect physical constraints while enabling timing improvements through intelligent resource allocation, cell orientation, and interconnect design. STA provides precise, constraint-driven feedback that guides incremental refinements toward timing closure, balancing the complex interdependencies among silicon area, manufacturability, performance, and cost. Mastery of these processes requires a detailed understanding of physical implementation techniques, parasitic modeling, and variability-aware strategies to rigorously meet design goals in advanced semiconductor technologies.

5.6. Resource and Power Optimizations

Optimizing RISC-V cores for area, power consumption, and performance requires a nuanced understanding of the trade-offs inherent to semiconductor design and application requirements. Central to these optimizations are architectural choices, circuit-level
techniques, and system-level strategies that collectively influence
efficiency and scalability across application domains, ranging from
deeply embedded systems to high-performance computing platforms.

Area Optimization Techniques

The silicon footprint of a RISC-V core directly impacts cost,
yield, and integration density within system-on-chip (SoC)
environments. To minimize area while maintaining functional
integrity, designers often employ techniques such as:

- **Microarchitectural Simplification**
  The RISC-V instruction set architecture (ISA), with its modular base and extensible standard extensions, enables selective inclusion of instructions to tailor the complexity of the
  datapath. Reducing the instruction decode complexity by
  eliminating less critical extensions or implementing only a
  subset of the integer multiplication and division units can cut
  logic gates and register file port counts, substantially reducing area.

- **Bit-Width Reduction**
  Where full 32- or 64-bit datapaths are not mandatory, nar-
  rowing register widths and datapaths to 16-bit (RVC compressed subset) or other custom widths can save consider-
  able silicon, particularly in embedded applications that process limited data sizes. This approach requires careful software co-design to ensure that type safety and data handling
  semantics align with reduced widths.

- **Resource Sharing and Pipeline Simplification**
  Multi-cycle functional units, such as the multiplier or di-
  vider, implemented with shared hardware resources rather
  than fully pipelined replicas, reduce area at the cost of increased latency. Similarly, shallow or non-pipelined designs
  provide modest performance but demand fewer stages and
  less control logic. This is especially beneficial in low-power
  or constrained-area environments where throughput is secondary.

- **Memory Architecture Optimization**
  On-chip memories, including instruction cache, data cache,
  and tightly coupled memories, often dominate chip area.
  Choosing appropriate cache sizes, associativity, and line
  sizes tuned to application workloads can balance area
  with performance. Employing scratchpad memories as
  software-managed fast storage reduces the complexity
  and area overhead of caches, while facilitating predictable
  real-time behavior.

Power Consumption Reduction

Power efficiency in RISC-V cores is paramount across embedded
and portable designs, and increasingly significant in data center
and high-performance computing due to thermal constraints and
operational cost.

- **Clock and Power Gating**
  Fine-grained clock gating disables the clock signal to inactive
  registers and modules, eliminating unnecessary switching activity. This method often yields significant dynamic power
  savings without affecting functional correctness. Power gating extends this concept by physically disconnecting power
  rails to idle blocks in deep sleep modes, reducing static leakage currents, crucial in ultra-low-power applications.

- **Voltage and Frequency Scaling**

173

Dynamic voltage and frequency scaling (DVFS) allows the core to operate at reduced voltage and frequency during periods of low workload or latency tolerance, quadratically or more reducing dynamic power consumption while incurring proportional performance degradation. Architectures must support this via adaptive clock domain controllers and voltage regulators, facilitating real-time power-performance trade-offs informed by software or hardware monitors.

- **Operand Isolation and Data Gating**
  Selective blocking of transitions within combinational logic paths when operands do not change or results will not be consumed prevents redundant switching, reducing dynamic power. Operand isolation can be statically analyzed at synthesis or dynamically controlled via hardware, particularly effective in datapaths processing sparse or predictable data patterns.

- **Adaptive Body Biasing**
  Adjusting transistor threshold voltage through body biasing allows devices to optimize leakage power versus performance dynamically. Forward body bias reduces threshold voltage for speed boosts under performance demand, whereas reverse bias reduces leakage during idle. Implementing adaptive body bias with RISC-V cores requires sophisticated on-chip monitoring and control circuits but yields valuable power optimization margins.

Performance Optimization Strategies

Maximizing performance within area and power constraints necessitates architectural and microarchitectural enhancements that optimize instruction throughput and minimize latency.

- **Pipeline Depth and Hazard Mitigation**
  Careful design of pipeline stages balances clock frequency

174

with hazard detection complexity. Deeper pipelines enable higher clock rates but introduce more hazards and stall penalties. Employing branch prediction, out-of-order execution, or speculative execution—in limited or aggressive forms depending on the target market—improves throughput without linear area or power increase.

- **Instruction-Level Parallelism (ILP)**
  Superscalar implementations issue multiple instructions per cycle, leveraging parallel functional units and register renaming to exploit ILP. While enhancing performance, these features significantly increase complexity, area, and power. Selective and configurable superscalar width allows tuning ILP according to application characteristics.

- **Custom Extensions and Functional Units**
  RISC-V's extensibility encourages implementation of specialized instructions or accelerators tailored to domain-specific workloads, such as digital signal processing (DSP) or cryptographic primitives. Integrating custom functional units closely with the core reduces data movement and harnesses instruction-level acceleration to elevate performance with modest area and power overhead.

- **Cache Hierarchy and Memory System Optimization**
  Performance is often bottlenecked by memory latency and bandwidth. Integrating multi-level cache hierarchies with intelligent prefetching policies, write-back buffers, and coherency mechanisms enhances effective memory throughput. Additionally, cache size and associativity tuning, as mentioned for area optimization, must consider latency impacts for a balanced design.

Tailoring RISC-V Cores Across Application Domains

Design priorities vary widely across domains, and the flexible nature of RISC-V facilitates adaptation through parameterization and modularity.

- **Embedded and IoT Applications**
  In deeply embedded contexts, stringent power and area constraints dominate. Core designs here favor low-complexity, single-issue pipelines, minimal or no caches, and use clock or power gating aggressively. The RISC-V E (embedded) base integer subset, coupled with compressed instructions (RVC), reduces both code size and hardware complexity. Often, hardware multi-cycle units replace parallel functional units for area and power savings.

- **Mobile and Portable Devices**
  Moderate performance combined with stringent power budgets typifies these applications. Superscalar pipelines with limited ILP, DVFS capabilities, and optimized cache hierarchies deliver responsive yet power-efficient behavior. Core implementations can benefit from adaptive voltage scaling alongside clock gating, while extending ISA support with vector extensions for media and AI workloads enhances performance without drastic energy penalties.

- **High-Performance and Server-Class Systems**
  At the higher end, RISC-V cores compete by exploiting aggressive microarchitectural techniques: deep pipelining, out-of-order execution, branch prediction, and extensive ILP. Robust multi-level cache hierarchies and advanced prefetching are mandatory. Power optimization shifts towards system-level solutions, including thermal management, predictive DVFS coordinated with workload characteristics and runtime adaptation. Resource allocation is less constrained, allowing for larger register files and wide issue widths.

Holistic Co-Optimization Methodologies

Contemporary RISC-V core design benefits from co-optimization approaches that span algorithm, software, architecture, and circuit domains. Profile-driven design, where application benchmark characteristics guide hardware feature inclusion or omission, enables targeted optimization. Hardware-software co-design frameworks embed compiler and runtime toolchain support for power- and performance-aware scheduling, facilitating dynamic management of core microarchitecture.

Domain-specific languages and customizable microcode layers empower software exploitation of specialized instructions or accelerators, further refining performance or energy consumption without hardware redesign. Simultaneously, leveraging formal methods and advanced verification ensures that aggressive resource optimizations do not compromise correctness or introduce subtle faults.

Summary of Proven Optimization Approaches

Recurring themes in resource and power optimization for RISC-V cores are judicious complexity management, modular scalability, and adaptive control. Key proven approaches include:

- Employing minimal microarchitectural complexity consistent with target performance.

- Exploiting fine-grained clock and power gating to eliminate unnecessary switching.

- Incorporating DVFS and adaptive body biasing for dynamic power-performance trade-offs.

- Leveraging compressed and custom instructions to reduce code and data footprint.

- Designing multi-level memory subsystems optimized for application workload patterns.

- Utilizing configurable pipeline depths and parallelism degrees matching target market needs.

177

- Integrating hardware accelerators and domain-specific extensions aligned with software tooling.

These approaches, embedded within the RISC-V ecosystem's flexibility, empower designers to tailor cores that satisfy diverse performance, area, and power envelopes. The calculated synergy among architectural, circuit, and software layers unlocks efficient implementations adapted to the stringent demands of modern computing across scales and sectors.

5.7. Verification and Validation Strategies

The verification and validation of RISC-V hardware necessitate a multifaceted approach, integrating simulation, formal methods, assertion-based verification, and hardware emulation to ensure both functional correctness and compliance with the ISA specification. Each methodology targets specific aspects of design robustness, collectively fortifying the hardware against subtle bugs, architectural inconsistencies, and implementation errors.

Simulation remains the foundational technique for hardware verification, allowing designers to exercise the processor design under a broad variety of workloads and scenarios. Cycle-accurate simulators, such as those built upon SystemVerilog or dedicated event-driven engines, enable detailed behavioral modeling while closely mirroring realistic timing characteristics. Stimulus generation leverages both directed test cases and constrained random testing to probe corner cases and general functionality, often incorporating test programs derived from established RISC-V compliance suites. Simulation environments typically integrate waveform viewing and coverage metrics, the latter quantifying state-space exploration and helping to identify untested regions of the design. Functional coverage targets include instruction decoding, pipeline control states, and exception handling pathways, providing a nuanced measure of verification completeness.

Formal verification augments simulation by applying mathematical rigor to prove correctness properties over all possible inputs, circumventing the incompleteness intrinsic to selective testing. Model checking tools, operating on hardware description languages such as Verilog or SystemVerilog, verify that the microarchitecture adheres to key invariants and safety properties stipulated by the RISC-V ISA. Examples include monotonicity of program counter increments, correctness of privilege mode transitions, and atomicity of certain instruction sequences. Equivalence checking compares RTL against higher-level ISA models to confirm functional alignment, often deploying tools like JasperGold or proprietary frameworks. The scalability challenges of formal methods necessitate a modular verification methodology, isolating pipeline stages, control units, and peripheral components into tractable formal modules. This modular approach enables compositional reasoning to scale proofs across the full processor design.

Assertion-based verification represents a pivotal methodology bridging simulation and formal techniques. Designers embed properties as SystemVerilog Assertions (SVA) or Property Specification Language (PSL) directives directly within RTL code. These assertions continuously monitor design signals and temporal sequences during simulation or emulation, instantly flagging violations of architectural assumptions or implementation constraints. Assertions capture temporal relationships, such as the requirement that data memory access returns valid data within a fixed latency, as well as functional conditions, like the consistency of register writes with decoded instructions. The dual utility of assertions-serving also as formal properties in model checking-streamlines verification by providing a unified specification framework. Assertion libraries, often curated by RISC-V consortium affiliates, constitute a vital resource to formalize canonical ISA behaviors and microarchitectural protocols.

179

Hardware emulation platforms close the loop by enabling pre-silicon validation under real-time execution conditions. Emulators based on FPGA prototyping or dedicated emulation appliances such as Cadence Palladium and Mentor Veloce accelerate design bring-up and system integration testing. Running a complete software stack-including operating systems, runtime libraries, and application binaries-on an emulated RISC-V core exposes bugs that manifest only under full-system interactions, such as cache coherence anomalies, interrupt timing irregularities, or subtle bugs in memory-mapped I/O. Emulation harnesses hardware speed and observability to enable long-duration test scenarios impractical in pure simulation. Advanced emulators also support hardware-in-the-loop (HIL) configurations, integrating peripheral models or even physical devices, thereby enabling comprehensive system validation. Frequent re-synthesis and regression testing ensure that incremental design changes maintain correctness without regression.

Integration of these methodologies forms a robust verification framework. Verification plans delineate coverage goals and verification tasks, orchestrating simulation campaigns guided by functional coverage data. Assertion-based verification enriches simulation-based defect detection while providing artifacts usable by formal engines for exhaustive proof. Formal verification addresses critical safety and security properties that cannot be exhaustively tested by simulation. Emulation validates system-level behavior and performance, providing a high-fidelity environment for software-hardware co-verification.

Comprehensive compliance to the RISC-V specification leverages standard test suites such as the RISC-V Architectural Test Suite (ATS), which define directed tests spanning ISA subsets and privileged instructions. Automated test runners execute these workloads within simulation and emulation platforms, verifying correct instruction execution, exception generation, and CSR functionality. Failures uncovered in this phase prompt root-cause analysis via waveform traces and assertion error logs. Compliance testing extends beyond ISA functionality to include memory ordering models and privileged architecture features, ensuring that the processor meets the strict timing and correctness criteria necessary for reliable deployment.

Performance verification also benefits from these strategies. Simulation and emulation tools measure pipeline throughput, branch prediction accuracy, and cache performance under representative workloads. Formal methods ascertain that pipeline hazards are correctly detected and resolved, maintaining data and control flow integrity without stalls or deadlocks. Assertion-based monitors detect unintended structural hazards or race conditions, critical for multiprocessor coherence correctness.

Debug capabilities integral to verification frameworks include trace buffers, cycle counters, and hardware breakpoints. These features permit intricate observation of pipeline states and event sequences, facilitating rapid identification of design anomalies. Assertion failures and formal counterexamples can be replayed and analyzed using these debug aids to isolate root causes effectively. Modern RISC-V verification environments often integrate these debug mechanisms with automated analysis scripts, reducing human effort and increasing verification throughput.

The verification and validation of RISC-V hardware depends on a harmonious application of simulation, formal verification, assertion-based checking, and hardware emulation, each compensating for the limitations of the others. Such synergy ensures that the processor not only executes the ISA specification correctly but also behaves reliably under the complex conditions encountered in real-world operation. This systematic approach provides the trustworthiness necessary for both academic exploration and commercial deployment of RISC-V processor implementations.

Chapter 6

Toolchains, Compilers, and Software Ecosystem

The true power of an architecture lies in more than hardware—it depends on a thriving software ecosystem. This chapter lifts the hood on RISC-V's toolchains and compiler support, showcasing the bridges that link silicon to modern software. Explore the compilers, debuggers, runtime libraries, and OS ports that empower developers to realize the full potential of open computing.

6.1. GCC and LLVM for RISC-V

The emergence of RISC-V as a prominent open instruction set architecture (ISA) has been significantly bolstered by the robust backend support available in the GNU Compiler Collection (GCC) and the LLVM compiler framework. Both toolchains have adapted rapidly to the RISC-V ecosystem, providing advanced code generation capabilities, comprehensive optimization passes, and modular infrastructures that enable efficient exploitation of RISC-V's architectural features. This section explores the implementation of RISC-V in the backend of these compilers, elucidating the mechanisms through which they facilitate high-performance code generation and drive widespread adoption.

Overview of Backend Support in GCC

GCC's RISC-V backend emerged as part of the upstream repository in 2015, contemporaneous with the initial specification of the RISC-V ISA. The GCC backend architecture adheres to the traditional multi-stage compilation model, with the backend comprising instruction selection, register allocation, and instruction scheduling components tailored specifically for RISC-V's modular instruction set. The backend is implemented using a combination of machine description (MD) files and target-specific C++ code.

The machine description files encapsulate the ISA semantics and register classes. They define instruction patterns used during instruction selection-transforming the compiler's intermediate representation (RTL, Register Transfer Language) into RISC-V machine instructions. GCC's RTL-based optimizations complement these descriptions by leveraging pattern-matching to substitute complex expressions with efficient instruction sequences exploiting compressed and extended instructions introduced in RISC-V variants (e.g., the C extension for compressed instructions).

The GCC RISC-V backend supports both 32-bit (RV32) and 64-bit (RV64) variants, with additional handling for privilege modes and floating-point extensions. Conditional compilation flags enable fine-grained control over supported instruction subsets, allowing developers to generate highly optimized binaries tuned to specific microarchitectural features. Such granularity is essential for addressing the diversity of RISC-V implementations, ranging from deeply embedded microcontrollers to high-performance general-purpose processors.

Beyond instruction selection, GCC implements RISC-V-specific optimization passes. For instance, peephole optimizations in GCC enhance the code sequence by reducing register pressure and identifying opportunities to replace multiple instructions with single fused operations where the hardware supports them. Moreover, GCC's linker relaxation feature can dynamically substitute longer instruction sequences with shorter compressed forms during the final linking phase, improving code density without sacrificing correctness.

LLVM's RISC-V Backend Architecture

LLVM's RISC-V backend distinguishes itself through its use of an intermediate representation (IR) designed for flexible target-specific transformations and its modular, reusable components. Unlike GCC's RTL, LLVM IR is a strongly typed, SSA-based (Static Single Assignment) representation, which facilitates more aggressive and global optimizations before target code emission.

The RISC-V LLVM backend encompasses several stages: instruction selection via TableGen-defined patterns, register allocation, instruction scheduling, and late-stage optimizations such as instruction combining and branch folding. TableGen, a domain-specific language integrated into LLVM, enables concise and declarative specification of RISC-V instructions, encoding formats, and constraints. This significantly accelerates backend development and maintenance while ensuring correctness in instruction selection.

LLVM's instruction selector uses a Directed Acyclic Graph (DAG) pattern matcher to translate IR to target instructions. RISC-V's relatively orthogonal instruction set simplifies the generation of efficient DAG nodes. Additionally, LLVM incorporates custom lowering rules to manage architectural features such as compressed instructions, floating-point operations, and atomic instructions in compliance with RISC-V's extensions.

185

Register allocation in LLVM for RISC-V relies on standard algorithms (e.g., basic graph-coloring) adapted to the RISC-V register file, which consists of 32 integer registers and a varying number of floating-point registers depending on the extension. Configurable allocator passes allow LLVM to optimize register usage based on calling conventions and hardware constraints, impacting both runtime performance and code size.

LLVM also features a robust selection of optimization passes that exploit RISC-V's capabilities. Loop unrolling, vectorization (where applicable), and speculative execution safety checks are all implemented with RISC-V considerations. For example, LLVM's MachineCombiner pass merges instruction sequences into compact, hardware-friendly forms such as compressed instructions, thereby enhancing performance and reducing binary sizes.

Optimizations Specific to RISC-V Features

Both GCC and LLVM recognize the modular nature of RISC-V, wherein the base integer ISA can be extended through optional components such as the M (multiply/divide), A (atomic), F and D (floating-point), and C (compressed) extensions. Compiler backends must therefore adapt dynamically to these features, enabling or disabling code sequences and optimizations accordingly.

Compressed instructions (C extension) are a particular focus: both GCC and LLVM can emit 16-bit instructions to reduce code size, critical in embedded systems or memory-constrained environments. This capability requires careful instruction selection and scheduling to ensure that smaller instructions do not impede pipeline throughput or introduce alignment hazards. GCC adopts a two-tiered approach, generating full-length instructions initially and enabling linker relaxation to compress them post-compilation. LLVM, in contrast, integrates compressed instruction selection directly into the instruction selection and combining phases, enabling earlier and more holistic optimizations.

Support for atomic operations and memory consistency models is another area where backend optimizations are crucial. Both compilers implement atomic intrinsic lowering that maps high-level concurrency constructs onto efficient RISC-V atomic instructions, considering memory fences and acquire-release semantics. These implementations ensure that multi-threaded applications can leverage RISC-V's atomic instructions without incurring unnecessary overhead.

Floating-point optimizations are governed by the presence of F and D extensions, with backend passes performing transformations such as constant folding, strength reduction, and instruction reordering to exploit hardware floating-point units fully. Both GCC and LLVM adopt target-aware vectorization strategies to improve floating-point throughput where applicable.

Facilitating Software Ecosystem Growth

The high-quality backend implementations in GCC and LLVM have been pivotal in enabling rapid uptake of RISC-V across a diverse software community. The mature support lowers barriers for application developers and tool vendors, providing immediate benefits such as debugging support, profile-guided optimizations, and cross-compilation capabilities.

Both toolchains interface seamlessly with ancillary tools in the RISC-V ecosystem, including assemblers (e.g., GNU Assembler and LLVM's integrated assembler), linkers, and debuggers such as GDB and LLDB. This end-to-end toolchain availability fosters robust testing and deployment workflows across multiple platforms and operating systems.

Moreover, the open-source nature of GCC and LLVM ensures that improvements to RISC-V backend support can be collaboratively developed, peer-reviewed, and propagated. This has resulted in continuous performance improvements, extended architectural support, and rapid responses to emerging RISC-V specifications

187

such as the Vector (V) extension.

Comparative Backend Characteristics and Future Directions

While both GCC and LLVM achieve effective code generation for RISC-V, their differing internal architectures manifest in distinct strengths. GCC's RTL approach lends itself well to mature, conservative optimizations that prioritize stability and portability. LLVM's IR and TableGen-based design facilitate more experimental and aggressive optimizations, enabling cutting-edge transformations and quicker adaptation to novel ISA features.

Ongoing development efforts in both backends focus on enhancing code density through better compressed instruction utilization, improving code scheduling to better match emerging RISC-V microarchitectures, and expanding support for vectorization and multi-threading extensions. Furthermore, integration with hardware performance counters and profiling tools continues to evolve, enabling fine-grained performance tuning.

GCC and LLVM provide comprehensive, evolving backend support for RISC-V that fully leverage its architectural modularity. These advancements are critical enablers of the ISA's practical adoption, reducing development time and improving the efficiency of compiled code for a broad array of applications.

6.2. Assembler, Linker, and Toolchain Internals

The process of transforming human-readable assembly instructions into executable machine code in the RISC-V ecosystem involves several tightly coupled components: the assembler, the linker, and related toolchain utilities. An in-depth understanding of their internal structure elucidates how source code evolves into an efficient, relocatable, and executable binary, emphasizing object file formats, relocation handling, and final binary generation.

The assembler serves as the foundation by translating assembly language into an intermediate representation known as object files. These object files contain machine instructions, data sections, symbol tables, and relocation records. The common object file format on most platforms employing RISC-V is the Executable and Linkable Format (ELF). The ELF format organizes information into headers, sections, and segments, facilitating modular management and linking of program components.

Within ELF, critical sections include the .text segment for executable instructions, .data and .bss segments for initialized and uninitialized data, respectively, and various metadata sections such as .symtab and .rela.* for symbol and relocation data. Symbols represent named entities like functions or global variables, binding symbolic references in code to concrete addresses. The assembler collects symbol definitions and references, encoding relocation entries where addresses or offsets are not yet known.

Relocation is fundamental to the linking process, enabling separate compilation units to be combined flexibly. A relocation entry describes how a particular reference in the code or data must be modified to point to the final address of a symbol after linking. For RISC-V, relocations must account for the architecture's instruction formats and immediate field sizes. For example, an R_RISCV_CALL relocation adjusts a 20-bit immediate in a JAL instruction to the final destination address. The relocation format specifies the type, offset within the section, target symbol, and additional addends when necessary.

The assembler's role extends beyond translation to precise encoding of instructions adhering to RISC-V's variable-length encoding constraints, especially in extensions such as compressed instructions (the C extension). It must also manage local symbol binding, ensuring that branch and jump instructions within a function remain correct relative to their offsets. Generation of debug symbols

189

and DWARF data further enriches object files, enabling source-level debugging post linking.

The linker orchestrates a more complex transformation by resolving symbolic references across all input object files and libraries, and producing a final executable or shared object. Central to this process is symbol resolution: identifying the definitive locations of all external symbols and consolidating duplicated or weak symbols into single definitions. The linker processes symbol tables from all inputs, prioritizing strong definitions and applying language linkage rules where applicable.

Relocation processing at the linker stage modifies instructions and data based on the final layout of the executable. The linker applies relocations by calculating the addresses of symbols within the mapped memory layout and patching immediate fields in instructions accordingly. This step requires a detailed understanding of RISC-V relocation types, including PC-relative jumps, absolute addresses, and GOT/PLT entries for dynamic linking. The linker must honor alignment constraints and instruction encoding rules, often performing instruction relaxation or trampolining when direct branch ranges are insufficient.

Handling global offset tables (GOT) and procedure linkage tables (PLT) is pivotal in supporting position-independent code (PIC) and dynamic linking on RISC-V. The GOT holds addresses of global variables and external functions, while the PLT enables late binding of function calls through runtime symbol resolution. The linker generates and populates these tables, instruments the code to reference them properly, and lays out the executable's sections to support these mechanisms.

RISC-V's object and executable formats are further influenced by linker scripts-user-defined specifications controlling section placement, memory mapping, and symbol assignments. The linker processes these scripts to allocate sections to proper memory regions, define entry points, and handle startup routines. Scripts also dictate how segments such as .init, .fini, and constructor/destructor sections are ordered, ensuring runtime initialization semantics.

The final executable binary format encapsulates all linked sections into a file image ready for loading into memory. The ELF headers provide the operating system or firmware loader with metadata about loadable segments, entry points, and program interpreter paths. Particularly in embedded RISC-V environments, the toolchain must generate binary or hex files usable by flash programmers or debuggers, converting among ELF, binary, and other formats through utilities like objcopy.

Integrated toolchains typically bundle the assembler, linker, and utilities such as objdump, readelf, and nm to inspect and manipulate these intermediate and final files. objdump disassembles the binary back into assembly, verifying correct translation, while readelf reports ELF internals useful for diagnosing symbol and relocation issues.

The optimizations embedded within assembler and linker steps also impact RISC-V binary generation. Instruction scheduling, branch prediction hinting, and alignment padding introduced at assembly or link time can improve performance on target processors. The linker's garbage collection of unused sections eliminates code and data not reachable from entry points, reducing executable size-particularly crucial in embedded contexts.

The assembler, linker, and associated tools form an interconnected toolchain that meticulously constructs RISC-V executables by interpreting architecture-specific constraints, object file standards, and program linkage semantics. Mastery of their internals provides critical insights for compiler developers, systems programmers, and embedded developers striving for precise control over the binary generation process, enabling efficient, correct, and optimized executables tailored to RISC-V platforms.

6.3. Debugging and Profiling Environments

The evolution of RISC-V as an open-standard instruction set architecture (ISA) has necessitated the development and refinement of debugging and profiling environments that cater to its unique characteristics. A robust toolchain for debugging and performance analysis is indispensable for developers aiming to ensure correctness, identify bottlenecks, and optimize software across diverse RISC-V implementations. This section surveys the current state of support in prominent tools such as GDB, QEMU, and various visualization platforms, highlighting their features, integration modalities, and practical applications in diagnosing issues and improving runtime performance.

The GNU Debugger (GDB) stands as a cornerstone for debugging in the RISC-V ecosystem, offering extensive support for RISC-V architectures with a focus on both 32-bit and 64-bit variants. GDB's ability to interpret RISC-V-specific debug symbols and handle its register sets equips developers with granular control over program execution. The debugger supports single-stepping, breakpoints, watchpoints, and remote debugging via the GDB Remote Serial Protocol (RSP), facilitating interaction with hardware targets or simulators. Modern iterations of GDB extend this with support for RISC-V's compressed instruction sets and privileged modes, enabling sophisticated investigation of kernel-level code and embedded firmware.

Remote debugging with GDB integrates seamlessly with hardware debug probes conforming to the RISC-V Debug Specification, such as those utilizing the RISC-V Debug Module Interface (DMI). These interfaces allow real-time inspection of processor state over JTAG or Serial Wire Debug (SWD), making it practical to halt execution, inspect registers, and modify memory on physical RISC-V boards. Furthermore, GDB's scripting capabilities using Python enable customized breakpoint actions and automated diagnostic routines tailored to the RISC-V platform's idiosyncrasies.

QEMU, as a versatile open-source emulator, plays a pivotal role in RISC-V software development by providing a virtual execution environment that mimics RISC-V hardware. Its support encompasses a wide spectrum of RISC-V profiles, including the standard ISA subsets and privileged extensions, enabling system emulation from bare-metal to full operating system stacks. QEMU's advantage lies in its flexibility to simulate various machine configurations without the need for physical hardware, thereby expediting early stage development and facilitating fault isolation under controlled conditions.

Profiling support within QEMU is realized through its built-in tracing and logging mechanisms. Developers can enable detailed tracepoints covering instruction execution, memory accesses, and peripheral interactions, producing granular data useful for performance tuning and behavioral analysis. QEMU also interfaces with external profiling tools, often via its integration with GDB for live debugging, furnishing a comprehensive environment for iterative performance refinement.

Profiling tools compatible with RISC-V leverage hardware performance counters defined by the architecture, accessible through performance monitoring units (PMUs) specified in the privileged architecture. The Linux `perf` tool, for instance, supports RISC-V processors by reading these counters to gather data on instructions retired, cache misses, branch mispredictions, and more. This low-overhead profiling facilitates hotspot detection and guides optimizations in compiler-generated code or runtime libraries. The combination of PMU-based profiling and trace collection from QEMU or hardware tracing infrastructure provides a layered perspective on system behavior.

Visualization platforms augment debugging and profiling by transforming raw data into interpretable insights. Tools such as Eclipse-based IDEs, VSCode extensions tailored for embedded RISC-V development, and standalone GUI applications enable graphical display of call graphs, execution timelines, and register state transitions. These platforms often integrate with GDB and perf data, allowing synchronized views of source code, disassembly, and performance metrics. Visualization aids in comprehending complex interactions, such as pipeline stalls or memory latency effects, which are challenging to infer from console outputs alone.

A critical aspect in using these environments is understanding the mapping between hardware and software abstractions. RISC-V's modular ISA design, with optional extensions and numerous implementation variants, demands flexible debugging workflows. Tools must accommodate differences in privilege levels, memory models, and custom extensions. This flexibility is evident in GDB's modular target definitions and QEMU's machine descriptors, allowing tailored debugging sessions that reflect actual deployment conditions. Profiling instrumentation likewise needs to consider variable performance counter availability and configuration.

To diagnose software faults, the integration of hardware watchpoints and trace buffers provides immediate visibility into erroneous writes or control flow deviations. Combining GDB's breakpoint capabilities with QEMU's instruction logging can isolate root causes in intricate scenarios such as kernel panics or real-time system failures. Moreover, simulators support checkpointing and reverse execution to rewind program state, enhancing the investigative process.

Performance optimization on RISC-V benefits from systematic profiling and iterative refinement facilitated by these toolchains. Identifying inefficient loops, costly memory accesses, or suboptimal instruction sequences gains precision when supported by direct counter feedback and visual performance analytics. Compiler flags generating detailed debug information further improve breakpoint reliability and stack unwinding, critical for analyzing deeply nested call structures typical in system software.

The ecosystem surrounding RISC-V debugging and profiling continues to mature with contributions focused on expanding trace capabilities, enhancing graphical dashboards, and standardizing telemetry interfaces. Advanced techniques such as hardware-assisted tracing via the RISC-V Embedded Trace Macrocell (ETM) and integration with system-level analysis platforms promise to elevate developer confidence and code quality.

Collectively, the robust support for RISC-V in GDB, QEMU, and visualization tools constitutes a powerful environment for diagnosing complex issues, conducting thorough performance studies, and confidently advancing software development. The synergy between these components ensures that both novice and expert developers can approach RISC-V platform intricacies methodically, leveraging precise instrumentation and insightful analytics embedded in the contemporary toolchain.

6.4. Runtime Libraries and ABI Compliance

The ecosystem surrounding RISC-V extends beyond its flexible instruction set architecture (ISA) to encompass a comprehensive suite of runtime libraries and application binary interface (ABI) standards that underpin compiler toolchains, system software, and application interoperability. These aspects are indispensable for ensuring the portability, stability, and performance consistency of compiled programs across diverse RISC-V implementations and toolchains.

At the core of executable environments for RISC-V targets lies the runtime library infrastructure, designed to provide essential support for application execution, initialization, termination, and interfacing with operating system services. The minimal runtime often includes the crt0 (C runtime zero) startup files, which prepare the environment prior to invoking the main() function and manage program exit. RISC-V toolchains, such as those based on GCC or LLVM, provide target-specific crt0 variants that comply with the

195

RISC-V privilege specification and the machine's ABI.

Beyond startup code, the runtime environment encompasses libraries to support dynamic memory allocation, thread-local storage, exception handling, and low-level atomic operations. Due to RISC-V's modular ISA design—with variable-width instruction subsets and optional extensions—runtime libraries must be carefully tuned to ABI conventions, instruction availability, and performance characteristics of individual profiles. Examples include:

- **libgcc**: The GCC low-level runtime support library containing compiler-rt routines for arithmetic operations, division algorithms, and exceptions.

- **compiler-rt**: A LLVM-related project with similar facilities, serving as a minimal runtime often integrated into the standard library.

- **libc**: The standard C library implementations adapted for RISC-V, which rely on runtime calls for system calls, I/O streams, and string/memory handling.

The prominence of the standard C library (`libc`) cannot be overstated, as it abstracts the interface between applications and the operating system kernel. On RISC-V platforms, several `libc` implementations have been ported or adapted, including but not limited to:

- **glibc**: The GNU C Library, renowned for full POSIX compliance and extensive internationalization, supporting RISC-V since GCC and glibc version updates circa 2019 onwards.

- **musl**: A lightweight, fast, and simple implementation targeting embedded and minimalist systems. Musl has been rapidly adopted for RISC-V due to its clean architecture and performance advantages.

- **uClibc-ng:** Tailored for embedded Linux systems with constrained resources, uClibc-ng supports RISC-V environments with smaller footprint requirements.

These libraries maintain source compatibility but diverge in design philosophy and complexity. Most importantly, each takes care to respect the RISC-V ABI specification, ensuring that the interfaces and internal function calls conform precisely to calling conventions, data representations, and system call conventions mandated for the target ISA.

The RISC-V ABI defines strict calling conventions to standardize function invocation semantics across binaries and libraries, enforcing interoperability between independently compiled code modules. The calling convention specifies how arguments are passed (registers vs. stack), where return values reside, and how the stack frame is constructed and destructed, along with register saving conventions.

For the prevailing RISC-V 64-bit (RV64) ABI (commonly referred to as the 1p64 and 1p64d configurations—64-bit long and pointer sizes, with and without double-precision floating-point support), the conventions include:

- Use of integer registers x10 to x17 (a0–a7) for passing up to eight integer or pointer arguments.

- Floating-point arguments passed in f10 to f17 registers when applicable.

- Return values are returned via a0/a1 for integers and f0/f1 for floating-point.

- Caller-saved registers include argument registers and temporaries; callee-saved specify x8–x9, x18–x27, and floating-point equivalents.

- The stack pointer (sp, or x2) must remain 16-byte aligned on function entry.

By adhering to these detailed rules, libraries compiled separately can link transparently and function without conflicts or undefined behavior arising from mismatched ABI expectations.

RISC-V ABIs formalize data type sizes, register usage, stack frame structures, and system call conventions. These specifications are essential for compilers, linkers, assemblers, loaders, and debuggers to cooperate seamlessly.

Key RISC-V ABI variants include:

- **ILP32**: 32-bit integers, longs, and pointers, used for embedded 32-bit RISC-V systems.

- **ILP32F** and **ILP32D**: 32-bit base with single-precision or double-precision floating-point support.

- **LP64**, **LP64F**, **LP64D**: 64-bit variants with optional floating-point extensions.

ABI stability means that programs compiled with the same ABI specification can interoperate, independently of optimization differences or compiler versions, facilitating stable linker behavior and reproducible builds. It also mitigates fragmentation in the software ecosystem by providing a common target for binary distribution.

Beyond function calls within the user space, runtime libraries must interact with operating system kernels through system calls. RISC-V prescribes a system call convention using the ecall instruction, with the call number passed in a7, and arguments in a0–a5.

Standardized library wrappers abstract system calls, matching the ABI calling conventions seamlessly to kernel interfaces. For example, the write() or mmap() calls in libc invoke ecall with the appropriate syscall numbers, preserving ABI constraints.

RISC-V defines atomic instructions as extensions (e.g., A extension for atomic instructions), which runtime libraries utilize to implement thread-safe primitives required by high-level synchronization constructs in C11 or POSIX threads. Functions such as spinlocks, atomic counters, and memory fences rely on these primitives through well-defined ABI interfaces, maintaining correctness across multi-threaded executions.

Runtime libraries implement these atomic operations following the RISC-V ISA specification so that compiled applications can achieve correct lock-free and concurrent behavior on compliant hardware, independent of vendor-specific microarchitectural optimizations.

Exception handling and signal processing mechanisms depend intimately on runtime support that conforms to RISC-V ABI and calling conventions. When a synchronous event (such as division by zero or illegal instruction) or asynchronous event (like a signal from the operating system) occurs, the runtime libraries provide the necessary frame setup and context switching to invoke user-level handlers.

These operations involve saving and restoring register state according to ABI conventions, handling stack frames appropriately, and ensuring that nested exceptions and signal handlers operate correctly without corrupting the program state. The runtime library functions for these behaviors are often implemented in assembly or compiler intrinsics finely tuned to the RISC-V ABI.

Variations among RISC-V compiler toolchains and runtime environments underscore the criticality of strict ABI compliance and the use of standardized runtime libraries:

- Ensuring cross-vendor binary compatibility requires consistent adherence to ABI and calling conventions.

- Runtime libraries provide abstracted interfaces accommodating ISA extensions dynamically, enabling extensibility
without breaking compatibility.

- Integration of system-level features such as threads, signals,
and atomic operations rely on ABI-compliant runtime functions.

Collectively, RISC-V runtime libraries and ABI specifications
construct a framework that empowers diverse compilation targets,
from embedded microcontrollers to high-performance 64-bit
general-purpose processors, to share a stable foundation for
executable code portability and reliable system behavior.

```
1  // Example: Simple RISC-V calling convention
        adherence (GCC-style)
2  // Function prototype: int add(int x, int y);
3
4  // Assembly to conform to RISC-V ABI:
5  add:
6      add a0, a0, a1    // a0 and a1 hold the first
        two integer args, sum into a0
7      ret              // return, result in a0
```

```
// Typical output from compiled function adhering to RISC-V ABI:

0000000000000000 <add>:
   0:   00b50533            add     a0,a0,a1
   4:   00008067            ret
```

This minimalistic example illustrates register use per the RISC-V
calling convention, where the first and second function arguments
arrive in registers a0 and a1, with the return value passed in a0.
All runtime libraries and compilers rely on such conventions to ensure interoperation and binary compatibility at the link and load
stages.

6.5. Operating System Support: Linux, RTOS, and Bare Metal

The adoption of RISC-V as a versatile and open processor architecture has necessitated comprehensive support across a spectrum of operating systems, ranging from fully featured Linux distributions to lightweight real-time operating systems (RTOS) and bare metal environments. The process of porting and optimizing these systems for RISC-V involves addressing architectural peculiarities, bootstrapping complexities, device support intricacies, and performance considerations unique to this evolving instruction set architecture.

Linux's modular design and widely portable nature have made it a prime candidate for deployment on RISC-V platforms. The porting effort typically begins with creating or adapting the Linux kernel to support the RISC-V privileged architecture, which specifies the execution environment, privilege levels, and hardware interfaces.

Key components involved in this porting include the implementation of low-level trap handling, context switching, and memory management units (MMU) support. The RISC-V privileged architecture defines several privilege modes-machine, supervisor, and user modes-each requiring tailored kernel routines to manage transitions and exceptions effectively. The CPU-specific startup code, often situated in assembly, configures the platform's virtual memory system and sets up page tables to leverage RISC-V's Sv32 or Sv39 virtual memory schemes depending on word size.

```
1  void setup_pagetable() {
2      // Allocate and configure root page table for
       Sv39 mode
3      root_pagetable = allocate_pagetable();
4
5      // Map kernel text and data sections
6      map_range(root_pagetable, KERNEL_BASE,
       KERNEL_PHYS, KERNEL_SIZE, PTE_R | PTE_X);
```

201

```
7
8      // Enable paging by writing to the satp
       register
9      uint64_t satp_value = MAKE_SATP(root_pagetable
       );
10     write_csr(satp, satp_value);
11 }
```

Device support within Linux on RISC-V necessitates additions and refinements to the kernel's device tree (DT) bindings. The DT communicates hardware topology and configurations to the kernel at boot time. RISC-V platforms are highly diverse, with widely varying peripheral sets and system-on-chip (SoC) implementations. Thus, the kernel code must accommodate differences in UARTs, timers, interrupt controllers, and other platform-specific hardware by either leveraging existing driver frameworks or integrating new drivers. For instance, the Platform-Level Interrupt Controller (PLIC) and Core Local Interruptor (CLINT) must be correctly initialized and integrated with the Linux interrupt subsystem.

Optimization of Linux on RISC-V includes both kernel and user-space efforts. On the kernel side, enabling and tuning features such as the RISC-V compressed instruction set extension (RVC) can reduce code size and improve instruction fetch efficiency. Kernel preemption, real-time patches (PREEMPT-RT), and scheduler tuning can enhance responsiveness and suitability for embedded or mixed-criticality workloads. On the user-space side, compiler optimizations (e.g., GCC or LLVM targeting RISC-V) must be utilized to generate efficient code sequences exploiting RISC-V-specific instructions such as atomic operations and vector extensions when available.

Real-time operating systems tailored for deterministic response and minimal latency form a critical layer in the RISC-V ecosystem, particularly for embedded and control applications. The porting of RTOSes such as FreeRTOS, Zephyr, and RT-Thread to RISC-V involves smaller footprints and tighter integration with hardware timers and interrupt subsystems when compared to full Linux systems.

Key to RTOS operation is the precise control of context switching, task scheduling, and interrupt handling. The RISC-V trap mechanism, encompassing synchronous exceptions and interrupts, must be mapped onto the RTOS kernel's interrupt service routines with minimal overhead. Porting efforts include implementing the machine-mode trap handler to redirect exceptions to supervisor mode or to kernel-managed handlers, depending on privilege configurations.

Timer support often relies on the Core Local Interruptor (CLINT), which provides the machine-mode timer interrupts used for periodic scheduling. Configuration of these timers must be accurate to achieve real-time deadlines. A common approach is configuring the machine timer compare registers (mtimecmp) and servicing timer interrupts to trigger scheduler ticks.

```
1  void machine_timer_isr(void) {
2      // Clear timer interrupt by setting next
       mtimecmp value
3      uint64_t next_tick = read_mtime() +
       TICK_INTERVAL;
4      write_mtimecmp(next_tick);
5
6      // Notify kernel scheduler of tick
7      rtos_tick_handler();
8  }
```

The integration of RISC-V-specific features such as hardware thread local storage (TLS) or custom instruction set extensions enables further optimizations. For example, the atomic memory operation instructions (AMO) permit lock-free synchronization primitives critical for RTOS efficiency. The modular nature of RTOS codebases facilitates selective enabling of such features based on the target RISC-V variant and application requirements.

Peripheral drivers in RTOSes are often customized to match minimalistic footprints, focusing on direct register access and interrupt-based I/O. The use of device trees is less pervasive than in Linux, so driver code frequently includes static hardware descriptors and initialization sequences hardcoded or generated during build time.

Bare metal environments leverage the raw hardware capabilities of RISC-V processors without an intervening operating system layer. Such programming is pervasive in deeply embedded systems, custom accelerators, or early-stage bootloaders.

Successful bare metal software design requires intimate knowledge of the CPU's privileged architecture, memory map, and peripheral registers. Before application logic can run, the bootstrapping process must configure the processor's execution environment-a task that includes setting machine-mode status registers, disabling interrupts, initializing stack pointers, and configuring memory protection if present.

```
1    .section .text
2    .globl _start
3  _start:
4    la sp, stack_top        # Initialize stack
     pointer
5    csrw mscratch, zero     # Clear machine scratch
     register
6    csrsi mstatus, MIE      # Enable machine
     interrupts
7    call main               # Jump to main
     application
```

Peripheral interaction is typically performed by direct memory-mapped I/O register accesses, often encapsulated in inline functions or macros to improve readability and maintainability. This direct control facilitates deterministic timing and reduced overhead, critical in real-time constraints or power-sensitive applications.

Bootstrapping procedures may involve configuration of external memories (such as DRAM controllers), initialization of clock and voltage domains, and powering up or resetting connected devices. The RISC-V Supervisor Binary Interface (SBI), often implemented as firmware or a minimal abstraction layer, can provide essential runtime services in multi-core or complex SoCs. When available, SBI provides a standardized interface to manage core startup, interrupts, and low-level platform features, easing bare metal programming complexity.

Optimization techniques at the bare metal level exploit RISC-V extensions and pipeline features. For example, leveraging the compressed instruction set reduces executable size, beneficial where limited memory exists. The use of hardware counters and performance monitoring units supports fine-grained profiling that can help tailor code sequences for minimal cycle counts and energy efficiency.

An overarching challenge in porting operating systems to RISC-V is the bootstrapping process, which must accommodate the architectural model where the system starts in machine mode at the highest privilege. Transitioning to lower privilege levels and initializing the runtime environment involves careful sequencing.

For Linux, the bootloader (such as U-Boot adapted for RISC-V) sets up initial device and memory configurations, then passes control to the kernel, often with supplementary arguments passed via device trees and firmware interfaces. This flexible interface helps abstract platform-specific details, although early-stage debugging may require detailed attention to trap vector correctness and CSRs (Control and Status Registers).

RTOS and bare metal environments typically begin in machine mode but configure the platform's privilege modes according to system complexity. For bare metal, no privilege demotion may occur, whereas RTOS kernels might execute in machine mode or implement a microkernel strategy involving supervisor or user modes.

Device support remains a critical pillar enabling operating systems to leverage the diverse hardware on RISC-V platforms. The modular Linux driver model permits the integration of a broad range of peripheral support, from network interfaces to storage controllers, accelerated by device tree descriptions.

In contrast, RTOS and bare metal drivers generally prioritize lean implementations optimized for minimal latency and code size. For example, interrupt handlers must be concise and non-blocking, with deferred processing often handled by software interrupts or by main application loops.

The PLIC and CLINT interrupt controllers form a common baseline for establishing interrupt routing and prioritization. However, many SoCs augment these with proprietary interrupt controller extensions or power management units, requiring either vendor-supplied drivers or community-supported code.

Several optimization strategies facilitate enhanced performance and system robustness for operating systems on RISC-V architectures:

- **Leverage ISA Extensions:** Utilize standard extensions such as A (atomic), C (compressed), and F/D (floating point) where appropriate, enabling both compact code and advanced instruction capabilities.

- **Tailor Privilege Levels:** Carefully configure privilege modes to balance security and performance. Running parts of the OS in supervisor mode or using user-mode execution for applications with hardware-enforced separation increases system integrity.

- **Efficient Trap Handling:** Optimize trap vector table layouts and minimize interrupt latency by reducing instruction counts in exception handlers and using fast context switch mechanisms.

- **Device Tree Accuracy:** Maintain precise and well-structured device tree descriptions to prevent ambiguous hardware configurations and improve driver auto-discovery and initialization.

- **Use Performance Counters:** Employ RISC-V performance counters for profiling critical code paths and tuning scheduler and driver behaviors under realistic load.

- **Cross-Compilation Toolchain:** Utilize optimized toolchains that target specific RISC-V variants, including those enabling link-time optimizations and profile-guided feedback.

The evolving RISC-V ecosystem continues to provide growing support and improvements to operating system compatibility and functionality. As the instruction set architecture matures and hardware implementations proliferate, the symbiotic advancement of OS ports and optimizations ensures that RISC-V stands as a compelling choice for a wide array of computing domains.

6.6. Cross-compilation and Bootstrapping

Cross-compilation and bootstrapping form the cornerstone of developing and deploying software across the heterogeneous landscape of RISC-V architectures. The process begins with constructing a reliable cross-toolchain capable of generating binaries for RISC-V targets from a host platform, which typically differs in architecture and operating system. This section delineates the systematic approach toward building such cross-toolchains, bootstrapping essential software stacks, and establishing a development environment conducive to scalability, from minimal embedded devices to full-featured multi-core systems.

Building a cross-toolchain suitable for RISC-V targets involves assembling components that can interoperate seamlessly: a compiler, assembler, linker, and standard C library. The GNU Compiler Collection (GCC) and LLVM/Clang are principal compiler choices, each offering support for various RISC-V ISA variants, extensions, and ABI conventions.

The initial step is procuring or building a cross-binutils package that includes assembler (`riscv64-unknown-elf-as`) and linker (`riscv64-unknown-elf-ld`), configured explicitly for the RISC-V target triple, such as `riscv64-unknown-elf` or `riscv32-unknown-elf`. Proper configuration flags ensure correct handling of the RISC-V privilege modes and architecture subsets (e.g., RV32IMAC, RV64GC).

Following binutils, constructing the GCC cross-compiler requires a staged approach. The compiler's build is often split into stages to circumvent dependency loops between the compiler and the standard C library. The compiler's first stage builds a minimal cross-compiler, capable of producing executables that use a stub C library or none at all. This stage leverages tools like `gcc-bootstrap` or compilers on the host with prebuilt headers for the target's libc.

Next, a standard C library such as `newlib` (for bare-metal environments) or `glibc` (for full OS deployments) must be compiled for the target. The libc build consumes headers and startup files tailored for the RISC-V environment. Accurate configuration ensures the library conforms to the target ABI (e.g., ILP32, LP64) and includes optimizations for specific ISA extensions or privileged modes.

After libc is available, the compiler can be re-built with libc support, enabling full-featured code generation. This two-pass compilation process addresses dependencies where the compiler requires libc headers and the libc needs a working compiler.

Cross-compilation toolchains may also incorporate debugging tools such as GDB built with RISC-V remote target support, and utilities like `readelf` and `objdump` for inspection of RISC-V ELF binaries. Integration with debugging stubs (e.g., OpenOCD or embedded GDB servers) enhances visibility during remote development.

Bootstrapping the software stack involves progressively building a minimal base and layering additional capabilities until a full development environment emerges. This approach is crucial in RISC-V environments, which vary from constrained embedded devices with limited memory to multi-core Linux systems.

At the lowest level, a firmware or bootloader is commonly the starting point, responsible for hardware initialization, memory setup, and loading the operating system or runtime environment. Popular open-source bootloaders supporting RISC-V include OpenSBI, which provides supervisor binary interface services, and U-Boot, capable of complex boot sequences.

Once bootloaders are operational, foundational runtime components such as the GNU C Library (glibc), musl, or newlib must be bootstrapped. The choice depends largely on the target environment; bare-metal applications rely on smaller, simpler C libraries (newlib), whereas full OS stacks employ glibc or musl with comprehensive POSIX support.

Bootstrapping typically involves cross-compiling these libraries for the RISC-V target and carefully aligning compiler flags, ABI compatibility, and processor features. For instance, selecting the correct floating-point ABI (`hard` versus `soft`) ensures runtime compatibility.

Higher layers include runtime environments, debuggers, and development tools. Cross-compiled development ecosystems like Buildroot and Yocto Project provide recipes for generating entire root filesystem images containing kernel, user-space utilities, interpreters, and package managers. These tools automate the bootstrapping process for large-scale deployment on RISC-V systems.

A smoothly functioning development environment integrates the cross-toolchain, bootstrapped software stack, and provisioned hardware or simulators. Key considerations revolve around uniformity, automation, and validation.

Integration of the cross-toolchain into popular build systems (e.g., Make, CMake, Bazel) requires setting appropriate target prefixes, sysroots, and path variables. Simultaneously, build environments need access to RISC-V headers, libraries, and runtime binaries. Including correct sysroot layout ensures consistent referencing of these resources and prevents accidental linking against host libraries.

Simulation tools such as QEMU provide early-stage development and testing environments that emulate RISC-V hardware, which is invaluable when physical boards are unavailable. Configured to match the target ISA subset and machine configuration, QEMU enables rapid iteration and debugging prior to hardware deployment.

For embedded systems, developers often employ in-circuit emulators or JTAG debuggers alongside OpenOCD or proprietary debugging servers. Cross-GDB debuggers configured for the RISC-V target allow interactive debugging from the host, crucial for diagnosing low-level issues in bootloaders or early runtime initialization.

Large-scale deployments spanning multiple RISC-V cores introduce further complexity. In such environments, cross-compilation must consider multilib configurations to support multiple ABIs or ISA variants transparently. Multilib toolchains enable generation of binaries optimized for each core configuration without requiring separate toolchains. Constructs for multi-core toolchains encompass cross-compilers capable of selecting correct instruction sets and extensions at compile time.

Automation frameworks, continuous integration systems, and containerized environments (e.g., Docker images containing RISC-V SDKs) streamline building, testing, and distributing software across development teams. Such infrastructure supports reproducible builds, cross-target testing, and seamless scaling from prototype hardware to production systems.

Several advanced considerations influence the robustness of cross-compilation and bootstrapping workflows for RISC-V:

- **ISA Diversity and Extensions:** The modular RISC-V ISA, with optional extensions (M, A, F, D, C, etc.), mandates tailored compiler and library support. Toolchains must be configured or built to enable appropriate extensions, ensuring generated binaries execute correctly and leverage performance features.

- **ABI and Endianness:** RISC-V supports multiple ABIs and is primarily little-endian by design, but tools must explicitly support these conventions. Consistency between compiler flags, linker scripts, and runtime libraries is essential to maintain binary correctness.

- **Linker Scripts and Startup Files:** Custom linker scripts define memory layout, section positioning, and entry points. Correctly authored scripts enable proper initialization sequences, exception handling, and support for bare-metal versus OS environments.

- **Cross-building Bootloaders and Kernels:** Bootloaders often require specialized cross-build environments with tightly controlled compiler flags. Kernel compilation for RISC-V may necessitate patches or configuration profiles to match the target hardware platform.

- **Multistage Bootstrapping and Self-hosting:** Some

211

projects aim for self-hosting toolchains where the RISC-V environment eventually builds its own compiler and toolchain. This requires iterative cross-compiler construction coupled with host-target coordination.

- **Performance Tuning:** Cross-compilers can be optimized for code size, speed, or debugging ease. Fine-grained control over target-specific flags (e.g., -march, -mabi, -mcmodel) refines generated code quality.

The typical sequence to build a minimal bare-metal cross-toolchain for RISC-V hardware (e.g., RV32IMAC) is outlined below. The example targets the riscv32-unknown-elf triple.

```
1  # Step 1: Build binutils
2  tar -xf binutils-2.xx.tar.gz
3  cd binutils-2.xx
4  ./configure --target=riscv32-unknown-elf --prefix
       =/opt/riscv32 \
5              --disable-nls --disable-werror
6  make -j$(nproc)
7  make install
8  cd ..
9
10 # Step 2: Download GCC sources
11 tar -xf gcc-10.xx.tar.gz
12 cd gcc-10.xx
13
14 # Step 3: Download newlib for libc
15 tar -xf newlib-4.xx.tar.gz
16
17 # Step 4: Configure and build GCC (bootstrap
       compiler)
18 mkdir build-gcc
19 cd build-gcc
20 ../configure --target=riscv32-unknown-elf --prefix
       =/opt/riscv32 \
21              --disable-nls --enable-languages=c,c
```

```
         ++ \
22                 --without-headers --disable-shared --
         disable-threads \
23                 --disable-libssp --disable-libmudflap
         --disable-libgomp
24 make all-gcc -j$(nproc)
25 make install-gcc
26 cd ..
27
28 # Step 5: Build newlib C library
29 mkdir build-newlib
30 cd build-newlib
31 ../newlib/configure --target=riscv32-unknown-elf
         --prefix=/opt/riscv32
32 make -j$(nproc)
33 make install
34 cd ..
35
36 # Step 6: Build complete GCC with newlib
37 cd build-gcc
38 make all -j$(nproc)
39 make install
```

This process results in a toolchain located under /opt/riscv32 capable of generating executables for bare-metal RISC-V devices with embedded C runtime support. Further cross-toolchains intended for operating system targets extend this process to include Linux kernel headers, glibc or musl libraries, and additional runtime components.

Robustness in cross-compilation and bootstrapping arises from meticulous alignment of toolchain components, ABI conformance, and layered integration of software stacks. The RISC-V ecosystem offers flexibility through modular tooling and open standards, but this requires careful management of version compatibility, configuration flags, and target-specific intricacies.

The evolution from embedded minimal systems to larger Linux-based deployments illustrates a continuum in complexity and tooling demands. Automation and containerization increasingly become mandatory to handle these complexities reproducibly.

Ultimately, a well-engineered cross-compilation and bootstrapping environment unlocks the full potential of RISC-V architectures, empowering diverse applications from resource-constrained IoT nodes to high-performance data center processors.

Chapter 7

Custom Extensions and Domain-Specific Accelerators

RISC-V's openness isn't just a promise—it's an invitation to innovate. This chapter empowers you to transcend generic computing by tailoring the architecture for groundbreaking workloads. Dive into the art and science of designing custom instructions, integrating vector units, and accelerating domains like AI, cryptography, and more, all while ensuring maintainable toolchain support and real-world verification.

7.1. RISC-V Extension Mechanism

The RISC-V instruction set architecture (ISA) was designed with extensibility as a core principle, enabling the addition of custom instructions and extensions without compromising the fundamental qualities of openness, simplicity, and compatibility. This extensibility relies on a rigorous formal process and careful technical considerations governing the definition, encoding, and naming of new instructions. Maintaining ecosystem coherence while fostering innovation requires adherence to predefined conventions to avoid instruction conflicts and guarantee forward and backward compatibility within implementations.

RISC-V's modular ISA framework divides the instruction set into a small base integer ISA (e.g., RV32I, RV64I) and optional standardized extensions such as multiplication/division (M), atomic operations (A), floating-point (F and D), and others. This modularity also facilitates implementation-specific extensions. The key design goal is to enable implementers to create custom functionality that seamlessly integrates with standard software and toolchains, preserving the integrity of the ISA as a unifying platform.

Crucial to this philosophy is the formal reservation of distinct opcode spaces for user-defined extensions. The base ISA defines several opcode fields as custom or reserved, indicating available encoding regions for non-standard instructions. Within these regions, custom instructions can be arbitrarily defined by individual organizations or hardware developers while ensuring no ambiguity in decoding.

Each RISC-V instruction is 32 bits in length in the base ISA, with fixed fields governing operand specification, operation type, and immediate encodings. Extensions rely on unused or reserved opcode values and functionally rich fields such as funct3 and funct7 to encode custom behavior. The encoding scheme separates opcode, register specifiers (rs1, rs2, rd), function codes (funct3, funct7), and immediate fields to facilitate compact and orthogonal instruction encodings.

Formally, custom instructions must occupy opcode spaces designated as custom-0, custom-1, custom-2, or custom-3, defined in the base ISA to avoid conflicts with future standardized instructions. For example, the opcode value 0001011b (binary 0001011) is

216

assigned for custom-0. Within this framework, the remaining bits (funct3, funct7, etc.) are allocated as needed to encode specific instructions uniquely.

Adhering to this directive avoids interference with the decoding of existing or future standard extensions, as the RISC-V privilege specification explicitly forbids usage of certain opcodes for non-custom purposes. As a result, operating system software, debuggers, and performance-monitoring tools can reliably interpret instruction streams without ambiguous interpretation.

Extensions in RISC-V are identified by short, mnemonic extension codes, typically single uppercase letters or pairs of letters, conforming to the established naming convention. Standard extensions adopt uppercase letters (e.g., "M" for integer multiplication and division, "A" for atomics), while custom extensions must avoid conflicts by using lowercase letters or combinations not reserved by the formal specification.

To maintain ecosystem compatibility, custom extension authors are encouraged to register unique extension identifiers with the RISC-V Foundation or relevant standards bodies, preventing duplication and facilitating community-wide awareness. This registry includes precise details of the opcode usage, instruction encodings, and semantic effects.

The selection of extension names and identifiers is governed by the principles of clarity and non-conflict:

- **Base Extensions:** Single uppercase ASCII letters reserved for standardized extensions.

- **Custom Extensions:** Lowercase letters or sequences, leveraging the vast namespace available.

- **Vendor-Specific Extensions:** Namespaces can be hierarchically assigned or namespaced by company or project to avoid collisions.

This structured naming system simplifies assembly language syntax, disassembler output, and software toolchain integration by enabling instruction mnemonics to include the extension identifier where necessary.

The process of designing a custom RISC-V extension involves several technical considerations:

- **Identification of Functional Requirements:** Designers must clearly define the operations the extension intends to support, including the instruction semantics, operand types, and side effects. This includes consideration of whether instructions will be arithmetic, logical, control flow, data movement, or system-oriented.

- **Allocation of Encoding Space:** Within the custom opcode space, a detailed encoding map must be designed. The allocation should minimize complexity, such as limiting the number of bits required for encoding, and avoid overlapping bit patterns for different instructions within the extension.

- **Compliance with Alignment and Atomicity:** Instructions must obey the RISC-V base ISA's alignment constraints and, for atomic or privileged instructions, must respect memory consistency and privilege-level protocols. Custom load/store operations or synchronization instructions need careful integration with existing memory models.

- **Integration with Register Files and Instruction Streams:** The extension must conform to the register operand conventions of the base ISA. This includes proper use of `rd`, `rs1`, `rs2` fields and consideration of new register types if applicable (e.g., vector registers in RISC-V Vector extension). Usage of reserved or architecturally undefined registers should be avoided unless explicitly expanded by the extension.

218

- **Software and Toolchain Support:** To maximize usability, custom extensions should be designed with simulator, assembler, compiler, and debugger support in mind. This requires definition of corresponding assembly mnemonics, immediate syntax, and ABI impact, including calling conventions and register usage policies.

Consider a hypothetical custom extension `custom-0` with opcode `0001011`. Within this opcode, seven bits (`funct7`) and three bits (`funct3`) may be used to differentiate instructions. Suppose the extension provides four instructions:

- `instr1` encoded with `funct7` = 0x01, `funct3` = 0x0

- `instr2` encoded with `funct7` = 0x02, `funct3` = 0x1

- `instr3` encoded with `funct7` = 0x04, `funct3` = 0x3

- `instr4` encoded with `funct7` = 0x08, `funct3` = 0x5

This encoding ensures orthogonality between instructions by defining unique `funct7`-`funct3` pairs. A formal specification must detail the bit fields used, behavior on exceptions or interrupts, and how the instructions interact with processor state such as flags.

Conflicts arise if two extensions claim the same encoding or if an extension uses a reserved encoding reserved for future standardized instructions. To prevent this:

- The RISC-V privileged architecture specifies which opcode spaces are permanently reserved or reserved for customization.

- Projects are advised to consult the RISC-V opcode allocation tables before defining encodings.

219

- Public documentation and community repositories provide annotation of assigned opcode regions and extension names.

Maintaining compatibility also requires ensuring that software handling instruction streams can recognize and correctly respond to custom instructions, either via graceful error handling, emulation, or tooling updates.

The existence of multiple custom extensions across different implementations risks fragmenting the software ecosystem. To mitigate this risk:

- Adherence to modular software design allows dynamic detection and fallback if a custom instruction is unsupported.

- Custom extensions that expose functionality overlapping existing standards are discouraged unless they provide significant performance or functional gains.

- Compilation toolchains increasingly support customizable backends, allowing conditional emission of custom instructions based on target capabilities.

Furthermore, the availability of user-level extension description languages and metadata permits software components to query processor capabilities at runtime, fostering portable yet optimized software.

While the base instruction width is 32 bits, RISC-V supports variable length instruction encoding (e.g., 16-bit Compressed instructions, 48-, and 64-bit-length instructions). Extensions must consider these variations:

- Custom instructions should be aligned with the extension's instruction-length policies.

- Instruction decoders must unambiguously resolve custom instructions regardless of length.

220

- ISA specification guidelines govern the use of reserved encodings for compressed or longer instruction forms.

Such considerations ensure that custom instructions remain interoperable with standard instruction fetch and decode pipelines.

The RISC-V extension mechanism's formal structure balances the imperative for innovation with the necessity of ecosystem stability. By prescribing rigorous opcode allocation and naming conventions, and emphasizing comprehensive specification of encoding details and semantic behavior, RISC-V maintains a robust, extensible platform. This approach enables diverse applications-from embedded microcontrollers to high-performance computing clusters-to benefit from tailored extensions without compromising the universality and openness of the architecture.

The rigorous technical process and formal considerations underpinning custom extension design are foundational to RISC-V's ongoing adoption and evolution in the global computing landscape.

7.2. Vector Processing and SIMD Extensions

Modern processor architectures increasingly exploit parallelism at multiple levels to improve computational throughput and energy efficiency. Among these parallelization schemes, vector processing and Single Instruction, Multiple Data (SIMD) extensions stand out as fundamental mechanisms that enhance the execution of data-parallel workloads by performing simultaneous operations on mul tiple data elements. This section explores the structural organization and architectural integration of vector and SIMD units, alongside performance optimization strategies and their implications for highly parallel computations.

Vector processing units (VPUs) are designed to operate on entire vectors—ordered sets of data elements—in parallel, rather than scalar units that process one data element per instruction cycle.

Early vector processors, such as those found in Cray supercomputers, implemented long vector registers and pipelines that processed vector elements sequentially but overlapped in a pipeline fashion to achieve high throughput.

Contemporary vector architectures organize registers as register files containing multiple vector registers, each capable of holding dozens to hundreds of elements. Supported element sizes typically include 8-, 16-, 32-, and 64-bit integers or floating-point values. The vector length (VL), representing the number of elements processed in one vector instruction, is often configurable, allowing the architectural state to be adapted to application demands. This parameterization enhances both flexibility and efficiency by enabling the reuse of the same instruction stream for varying vector sizes.

Functional units within a VPU include vector arithmetic logic units (ALUs), vector load/store units, and vector permute and reduction units. These units are pipelined to support continuous data flow and minimize latency. Vector memory instructions perform contiguous or strided memory accesses, exploiting spatial locality and prefetch mechanisms to maintain a steady data supply.

SIMD is a class of parallelism that enables a single instruction to operate simultaneously on multiple data elements stored in packed vector registers. Unlike classic vector processors that treat vectors as first-class objects, SIMD units often work within a more general-purpose register file in traditional scalar CPUs, using extended register widths and instructions to accomplish data-level parallelism.

The integration of SIMD extensions into CPUs involves several critical architectural decisions:

- **Register File Extensions:** Standard scalar registers are augmented or replaced by wider vector registers, e.g., from 128 bits in SSE to 256 bits in AVX and 512 bits in AVX-512 on x86 architectures, allowing a single SIMD register to hold multiple data elements and thus significantly increase parallel throughput.

- **Instruction Set Extension:** New SIMD instructions are incorporated to perform arithmetic, logical, permute, and memory operations across packed data elements. These instructions maintain the single-instruction semantic while extending operand width and complexity.

- **Data Alignment and Memory Access:** Efficient SIMD execution depends heavily on aligned memory accesses and the ability to load/store vector registers atomically or in few cycles. Architectures often specify alignment requirements or provide instructions for unaligned access with performance trade-offs.

- **Pipeline and Execution Units:** SIMD execution units are integrated within the CPU pipeline, often sharing resources with scalar units but optimized for wide data paths and parallel ALU operations. Multiple SIMD units may operate in parallel to increase throughput.

This integration enables existing scalar cores to gain substantial vector processing capabilities without necessitating separate vector pipeline architectures, facilitating broader applicability and ease of adoption in diverse workloads.

Maximizing performance using vector and SIMD extensions involves multiple strategies that encompass both hardware design considerations and compiler or programmer-level optimizations.

Data Layout and Memory Access Patterns

Effective vectorization requires data to be organized contiguously in memory to exploit wide load/store instructions. Data structures are often transformed from an Array of Structures (AoS) to a Structure of Arrays (SoA) format, enabling sequential access of homogeneous data elements without expensive gather/scatter operations. Coalescing accesses to avoid cache line splits and leverag-

223

ing prefetch instructions are fundamental for sustaining memory bandwidth to the vector units.

Alignment and Padding

Data alignment to SIMD register widths is critical for achieving peak throughput. Misaligned accesses either incur performance penalties or require additional microarchitectural handling. Padding data structures to ensure proper alignment or using compiler-specific alignment directives enhances data loading efficiency. Some SIMD instruction sets offer dedicated unaligned load/store instructions, but these typically have greater latency or lower throughput.

Instruction-Level Parallelism and Dependency Management

Vector instructions inherently process multiple data elements concurrently; however, dependencies within vector instructions, such as reductions or cross-lane operations, can introduce serialization points. Combining multiple independent vector operations to keep SIMD units fully occupied and employing techniques such as loop unrolling and software pipelining can minimize these bottlenecks.

Masking and Predication

Modern SIMD architectures support per-element masking that enables selective operation on vector elements within the same instruction, facilitating conditional execution without scalar branching overheads. Mask registers control which lanes participate in arithmetic or memory operations, optimizing utilization and enabling efficient handling of boundary conditions or irregular data lengths.

Recent advances in vector and SIMD extensions extend beyond simple wide parallelism to support complex computation patterns and improve programmability.

Gather/Scatter Memory Operations

Traditional SIMD instructions assume contiguous memory layouts; however, many applications exhibit irregular or sparse data access patterns. Gather and scatter instructions permit vectorized loading and storing from/to non-contiguous memory locations based on vector-indexed addresses. Although these operations involve higher latency, their availability reduces the need for scalar loops, improving overall vectorization efficiency.

Vector Predication and Control Flow

In architectures such as ARM's Scalable Vector Extension (SVE), vector length agnostic programming allows the same code to execute efficiently across a range of hardware vector widths. Predication enables vectorized conditional execution, reducing branch misprediction penalties and enabling more compact code.

Vector Reduction and Horizontal Operations

Performing reductions (sum, min, max) or horizontal operations across vector elements requires communication between SIMD lanes. Architectures provide specialized instructions to implement these efficiently via tree-like reduction circuits or shuffle operations. These instructions are essential for many scientific and machine learning workloads.

Mixed Precision Computation

To reconcile precision and performance, many SIMD extensions support mixed precision computing, allowing simultaneous arithmetic on varying precision levels, such as half-precision floating-point mixed with single or double precision. This capability benefits high-throughput domains like AI inference, where reduced precision yields significant speedups without sacrificing accuracy.

In workloads exhibiting data parallelism, such as multimedia processing, cryptography, scientific simulation, and machine learning, vector and SIMD units often serve as primary performance accelerators.

Throughput Gains

By processing multiple data elements per instruction, vector and SIMD mechanisms increase instruction throughput proportionally to the vector width, subject to memory bandwidth and dependency constraints. For example, a 256-bit SIMD unit operating on 32-bit floats can achieve an ideal $8\times$ performance improvement over scalar execution for throughput-bound kernels.

Energy Efficiency

Vectorized execution amortizes instruction decode and fetch overhead over multiple data elements, resulting in improved energy efficiency per operation compared to scalar equivalents. This efficiency is crucial in power-constrained environments, such as mobile and embedded systems.

Compiler and Programmer Requirements

Exploiting vector and SIMD extensions demands explicit support from compilers or manual optimization by programmers. Compilers use vectorization heuristics to translate loops into SIMD instructions, relying on alias analysis, loop dependence analysis, and profiling. When automatic vectorization falls short, programmers employ intrinsics or assembly-level instructions to explicitly harness SIMD capabilities.

Limitations and Challenges

While vector and SIMD extensions provide powerful tools for parallelism, certain computations with irregular data dependencies, control flow, or limited data-level parallelism may have limited benefits. Moreover, architectural constraints such as register file size, pipeline depth, and memory subsystem limitations can bound achievable performance.

Vector processing and SIMD extensions represent an essential layer of parallelism integrated within modern CPU architectures. By extending register widths, instruction sets, and pipeline resources, they enable efficient execution of data-parallel workloads with significant improvements in throughput and energy consumption. Their performance benefits rely on complementary software and hardware mechanisms that optimize data layout, alignment, masking, and instruction scheduling. Emerging architectural features such as gather/scatter, predication, and mixed precision support continue to broaden the applicability and effectiveness of vector and SIMD paradigms in diverse computational domains.

7.3. Cryptographic and Security-focused Extensions

Modern computing architectures increasingly integrate specialized cryptographic and security-focused extensions to address the growing demand for hardware-accelerated security primitives and trustworthy execution environments. These extensions enhance both performance and security guarantees, facilitating rapid cryptographic computations while mitigating software attack vectors. The progression from general-purpose instruction sets to domain-specific hardware support plays a pivotal role in safeguarding sensitive data and improving throughput in security-critical applications.

At the core of cryptographic hardware extensions are instructions dedicated to accelerating fundamental primitives such as symmetric encryption, hashing, modular arithmetic, and public-key operations. Traditional software implementations of these algorithms, while flexible, suffer from inefficiencies that hinder their deployment in latency-sensitive environments. Purpose-built hardware instructions enable significantly reduced cycle counts and energy consumption.

A fundamental example is the inclusion of instructions for AES (Advanced Encryption Standard) round transformations. The AES algorithm, widely adopted for confidentiality, involves a series of permutation and substitution operations over data blocks. Hardware-accelerated AES instructions implement the SubBytes, ShiftRows, MixColumns, and AddRoundKey steps directly within the processor datapath. This approach eliminates the overhead of software-based table lookups and bit manipulations while ensuring constant-time execution, thereby mitigating side-channel attacks based on timing variations. For instance, Intel's AES-NI instruction set provides the AESENC and AESDEC instructions to perform single AES encryption and decryption rounds respectively, substantially boosting throughput in cryptographic libraries.

Complementary to symmetric-key accelerators, hashing algorithms receive dedicated support through hardware instructions implementing compression and permutation functions. The SHA (Secure Hash Algorithm) family is commonly targeted, with instructions that compute SHA-1 or SHA-256 message schedule updates and compression rounds natively. These primitives reduce CPU load in digital signature verification, certificate handling, and integrity checks. The hardware instructions typically correspond directly to transformations such as Ch, Maj, and Sigma functions, accelerating iterative processes fundamental to hash computations.

Public-key cryptography benefits from hardware extensions aimed at accelerating modular exponentiation and elliptic curve operations. Since these cryptographic schemes underpin protocols like TLS and digital signatures, improving modular multiplication and reduction performance has wide-reaching implications. Some architectures incorporate dedicated modular arithmetic units or instructions that perform Montgomery multiplication, enabling faster modular exponentiations without resorting to cumbersome software multiplication and division sequences. Elliptic curve cryptography (ECC) extensions may provide point multiplication primitives, facilitating scalar multiplication on curves directly in hardware, thereby enhancing efficiency in operations such as key exchange and signing.

Beyond accelerating cryptographic primitives, specialized instructions enable secure computing and memory protection. Hardware support for trusted execution environments (TEEs) and isolated enclaves relies on security extensions that manage secure contexts with hardware-enforced access controls. Instructions for securely switching context or for cryptographic sealing of memory regions provide robust defenses against software attacks, including code injection and privilege escalation. For example, Intel SGX (Software Guard Extensions) introduces enclave creation and management instructions to establish protected memory areas, resistant to inspection and tampering even under powerful adversaries.

Additional security-focused instructions address random number generation and integrity verification. Cryptographically secure random number generators (CSRNGs) embedded in hardware expose instructions to retrieve entropy with low latency and high quality, critical for key generation and nonces. Integrity verification instructions, such as those that compute and check message authentication codes (MACs), help automate and offload authentication tasks.

The design of these extensions entails careful consideration of trade-offs between complexity, flexibility, and exposure to new attack surfaces. Hardware implementations must resist side-channel leakage, including timing, power, and electromagnetic emanations. Techniques such as constant-time logic, balanced circuits, and masking are integrated within the microarchitecture for critical instructions. Furthermore, the extension interfaces are designed to avoid leakage of sensitive data through register state or interrupt behavior, necessitating secure exception handling and context preservation.

From an architectural perspective, cryptographic and security extensions influence processor pipeline design and instruction scheduling. Special-purpose instructions often require additional functional units or modified datapaths. For example, AES round instructions perform parallelizable byte-level transformations in combinational logic, necessitating fine-grained datapaths aligned with the AES state matrix. Similarly, modular arithmetic instructions may introduce longer-latency multiply-accumulate stages that must integrate seamlessly into pipelined operation without excessive stalls.

Integration in the software development ecosystem is facilitated through compiler intrinsics and instruction set extensions. Compilers expose these specialized instructions to high-level languages via intrinsic functions, allowing cryptographic libraries to transparently benefit from hardware acceleration without hand-written assembly. This abstraction improves maintainability and portability while maximizing security, as hardened algorithms implemented via hardware instructions reduce reliance on error-prone software routines.

The effectiveness of these cryptographic extensions is evidenced by widespread adoption in both server-grade and embedded processors. Mobile devices incorporate accelerators for AES and SHA to enable secure communications and digital rights management at low power. Data center CPUs utilize hardware cryptography and trusted execution environments to protect virtual machine isolation and data confidentiality. Customizable security instructions within RISC-V and other open ISAs illustrate the emerging trend of domain-specific hardware extensions tailored to application-specific security requirements.

Cryptographic and security-focused hardware extensions significantly enhance the performance and trustworthiness of security-sensitive applications by embedding essential cryptographic functions directly into the processor pipeline. These extensions combine algorithm-specific instruction sets with architectural innovations and microarchitectural countermeasures to deliver high-throughput, side-channel resistant implementations. As cybersecurity demands evolve, hardware-accelerated cryptography re-

230

mains a critical element in the design of resilient, efficient computing platforms.

7.4. AI and Machine Learning Accelerators

The remarkable progress in artificial intelligence (AI) and machine
learning (ML) techniques has precipitated an urgent demand for
computational platforms optimized to handle large-scale and complex workloads efficiently. General-purpose processors, while versatile, are increasingly inadequate to meet the stringent latency,
throughput, and power constraints inherent to modern inference
and training tasks. This has catalyzed the development of specialized AI/ML accelerators, composed of tailored architectural elements and tightly integrated co-processors that provide significant
gains in performance and energy efficiency.

At the architectural level, AI accelerators embody a divergence
from traditional CPU paradigms by emphasizing massive parallelism, data reuse, and specialized numerical formats. The canonical pattern manifests in a hierarchy of execution units tightly coupled with on-chip memory subsystems optimized for the dataflows
characteristic of machine learning algorithms. These execution
units primarily consist of matrix multiply-accumulate (MAC) arrays, vector processors, and tensor cores, each engineered to exploit the dense linear algebra operations ubiquitous in neural network computations.

Matrix Multiply Units or systolic arrays have become archetypal
building blocks in deep learning accelerators. A systolic array is a
spatially arranged network of processing elements (PEs) that co-
operatively compute matrix products by propagating partial sums
rhythmically across the array. This architecture profoundly minimizes costly data movement and alleviates external memory bandwidth constraints by enabling high throughput with low floating-
point operations per byte (FLOP/byte). For example, Google's Ten-

231

sor Processing Unit (TPU) employs an extensive systolic array tailored for accelerating large matrix multiplications arising in both convolutional and fully connected layers.

Vector processing units specialize in parallelizing element-wise operations and smaller matrix kernels. These units are highly effective in supporting the non-linear activation functions, normalization operations, and other primitives that supplement the core linear computations in ML models. By embedding dedicated hardware for non-linearities such as ReLU, sigmoid, and tanh, accelerators reduce the instruction overhead and improve pipeline efficiency.

The emergence of reduced-precision arithmetic formats-such as 16-bit floating point (FP16), bfloat16, and integer quantizations-has additionally shaped the design of AI accelerators. Lower bit-width operations reduce compute complexity and memory bandwidth requirements without significant loss in model accuracy. Consequently, many accelerators incorporate mixed-precision pipelines that dynamically switch between precision modes. NVIDIA's Tensor Cores, for instance, perform mixed-precision matrix multiplications, combining FP16 inputs with FP32 accumulation, achieving notable gains in throughput and energy efficiency.

Central to the efficiency of AI accelerators is the design of on-chip memory hierarchies that accommodate the large volume of data reuse inherent in neural network inference and training. These hierarchies typically consist of multi-level register files, scratchpad memories, and caches tailored to frequent access patterns. Locality-aware dataflow designs aim to maximize reuse of weights and activations within the accelerator's high-bandwidth internal memory, drastically mitigating the latency and power cost of off-chip DRAM accesses.

Several common dataflow patterns have emerged to optimize these data movements, notably weight-stationary, output-stationary, and row-stationary dataflows:

- *Weight-stationary* dataflows pin the weight data within the PEs while streaming through input activations and accumulating partial sums externally. This minimizes weight fetches, advantageous for models with large static weight parameters such as convolutional neural networks (CNNs).

- *Output-stationary* dataflows focus on maintaining partial sums for output activations within PEs to reduce write-back traffic, beneficial when the output size is small relative to the input.

- *Row-stationary* dataflows, a generalized scheme, attempt to balance reuse across weights, inputs, and partial sums by dynamically adapting to workload characteristics, thus improving both energy and performance efficiency.

Beyond single-chip accelerators, integration with host processors constitutes a critical design dimension. These accelerators often function as tightly coupled co-processors, interfacing through high-bandwidth on-chip interconnects or coherent memory systems, allowing low-overhead task offloading and synchronization. The interface design influences achievable latency and throughput, a key consideration especially for real-time inference applications.

Recent designs leverage heterogeneous architectures where domain-specific accelerators complement general-purpose cores within unified systems-on-chip (SoCs). This approach enhances flexibility and programmability, allowing workloads to be partitioned strategically based on computational intensity, latency requirements, and precision sensitivity. For instance, a CPU may orchestrate control flow and handle irregular computations, while the AI accelerator manages bulk matrix operations.

In the context of training workloads, accelerators must also support highly parallel and dynamic operations such as backpropagation, gradient accumulation, and parameter updates. This ne-cessitates architectures that accommodate frequent synchroniza-tion and support efficient distributed computing paradigms when scaling across multiple nodes. High-bandwidth interconnects and scalable memory hierarchies play pivotal roles, as training datasets and model sizes can exceed single-chip capacities.

Emerging paradigms such as in-memory computing and analog accelerators seek to further bridge the gap between compute and memory by performing computations directly within memory ar-rays, thereby circumventing the von Neumann bottleneck. While these approaches promise potential leaps in efficiency, they intro-duce new challenges related to precision, noise, and programma-bility, which ongoing research aims to resolve.

Throughout contemporary AI/ML accelerator architectures, the interplay of specialization and programmability remains critical. Complete fixed-function accelerators yield high efficiency but lim-ited adaptability to evolving models and operations. Conversely, fully programmable designs afford broader applicability at the cost of performance overhead. The state-of-the-art continually refines this trade-off, employing domain-specific instruction set architec-tures (ISAs), configurable data paths, and software abstractions such as compiler frameworks and runtime libraries to strike an ef-fective balance.

The architectural landscape of AI and machine learning acceler-ators is characterized by the strategic deployment of specialized execution units-systolic arrays, tensor cores, and vector units-closely integrated with intelligent memory hierarchies and adapt-able dataflows. These designs cater precisely to the computational motifs of neural network workloads, delivering substantial acceler-ation in both inference and training phases. As machine learning models grow in complexity and demand escalates across applica-tions, continued innovation in accelerator microarchitectures and system integration will remain pivotal to sustaining scaling in AI performance and efficiency.

7.5. Compiler and Toolchain Support for Extensions

Extending processor instruction sets with custom instructions introduces significant challenges and opportunities for software toolchains. The primary objective is to enable compilers, assemblers, and debuggers to natively recognize, generate, and manipulate these instructions, thereby maintaining a seamless development process for programmers and system integrators. Achieving this requires a coordinated adaptation across the entire compilation and debugging pipeline to ensure efficient code generation, accurate debugging, and interoperability with existing software components.

A critical initial step in toolchain adaptation involves extending the compiler's instruction selection phase. Most modern compilers, including widely used frameworks such as LLVM and GCC, use an intermediate representation (IR) that abstracts machine instructions. Support for custom instructions necessitates enriching the compiler backend's machine description to define new opcode semantics, operand types, and instruction constraints. This is typically realized through customizing the instruction patterns in the compiler's backend description files-such as TableGen definitions in LLVM or machine description files in GCC-that govern instruction selection mechanisms. Incorporating these custom patterns enables the compiler's instruction selector to recognize opportunities for applying new instructions during the IR-to-assembly lowering stage, potentially guided by target-specific optimization passes targeting improved performance or code density.

Integrating custom instructions also requires careful consideration of the instruction scheduling and register allocation components of the compiler backend. The new instructions may possess unique latency, resource usage, and operand constraints that differ from standard instructions. Annotating these characteristics accurately within the compiler allows the scheduler to optimize instruction ordering and the register allocator to manage register pressure effectively. For example, a custom multiply-accumulate instruction might accelerate certain numerical kernels but impose specific register usage patterns. Failing to model these factors risks generating suboptimal or incorrect code. Consequently, extending the compiler's cost models and latency tables to incorporate custom instruction behavior becomes essential to maintaining correctness and efficiency.

Assemblers must be adapted correspondingly to recognize the syntax and binary encoding of custom instructions. This involves extending the instruction encoding tables and parser grammar. Assemblers such as GNU as or LLVM's integrated assembler rely on instruction definitions specifying mnemonic names, operands, and encoding formats. By augmenting these definitions, the assembler can accurately encode custom instructions from assembly source code into machine code. Additionally, the assembler syntax should support any new operand types or addressing modes introduced by the custom extensions to maintain syntactic clarity and ease of use.

Complementing the assembler modifications, disassemblers and binary utilities require updates to decode and display custom instructions correctly. Without decoder support, debugging and binary inspection tools may interpret the custom instruction opcodes as unknown or invalid, impairing developers' ability to analyze and optimize the generated code. Modifying disassembler tables ensures that instruction traces, backtraces, and profiling outputs correctly represent the presence and semantics of extensions, which is crucial for effective debugging and performance tuning.

Debuggers themselves demand enhancements to handle the semantic and operational implications of custom instructions. Since debugging often involves stepping through individual instructions, breakpoint management, and register inspection, the debugger's architecture must be aware of custom instructions' effects on program state. For instance, instructions that manipulate specialized registers or trigger hardware events necessitate extending the debugger's register models and possibly its execution control logic. This enables functionalities such as correct single-stepping over custom instructions and accurate register value display during debug sessions.

Moreover, symbol and debug information formats (e.g., DWARF) occasionally require extensions to represent new architectural features introduced by custom instructions. For example, custom instructions may operate on user-defined registers or introduce new execution contexts. Enhancing debug metadata to include these constructs ensures that source-level debugging remains coherent, supporting accurate variable location mapping and call stack unwinding in the presence of extensions.

Maintaining seamless integration of custom instructions within high-level language toolchains often involves augmenting compiler intrinsic functions or built-in functions. Intrinsics serve as explicit calls to architectural features unavailable through standard language constructs. By defining intrinsics corresponding to custom instructions, compiler frontends provide programmers with controlled access to extensions while preserving portability and safety. These intrinsics then map directly to the custom instructions during lowering, enabling optimized usage without inline assembly. Such intrinsics typically require modifications to language-specific frontend passes to expose them effectively.

Automated testing and verification of toolchain extensions are crucial to ensure robustness and correctness. Custom instructions introduce new code paths in compilation and debugging components, demanding thorough validation through unit tests, integration tests, and conformance suites. Cross-validation of generated machine code against hardware simulators or FPGA prototypes enables detection of discrepancies early in the development cycle. Incorporating regression testing pipelines that exercise custom instruction support minimizes the risk of regressions and promotes continuous improvement.

In complex system environments, tooling support must often span multiple abstraction layers, including just-in-time (JIT) compilers and virtual machines. Enabling JIT compilers to emit custom instructions requires runtime code generation components to recognize and encode these instructions dynamically. This may involve extending the JIT backend's instruction selection and encoding logic similarly to static compilers, along with mechanisms to query processor features at runtime for guard conditions to ensure safe usage of extensions.

Supporting multiple toolchains concurrently presents additional challenges, as each toolchain may have differing conventions and internal architectures. Hence, maintaining portability of custom instruction definitions across toolchains increases the sustainability of the extensions. Adopted strategies include standardizing instruction semantics in intermediate representations, using common description formats (e.g., LLVM TableGen files), and isolating architecture-specific definitions to manageable modules. Such modularity facilitates broader adoption and simplifies maintenance.

Interfacing with operating system and runtime components further influences toolchain support. Certain custom instructions may interact with privileged processor modes or require kernel awareness (e.g., for saving/restoring extended register sets). Compilers and debuggers must coordinate with operating system abstractions to ensure consistency. For example, debugging support may require kernel modules or drivers to expose processor state related to extensions, necessitating careful interface design between user-level tools and system software.

Finally, documentation and developer support materials are essential components of a successful toolchain adaptation strategy. Defining clear specifications for custom instructions-including instruction syntax, semantics, encoding, and constraints-provides the foundation for effective toolchain modifications. Well-documented APIs, intrinsic definitions, and guidelines for writing inline assembly or intrinsics greatly assist developers in leveraging extensions productively.

Supporting custom instructions through compiler and toolchain adaptations involves comprehensive modifications across instruction selection, encoding, scheduling, debugging, and runtime integration. These efforts enable developers to access hardware enhancements transparently within established programming environments, preserve software portability and maintainability, and ultimately deliver optimized performance on extended architectures.

7.6. Co-verification and Compliance Testing

Co-verification and compliance testing are pivotal processes that ensure custom extensions integrated within complex hardware or software ecosystems meet stringent functional and security requirements. These processes employ a rigorous combination of simulation, formal methods, and hardware-software co-design strategies, unified by comprehensive tools and methodologies that systematically validate and certify the intended behavior of custom extensions.

At the core of co-verification is the synchronized validation of hardware and software components, ensuring that extensions operate correctly within the overall system context. Custom extensions frequently alter or augment baseline instruction sets, introduce specialized processing units, or modify memory and peripheral interfaces. This complexity demands coordinated verification flows

239

where hardware models, firmware, device drivers, and higher-level software undergo collective evaluation. Such joint workflows typically detect integration issues, mismatches in assumptions, or inconsistencies between specification and implementation.

The initial stage in co-verification involves specifying the custom extension's functional intent in formal or semi-formal languages, coupled with a reference architectural model. This reference model encapsulates the precise semantics of the extended instruction set architecture (ISA) or the augmented hardware behavior. These models are commonly constructed using hardware description languages (HDLs) such as SystemVerilog or formal specification languages like SystemC or the RISC-V ISA formal semantics framework. This foundational step ensures traceability between original requirements and their manifestations in implementation and testing artifacts.

Functional verification primarily relies on simulation-based techniques, where the design-under-test (DUT) hardware model and corresponding software stacks execute carefully crafted test programs. Verification environments often utilize hardware simulation tools augmented with co-simulation capabilities, allowing concurrent execution of firmware or operating system components in software simulators. The test suites used in this phase typically derive from standardized compliance tests, custom validation routines, and coverage-driven random tests.

Compliance suites are essential for validating that custom extensions conform to architectural specifications and interoperate seamlessly with existing ecosystem components. These suites encompass tests assessing instruction-level behavior, exception handling, memory consistency, peripheral integration, and security properties. For example, the RISC-V Foundation provides an official compliance test suite that extends to custom instructions, enabling systematic evaluation of ISA extensions. Compliance test results serve as measurable certification benchmarks indicating functional correctness and adherence to architectural constraints.

Reference models, whether golden RTL blocks or formal models, act as oracles during test execution. They generate expected outputs and side-effect states against which DUT responses are compared. These models reduce reliance on manual inspection and enable automated pass/fail determinations in extensive test campaigns. Formal verification augmentations, such as equivalence checking and property verification, complement simulation by exhaustively proving correctness properties and corner-case behaviors that are challenging or infeasible to validate through testing alone.

Security correctness of custom extensions demands dedicated attention beyond functional verification. Extensions often introduce novel access control mechanisms, encryption accelerators, or privileged instructions that, if improperly designed, could lead to vulnerabilities or unauthorized state modifications. Security compliance testing evaluates whether the extension maintains system confidentiality, integrity, and availability constraints. This evaluation employs threat modeling, penetration testing, and side-channel analysis tools integrated within the co-verification flow.

Security validation also involves property checking and assertion-based verification methodologies, where security-critical properties are expressed as formal assertions monitored during simulation. Examples include ensuring that sensitive registers are accessible only in privileged modes or that speculative execution of new instructions does not leak information. Such assertions may be embedded directly in the HDL source or incorporated within external verification wrappers.

Certification of custom extensions often requires demonstrating compliance with regulatory or industry standards, necessitating traceable evidence of the entire verification process. Verification artifacts-including test plans, coverage reports, test execution logs, and formal proof certificates-form the documentation basis for certification authorities. Automated compliance reporting frameworks link execution outcomes with standards requirements, facilitating audits and reducing manual efforts.

Tools enabling co-verification and compliance testing are multifaceted and include integrated development environments (IDEs) with debugging, profiling, and trace capabilities; hardware/software co-simulation platforms; formal verification engines; and coverage analysis utilities. Emulators and FPGA prototyping platforms add validation layers, enabling near-real-time execution of custom extensions under realistic workloads and environmental conditions. These platforms support fine-grained performance, power, and security analysis, all essential for high-assurance designs.

The integration of continuous integration/continuous deployment (CI/CD) methodologies into the co-verification process has enhanced the efficiency and rigor of compliance testing cycles. Automated execution of compliance suites, triggered by code changes, ensures early detection of regressions and design deviations. Furthermore, employing containerization and cloud-based verification infrastructures allows parallel execution of extensive test campaigns, reducing verification turnaround times and increasing confidence in extension quality.

Verification coverage metrics remain fundamental for measuring completeness and identifying verification gaps. Functional coverage tracks exercised scenarios related to custom extension features, while code coverage monitors exercised RTL paths. Security coverage extends to simulated and tested attack scenarios to assess robustness. Achieving high coverage levels strongly correlates with reduced field failures and improved extension dependability.

Co-verification and compliance testing of custom extensions constitute an advanced, multidisciplinary effort that combines functional correctness verification, security assurance, and regulatory compliance in an integrated environment. Reliance on standard-

242

ized compliance suites and authoritative reference models ensures repeatability, reproducibility, and trustworthiness of verification outcomes. The synergy of formal methods, dynamic simulation, and hardware/software co-emulation produces a comprehensive validation infrastructure essential for deploying custom extensions that are both functionally correct and secure.

7.7. Case Studies in Custom Silicon

Custom silicon design leveraging RISC-V extensions has yielded compelling breakthroughs across a diverse spectrum of application domains. The intrinsic modularity and extensibility of the RISC-V ISA create a natural foundation for architecting domain-specific accelerators, enabling tailored performance, efficiency, and security enhancements. This section examines salient real-world examples where bespoke RISC-V extensions have translated into tangible improvements, highlighting architectural decisions, implementation strategies, and the resulting impact on system metrics.

Low-Power IoT Edge Processing: Khronos Devices

Khronos Devices, a leading provider of ultra-low-power IoT endpoints, integrated custom RISC-V instruction extensions within their sensor-hub microcontrollers to optimize data acquisition and preprocessing. The baseline design comprised a 32-bit RV32IM core, augmented with custom fixed-point arithmetic units and specialized bit manipulation instructions tailored for sensor fusion algorithms. By extending the ALU with parallel dot-product operations and vectorized threshold checks directly encoded in novel ISA instructions, Khronos achieved an average $3\times$ speedup in sensor data filtering and compression tasks compared to pure software implementations.

From a power perspective, these hardware extensions enabled clock gating and early exit conditions in computation, reducing active cycles significantly. The die area overhead was constrained to under 10% by careful instruction encoding reuse and localized arithmetic unit modifications. Khronos' design process emphasized early co-verification of hardware and software changes, ensuring seamless integration with existing compiler backends and runtime environments. This experience underscores the value of close collaboration between hardware architects and software developers to fully exploit custom ISA advantages in energy-constrained embedded scenarios.

High-Performance Cryptography Acceleration: Securisync

Securisync, a semiconductor company specializing in secure communications, deployed custom instructions to accelerate cryptographic primitives within an RV64G core framework. Recognizing that conventional RISC-V instructions inadequately optimized finite field arithmetic and modular exponentiation, Securisync introduced an extension set incorporating multi-precision multiply-accumulate operations and bit-level permutation instructions designed specifically for elliptic curve and RSA algorithms.

Notably, the custom instructions enabled execution of modular reduction sequences in significantly fewer CPI (cycles per instruction) compared to software libraries on standard cores. When integrated with a tailored hardware multiplier pipeline, the resulting silicon implementation demonstrated a $5\times$ throughput increase in cryptographic throughput while maintaining low leakage currents through fine-grained clock and power gating of specialized units.

Securisync's success hinged on the formal verification of the extended ISA semantics, guaranteeing secure instruction behaviors immune to side-channel leakage that could otherwise compromise cryptographic integrity. The project also illuminated the critical interplay between microarchitecture tuning and ISA design balancing instruction complexity against pipeline depth to preserve high clock frequencies and minimize latency in security-sensitive operations.

AI Inference Acceleration: NeuVector Processor

NeuVector's AI inference engine implemented a custom RISC-V core augmented with vector and matrix computation units embodied as ISA extensions. The design integrated a lightweight vector processing unit (VPU) supporting packed integer operations and fused multiply-add instructions optimized for sparse neural network layers. Custom instructions for dynamic quantization and activation function approximation further enhanced inference speed and memory efficiency.

Hardware-software co-design efforts focused on compiler intrinsics exposing these instructions to machine learning frameworks, enabling efficient mapping of convolutional kernels and recurrent layers directly onto hardware. Silicon prototypes demonstrated a 4.2× improvement in inference latency and a 3.6× reduction in power consumption compared to standard RV64GC cores executing the same workloads.

Key challenges encountered included managing increased instruction set complexity without impacting trigger-based debugging and profiling capabilities, along with integrating novel instructions into the existing memory hierarchy for seamless cache coherency. NeuVector's case exemplifies the transformative potential of RISC-V-based custom extensions in domain-specific AI acceleration platforms, combining architectural flexibility with scalable parallelism.

Real-Time Signal Processing: Wavecore DSP

Wavecore's real-time digital signal processing solution employs a custom RISC-V core extended with a suite of instructions for cyclic redundancy checks (CRC), fast Fourier transform (FFT) butterfly operations, and windowing functions. These specialized instructions encode hardware-accelerated loop unrolling and bit-reversal permutations to expedite spectral analysis, essential in wireless

245

communication and radar systems.

The silicon implementation benefits from an instruction set architecture that supports variable-length immediate fields, enabling compact encoding of control-flow optimizations critical in DSP kernels. Wavecore reports an overall $3.8\times$ speedup in signal processing tasks, with deterministic latency guarantees-imperative for timing-sensitive applications.

By leveraging RISC-V's open nature, Wavecore implemented iterative design refinements through rapid retargeting of toolchains and simulation environments. The project illustrates how incremental custom extensions can significantly boost domain-specific performance while maintaining compatibility with standard core components, easing system integration.

Security-Enhanced Microcontrollers: Sentinel IC

Sentinel IC developed a family of microcontrollers embedding custom RISC-V security extensions aimed at thwarting both invasive and non-invasive attacks. This included instructions for secure context switching, shielded memory access, and hardware-enforced pointer validation. The extensions facilitated trusted execution environments (TEE) and secure boot sequences within embedded environments.

Integrating these security-focused instructions required non-trivial modifications to privilege levels and pipeline hazard management, with particular attention to secure state transitions and side-channel resistance. Sentinel's verification process combined formal methods with hardware fault injection testing to validate robustness.

The resulting silicon showcased a $2.5\times$ improvement in the speed of cryptographic protocol authentication phases and a significant reduction in attack surface due to compartmentalized execution flows. Sentinel's implementation reinforces the criticality of ISA-level security primitives as foundational building blocks for modern trustworthy computing systems.

Lessons Learned and Best Practices

The examined case studies collectively reveal a consistent set of principles facilitating effective custom silicon development using RISC-V extensions:

- **Early Hardware-Software Co-Design:** Close collaboration between ISA designers, microarchitects, and compiler engineers from the outset enables practical, fully optimized instruction sets and reduces costly redesign cycles.

- **Minimizing ISA Complexity Growth:** Leveraging encoding space efficiently and reusing existing opcode slots avoids excessive decoder complexity; simpler instructions with well-defined semantics integrate more seamlessly into pipelines.

- **Comprehensive Verification and Validation:** Formal semantic verification combined with hardware-level stress testing and side-channel analysis is essential, especially when security or critical real-time requirements are involved.

- **Toolchain and Ecosystem Support:** Early adaptation of compilers, debuggers, and simulation tools to recognize and correctly handle custom extensions ensures smooth software development workflows and debugging fidelity.

- **Iterative Prototyping and Feedback Loops:** Rapid prototyping on FPGA or emulation platforms provides early functional insights, enabling incremental refinement of ISA features and microarchitectural designs.

- **Focus on Application-Specific Metrics:** Custom extensions yield the greatest benefits when clearly guided by target application performance, power, or security metrics rather than generic optimization goals.

247

Across these projects, the RISC-V ecosystem's openness and modularity have proven invaluable in fostering innovation through custom silicon. The capacity to extend the ISA with targeted, efficient instructions tailored to precise workloads epitomizes the advantage of open architecture principles for driving next-generation chip design.

The experiences documented impress upon practitioners that thoughtful and judicious incorporation of custom RISC-V extensions can unlock orders-of-magnitude benefits across diverse domains, from edge compute to high-performance acceleration and embedded security. These case studies collectively chart a roadmap for organizations seeking to harness the modularity and flexibility of RISC-V to realize silicon solutions with uncompromised specialization and optimized resource utilization.

Chapter 8

Security, Reliability, and Robustness

In an era of pervasive threats and uncompromising demands for uptime, the trustworthiness of a computing platform is paramount. This chapter explores the technologies, strategies, and best practices that fortify RISC-V systems against attack, data corruption, and unpredictable failures. Discover how integrating security and reliability from the ground up equips RISC-V to power mission-critical and safety-sensitive applications.

8.1. Threat Modeling RISC-V Systems

Threat modeling RISC-V systems demands a comprehensive, multi-layered analytical framework, systematically dissecting potential adversarial interactions at the Instruction Set Architecture (ISA), microarchitecture, and System-on-Chip (SoC) levels. This approach illuminates critical attack surfaces and valuable assets, thereby establishing a foundation for targeted defense mechanisms essential to the security posture of increasingly complex RISC-V deployments.

At the ISA level, the threat landscape emerges from the architectural definition that abstracts hardware features into a programmer-visible interface. The RISC-V ISA, defined by a modular specification with a base integer instruction set and numerous optional extensions, inherently shapes the attack surface by virtue of its design choices and extensibility. Threat modeling here initially involves enumerating architectural features accessible to software and privileged modes, including instruction formats, privilege levels (user, supervisor, machine), and memory management constructs such as paging and address translation. The open-source nature of RISC-V encourages custom extensions, which, while promoting innovation, introduces variability in security guarantees. Each extension represents a potential vector for exploitation if inadequate validation or unintended interactions occur.

Fundamental to the ISA threat model is the classification of critical assets. These encompass registers holding security-sensitive information (e.g., control and status registers such as `mstatus`, `medeleg`, `mideleg`), memory regions with privilege-dependent access, and machine mode instructions permitting system control. Attack vectors at this layer may exploit incorrect privilege escalation paths, instruction misinterpretation, or subtle side effects caused by asynchronous interrupts and exceptions. For instance, adversaries might manipulate privilege transitions to bypass access controls or trigger race conditions during context switches.

Subsequent analysis at the microarchitecture layer must integrate an understanding of the hardware implementation nuances underpinning the ISA semantics. The microarchitecture entails all implementation-specific components such as pipelines, caches, branch predictors, and execution units, which collectively determine performance and influence side-channel exposure. Threat

250

modeling here demands granular dissection of timing, power, and electromagnetic behavior, as these physical characteristics furnish indirect leakage channels exploitable via microarchitectural attacks like Spectre, Meltdown, and rowhammer variants.

Key assets identified at this stratum include microarchitectural buffers, speculative execution logic, and privilege escalation circuits. An attacker proficient in leveraging microarchitectural vulnerabilities can induce speculative execution of unauthorized instructions or infer privileged state by monitoring covert channels. An accurate threat model incorporates formal reasoning about pipeline stages, reorder buffers, and speculative control flow, emphasizing how speculative side effects may deviate from ISA-defined behavior. Additionally, microarchitectural resource sharing within multicore or multithreaded cores introduces interprocess leakage pathways, necessitating analysis of cache partitioning, flush mechanisms, and access arbitration policies.

At the SoC level, threat modeling broadens to encompass heterogeneous hardware blocks integrated alongside the RISC-V core, including peripheral controllers, direct memory access (DMA) engines, interconnect fabrics, and firmware components. The complexity and diversity of SoC subsystems amplify the attack surface and challenge defense strategies. Peripheral interfaces often function with varying privilege boundaries or incomplete validation, potentially enabling adversaries to inject malicious transactions or escalate privileges through bus mastering or malformed requests.

Assets in SoC threat modeling encompass configuration registers, debug interfaces, firmware code stored in non-volatile memory, and communication channels between components. Attack surfaces emerge from exploitable misconfigurations, unprotected debug ports (e.g., JTAG), and insecure firmware update mechanisms. Moreover, complex interactions between firmware and hardware subsystems raise the specter of supply-chain attacks, persistent malware, or hardware Trojans. Accurately modeling risks requires

251

detailed knowledge of the SoC integration, inter-component trust assumptions, and the operational environment.

Methodologically, a robust threat modeling process invokes structured frameworks such as STRIDE (Spoofing, Tampering, Repudiation, Information disclosure, Denial of service, Elevation of privilege), adapted to each abstraction level. The identification phase enumerates possible threats by assessing data flows, trust boundaries, and asset exposures. RISC-V-specific considerations include the implications of open ISA extensibility, variable privilege modes, and the modular SoC landscape.

Attack surface analysis benefits from leveraging formal specification artifacts and design documentation wherever available to construct precise attack graphs that relate adversarial capabilities to potential vulnerabilities. Hardware description languages combined with verification tools aid in uncovering corner cases arising from combinatorial and sequential logic interactions. Similarly, static analysis of firmware and bootloaders supplements the threat enumeration for SoC-level firmware-based exploits.

The interdependence across abstraction levels necessitates a coalesced view where threats identified at one layer propagate or amplify risks at others. For example, a microarchitectural side-channel vulnerability can enable leakage of privileged information defined in the ISA, while insecure firmware management on the SoC permits injection of compromise that subsequently manipulates microarchitectural state. Accordingly, a layered defense-in-depth strategy informed by threat modeling ensures protections are aligned with the most critical and exploitable assets.

Quantitative aspects integrate into threat modeling through attack surface metrics and risk scoring, assessing exposure, exploitability, and impact parameters. Metrics such as the number of entry points, complexity of exploit execution, and potential damage to confidentiality, integrity, and availability guide prioritization of mitigation efforts. This systemic quantification aids designers and defenders in balancing security trade-offs against performance, cost, and flexibility inherent in RISC-V system implementations.

The dynamic and evolving nature of RISC-V ecosystems, coupled with extensive customization capabilities, places a premium on continuous threat reassessment throughout design, development, and deployment phases. Automated tooling capable of extracting threat-relevant information from ISA specifications, RTL codebases, and SoC integration scripts presents promising avenues to scale threat modeling efforts efficiently.

In summation, an effective RISC-V threat model intricately maps vulnerabilities across the ISA, microarchitecture, and SoC layers, aligning identified attack surfaces and assets with adversary goals and system trust assumptions. This foundational analysis not only illuminates existing risk vectors but also anticipates emergent threats, thereby empowering resilient architectural and implementation choices central to securing modern RISC-V-based computing platforms.

8.2. Secure Boot and Chain of Trust

Establishing a secure boot process is fundamental to the security posture of modern computing systems, providing a hardware-rooted foundation that ensures only trusted and authenticated code is executed from system initialization onward. The core concept underpinning this security model is the *chain of trust*, which links a series of verifications starting from immutable hardware elements through successive layers of firmware and boot code, culminating in the operating system and application software. The primary objective of secure boot is to prevent unauthorized or compromised code from executing during the early phases of system startup, thereby mitigating a wide range of attacks such as bootkits, rootkits, and firmware tampering.

At the base of the chain of trust lies the *hardware root of trust* (RoT), an immutable piece of logic embedded in silicon or fused within the device during manufacturing. This RoT is designed to be tamper-resistant and is responsible for verifying the authenticity and integrity of the initial program load (IPL) code. Typically, the RoT consists of a minimal bootloader or verification engine embedded in read-only memory (ROM) inside a trusted execution environment (TEE) or secure enclave. The integrity of this root element is critical, as it acts as the trust anchor upon which all subsequent verification steps depend.

The boot verification process mandates that each boot stage cryptographically authenticates the next stage before transferring control, thereby chaining trust from the RoT outward to the full software stack. Authentication typically involves verifying digital signatures or message authentication codes (MACs) using embedded public keys or symmetric keys provisioned securely within the hardware. The initial bootloader code is stored in non-volatile memory (e.g., ROM or firmware flash) and signed by the platform vendor or device manufacturer employing asymmetric cryptography. Upon system power-on, the RoT performs a signature check against this code, rejecting and halting the boot process if verification fails.

Once the initial bootloader is verified and executed, it performs a similar verification on the subsequent bootloader or firmware stage, which may include components such as the Unified Extensible Firmware Interface (UEFI) firmware or a trusted execution environment loader. This multilevel verification paradigm is often implemented via well-defined mechanisms, such as the Intel Boot Guard or ARM Trusted Firmware, which embed platform-specific hardware modules to facilitate cryptographic verification. Secure boot architectures leverage cryptographic hash functions and digital signatures, stored certificates, and hardware-protected key storage mechanisms (e.g., fuses, eFuses, or secure elements) to ensure the confidentiality and integrity of keys.

A crucial factor in the chain of trust is the *measured boot* variant, which supplements authentication with the measurement and reporting of code integrity. Each boot stage computes a cryptographic hash of the loaded binary and securely extends this measurement into hardware-protected platform configuration registers, such as Platform Configuration Registers (PCRs) compliant with the Trusted Platform Module (TPM) specification. This measurement log acts as an attestation of system integrity, and can be used to verify remotely or locally that the platform has not been tampered with during boot. Combined with attestation protocols, measured boot provides stronger guarantees and the ability to enforce policy-based access to encrypted or sensitive resources based on boot integrity.

The design of secure boot mechanisms requires careful consideration to prevent common pitfalls and attacks. For instance, rollback attacks, wherein old signed but vulnerable firmware is installed, are mitigated through monotonic version counters or anti-rollback protection integrated within the hardware RoT. Additionally, secure boot must resist key extraction or compromise by employing hardware security modules with physical tamper-resistance and deploying robust key provisioning and lifecycle management workflows.

A typical boot sequence in a system with secure boot and chain of trust proceeds as follows:

1. **Power-on and reset**: The processor begins execution in a privileged mode from a fixed memory location within the ROM-resident RoT.

2. **Root of trust verification**: The embedded RoT verifies the digital signature of the Initial Bootloader Code stored in non-volatile memory.

3. **Loader chaining**: Following successful verification, control passes to the initial bootloader, which in turn verifies the

255

signature and integrity of the next stage, such as a secondary bootloader or firmware.

4. **Measured boot measurement**: Each stage additionally computes a cryptographic hash of the loaded code and extends it into secure hardware PCRs, creating an irrevocable record of the system state.

5. **Operating system verified boot**: The final stage verifies the operating system kernel and critical drivers, often leveraging the TPM or other secure elements for both verification and attestation.

These steps collectively form a continuous and unbroken chain of cryptographic verifications, ensuring that all boot components are authentic and authorized, thus preventing the system from executing untrusted or unauthorized code.

A concrete example of secure boot implementation can be found in the UEFI Secure Boot specification. In this architecture, the platform's firmware includes a database of trusted public keys and signatures, often stored in a secure variable storage with hardware-backed protection. During boot, the firmware verifies each executable image (driver, bootloader, OS loader) by checking the embedded signature against these trusted keys. If verification fails, the boot process is halted or redirected to a recovery mode, preventing further boot progression. Additionally, Secure Boot supports customizable key enrollment, allowing platforms to maintain strong security while accommodating software updates and ecosystem dynamics.

Further strengthening the chain of trust, custom hardware features such as Intel Boot Guard embed secure microcontrollers within the silicon that enforce a hardware-locked verification policy, reducing the attack surface by eliminating the possibility of disabling signature enforcement. ARM TrustZone technology partitions the CPU execution environment into secure and non-secure worlds, providing dedicated runtime environments for verification tasks and secure key storage. These capabilities illustrate the symbiotic relationship between hardware-enforced security features and the secure boot chain.

The cryptographic foundations underlying secure boot rely heavily on asymmetric key algorithms such as RSA or elliptic curve cryptography (ECC) for signature generation and verification, and cryptographic hash functions like SHA-256 for data integrity checks. Hardware implementations optimize these operations with dedicated cryptographic engines and secure key storage, minimizing performance impact and enhancing resistance to side-channel attacks. The immutable nature of the root key set is often assured by fuse programming or embedded secure storage that prevents post-manufacturing modification.

In essence, secure boot with chain of trust mechanisms transforms the boot process into a rigorously verified sequence, anchored in hardware that cannot be altered or bypassed through software means alone. Attacks aiming to subvert system integrity must now contend with hardware-enforced cryptographic barriers, secure key storage, and verifiable measurement logs. This holistic security approach forms the foundation for secure computing platforms, facilitating trusted execution environments, measured boot attestation, and compliance with security standards critical to enterprise, industrial, and consumer systems alike.

```
1  function verify_image(image, trusted_db):
2      signature = extract_signature(image)
3      public_key = find_key_in_db(trusted_db,
       signature.key_id)
4      if public_key is None:
5          return False
6      hash = sha256(image.code)
7      return verify_signature(public_key, signature,
       hash)
8
9  function secure_boot_process():
```

```
10   trusted_db = load_trusted_key_database()
11   boot_images = get_boot_sequence()
12   for image in boot_images:
13       if not verify_image(image, trusted_db):
14           halt_boot("Verification failure")
15       pcr_extend(hash(image.code))
16       load_and_execute(image)
```

```
Verification failure triggers boot halt:
Secure Boot Validation: FAIL
System halted to prevent unauthorized code execution.
```

8.3. Hardware Security Extensions

Hardware security extensions represent a critical evolution in the
protection of computing platforms, particularly in the context of
RISC-V architectures. These extensions aim to enforce robust security policies directly in hardware, mitigating a broad class of
software and hardware vulnerabilities. The modular and open-
source nature of RISC-V facilitates the integration of customized
security features including memory isolation mechanisms, side-
channel attack countermeasures, and trusted execution environments (TEEs). Each of these dimensions addresses unique vectors
of potential compromise and collectively constitute a layered defense strategy.

Memory Isolation Mechanisms

Memory isolation remains a cornerstone of hardware security, preventing unauthorized code or data from being accessed or cor-
rupted. RISC-V implementations typically leverage the Physical
Memory Protection (PMP) unit and the Supervisor Memory Management Unit (S-MMU) to establish hardware-enforced memory
boundaries at different privilege levels.

The PMP provides fine-grained control over physical memory regions by permitting specifications of access permissions—read,

258

write, execute—on segments of physical address space. This configuration is typically managed through a set of address and configuration registers that map to contiguous or discontiguous memory ranges. By enforcing PMP rules, software running in machine mode can restrict device drivers or other less-trusted machine-mode software from accessing sensitive memory, thus reinforcing security at the lowest privilege level. The granularity of PMP regions and the number of entries vary by implementation but generally allow segmentation into regions as small as 4 bytes to as large as the entire address space.

The S-MMU supports virtual memory mechanisms for supervisor-mode software through translation and protection. It provides address translation between virtual and physical memory while implementing page-based protection attributes. This isolation ensures that processes running at supervisor level cannot access each other's memory without explicit permissions, thus protecting against unauthorized inter-process access. When combined with PMP, the S-MMU delivers multi-layered memory protection, with PMP governing physical memory access and S-MMU managing virtual memory contexts. Both these mechanisms together create hardware-enforced isolation domains essential for multi-tenant operating systems and secure runtime environments.

Side-Channel Attack Countermeasures

Side-channel attacks exploit physical leakages such as timing variations, power consumption, electromagnetic emissions, and cache behavior to infer confidential information. Preventing these attacks necessitates hardware designs that reduce or randomize observable side-channel signals while maintaining computational efficiency.

RISC-V hardware extensions introduce countermeasures tailored to reduce timing side channels. These include constant-time instruction execution units, where cryptographic operations are re-timed or balanced to ensure that execution time does not depend on secret data. For example, an arithmetic logic unit (ALU) can be designed to operate in a data-oblivious mode when performing cryptographic primitives.

Cache side-channel defenses are particularly critical given the pervasiveness of cache timing attacks. Microarchitectural features such as cache partitioning and cache locking can be implemented to isolate or harden critical data. Cache partitioning divides cache into non-overlapping regions assigned to distinct execution contexts, eliminating contention-based leakage. Cache locking holds critical cache lines fixed, preventing eviction timing variations. Some RISC-V implementations integrate cache randomization techniques, which remap cache indices or tags pseudorandomly, thus frustrating an attacker's ability to correlate memory accesses with cache hits or misses.

Power analysis resistance is achieved through hardware-balanced logic styles and noise insertion. Dual-rail precharge logic, which balances the power consumption irrespective of data values, can be incorporated at the circuit design level. Additionally, randomized clock gating and intentional switching activity introduce noise to power traces, complicating differential power analysis efforts.

The modularity of RISC-V allows selectively integrating these countermeasures into the pipeline and datapath components without wholesale redesign, permitting tailored trade-offs between security, power, and performance.

Trusted Execution Environments

Trusted Execution Environments (TEEs) provide isolated environments with strong assurance that code and data are shielded from external interference, including privileged software such as operating systems and hypervisors. For RISC-V, security extension proposals such as the *RISC-V Secure* and *RISC-V Keystone* frameworks enable structured TEEs through architectural and platform-level support.

One fundamental architectural primitive for TEEs in RISC-V is the concept of multiple privilege levels beyond the traditional M (Machine), S (Supervisor), and U (User) modes. The addition of a *Secure* or *Trusted* execution level enables the implementation of isolation boundaries enforced in hardware. These boundaries guarantee that sensitive workloads execute in a domain inaccessible to untrusted software.

Keystone, an open-source framework for RISC-V TEEs, leverages PMP for physical memory isolation and introduces secure eXtensible Firmware Interface (EFI) layers to bootstrap trusted domains. Keystone supports secure enclaves containing critical code, isolated heap, and stack, combined with cryptographic attestation to verify enclave integrity remotely. Attestation is particularly important to establish hardware-rooted trust, typically via unique device identifiers embedded in fuses or read-only memory, enabling proof that code is running in a genuine enclave on authentic hardware.

Architecturally, TEEs on RISC-V may incorporate specialized instructions for secure context switching, cryptographic accelerators, and secure storage. Hardware-enforced monotonic counters and tamper-resistant key storage help resist rollback and physical attacks. Secure debug features ensure developer visibility without compromising security policies.

Support for asynchronous events within TEEs is another challenge addressed by RISC-V extensions. Interrupts targeting trusted domains must be carefully mediated to avoid leakage of secure state while preserving responsiveness. Some implementations employ a dedicated secure interrupt controller, isolating secure events from normal interrupts.

Emerging Trends and Challenges

As RISC-V adoption expands, emerging hardware security features increasingly emphasize composability and configurability. The modular ISA design enables vendors and system designers to add or remove security extensions as dictated by application needs, from embedded IoT devices to cloud-grade processors. This leads to wide variability but also mandates rigorous security certification frameworks.

Industry efforts under the RISC-V Foundation, including the development of the Zkr instruction set for cryptographic accelerators and proposals for side-channel resistant cryptographic instructions, are pushing forward the state of hardware-based security.

Additionally, integration of formal verification techniques at RTL and microarchitecture levels is becoming more prevalent to prove the correctness of security properties such as non-interference and memory isolation. These verification methods are crucial to establish trustworthiness for hardware designed in an open-source ecosystem.

Power and area overheads induced by security extensions present ongoing design trade-offs. Balancing these against security gains requires co-design with software, for example by enabling OS schedulers to assign security domains efficiently and instrumentation to detect anomalous side-channel signals.

The rich set of hardware security extensions available and emerging for RISC-V provides a flexible foundation for secure computing. Memory isolation units, side-channel countermeasures, and trusted execution environments each contribute unique protections, which when properly integrated, deliver robust systems capable of withstanding sophisticated threat models in diverse deployment scenarios.

8.4. Fault Tolerance and Error Correction

Fault tolerance is a foundational principle in the design of dependable computing systems, ensuring uninterrupted service despite the presence of hardware faults. As integrated circuits and system architectures become increasingly complex, the probability of transient and permanent errors arising from physical imperfections, environmental disturbances, or aging components escalates correspondingly. Effective fault tolerance mechanisms leverage a combination of error-detecting and error-correcting codes (ECC), redundancy strategies, and recovery protocols to detect, report, and correct faults without compromising system integrity or performance.

Error-correcting codes represent one of the most direct and mathematically grounded approaches to fault tolerance. These codes add controlled redundancy to data representations to enable the system to identify and rectify errors autonomously. At the hardware level, ECCs are widely employed in memory subsystems such as DRAM, caches, and registers, where single-bit flips or multibit errors can have catastrophic consequences. The classic Hamming code [?] initiates this lineage by providing single-error correction and double-error detection (SECDED) capabilities using a parity check matrix constructed systematically. More advanced codes, such as Bose–Chaudhuri–Hocquenghem (BCH) codes and Reed-Solomon codes, extend error correction capacity to multi-bit bursts, benefiting storage systems and communication channels particularly where error patterns are non-random and bursty.

Implementation of ECC involves encoding data prior to storage or transmission, embedding parity bits per the chosen algorithm. When data is retrieved, a syndrome calculation evaluates parity constraints; a zero syndrome indicates error-free data, whereas a non-zero syndrome identifies a specific error pattern location that can be corrected using the decoding algorithm. The syndrome vector **s** is typically computed as

$$\mathbf{s} = \mathbf{r} \cdot \mathbf{H}^{\top},$$

where **r** is the received codeword vector and **H** is the parity-check matrix. Correcting errors necessitates mapping the syndrome to an error pattern, often through look-up tables or algebraic decoding procedures.

```
1  uint8_t calculate_syndrome(uint8_t received,
       uint8_t parity_mask) {
2      uint8_t syndrome = 0;
3      // XOR bits according to parity mask
4      syndrome ^= __builtin_parity(received &
       parity_mask);
5      return syndrome;
6  }
```

Complementary to ECC at the data level, spatial and temporal redundancy strategies increase fault tolerance by replicating critical system components or computations. Spatial redundancy, as implemented in Triple Modular Redundancy (TMR), duplicates hardware modules thrice and derives correct outputs through majority voting. This masks single module failures effectively and is prevalently employed in safety-critical domains such as avionics and nuclear controls. In contrast, temporal redundancy re-executes computations multiple times using the same hardware module, comparing results across runs to detect transient faults. Time redundancy, while resource-efficient in terms of hardware area, introduces latency and is thus applied judiciously.

Redundancy's principal challenge lies in balancing system complexity, cost, power, and performance overhead against the desired fault coverage. Advanced fault-tolerant architectures may combine spatial and temporal redundancy alongside ECC to form a layered defense. For instance, memory controllers may utilize ECC to correct single-bit errors at runtime while employing row sparing—a form of hardware redundancy—to replace permanently

264

faulty memory rows.

Beyond detection and correction, dependable system operation requires effective fault reporting and recovery protocols. Faults detected during runtime must be logged and propagated to higher system levels for appropriate action, such as initiating error recovery routines or system reconfiguration. Monitoring subsystems typically use hardware error status registers and interrupt mechanisms to report anomalies to operating system or hypervisor layers.

Recovery protocols encompass error containment, rollback, restart, and graceful degradation mechanisms. At the simplest level, a memory controller correcting an ECC-detected error continues operation transparently. For more severe or unrecoverable faults, checkpointing mechanisms allow systems to roll back to previously saved consistent states, minimizing data loss and downtime. Checkpoint intervals involve trade-offs between overhead and recovery latency and must be designed considering system workload patterns and fault rates.

In distributed systems, consensus-based recovery protocols integrate fault tolerance at the network and application layers. These protocols rely on replicated state machines and majority agreement algorithms such as Paxos or Raft to mask node failures and communication errors. Even within individual computing nodes, recovery employs techniques like guard bands, error buffering, and fault isolation to prevent fault propagation.

An effective fault-tolerant system design also incorporates fault classification and prediction techniques. Differentiating between transient, intermittent, and permanent faults enables tailored response strategies. Transient faults typically result from environmental phenomena such as cosmic rays or electromagnetic interference and can be corrected via ECC or transient error mitigation. Permanent faults caused by hardware wear-out or manufacturing defects necessitate isolation or hardware replacement. Intermittent faults, often precursors to permanent failures, can be monitored through online health diagnostics for proactive fault management.

Hardware fault models guide the design and verification of fault-tolerance mechanisms. Common models include stuck-at faults, bridging faults, and transient pulse faults. Simulating fault injection under these models validates the efficacy of ECC schemes and redundancy architectures. Simulation frameworks often integrate fault injection at RTL or gate-level to evaluate system responses comprehensively.

```
1  // Inject stuck-at-1 fault on signal 'data_out'
2  always @(posedge clk) begin
3      if(fault_enable) begin
4          data_out <= 1'b1; // Fault forces line
           high
5      end else begin
6          data_out <= data_in;
7      end
8  end
```

Techniques such as scrubbing are used to maintain data integrity in memories afflicted by soft errors. Scrubbing continuously reads memory contents and corrects detected errors using ECC before they accumulate into uncorrectable levels. This background maintenance is critical for large memories operating in radiation-prone environments, such as spacecraft avionics memory.

The integration of fault tolerance in modern processors extends beyond simple ECC. Emerging technologies incorporate specialized hardware monitors, error propagation containment, and adaptive redundancy schemes responsive to environmental conditions and workload stress. For example, dynamic voltage and frequency scaling combined with fault detection can shift operating points to regions of higher reliability, optimizing the trade-off between energy efficiency and fault resilience.

Fault tolerance in hardware systems harnesses a synergy of error-correcting codes, redundancy techniques, and layered recovery protocols to enable robust, dependable operation in the presence of faults. The ongoing evolution of semiconductor technologies and system complexities necessitates continual refinement of these strategies to safeguard critical infrastructures and maintain system availability.

8.5. Formal Verification for Security Assurance

The increasing adoption of RISC-V as an open and extensible instruction set architecture (ISA) has catalyzed significant interest in the formal verification of its hardware implementations, particularly regarding security assurances. Unlike software verification, formal verification applied to RISC-V hardware demands rigorous mathematical proofs to confirm adherence to strict correctness and security properties. These proofs provide compelling evidence that the design and its extensions—ranging from privileged modes to custom instructions—are free from classes of vulnerabilities and implementation flaws that could be exploited by adversaries.

The foundation of formal verification in RISC-V hardware rests on the precise mathematical modeling of the processor microarchitecture and its operational semantics. At the ISA level, the formal semantics of RISC-V serve as a canonical reference, specifying the exact behavior of each instruction. Formal methods exploit these semantics to establish functional equivalence, ensuring that the hardware implementation conforms exactly to its specification. However, security properties extend beyond functional correctness; they encompass non-interference, information flow integrity, access control policies, and resilience to side-channel attacks. Consequently, formal verification workflows must incorporate not only refinement and equivalence checking but also property checking against detailed models of threat scenarios.

Industry-standard tools for formal verification in hardware design have matured significantly, with several supporting the RISC-V ecosystem explicitly or through extensibility. Tools such as Cadence JasperGold, Synopsys VC Formal, and open-source platforms like Coq, Isabelle/HOL, and the RISC-V Formal Verification framework (riscv-formal) form the backbone of modern verification toolchains. These tools facilitate property specification, model checking, theorem proving, symbolic simulation, and equivalence checking. A typical workflow integrates synthesis-level property verification with cycle-accurate reference models, culminating in end-to-end proofs of security-critical properties.

To illustrate, consider the formal verification of the RISC-V privileged architecture's isolation properties. The privileged specification defines multiple privilege levels (user, supervisor, machine) with precise access rights to memory and control registers. Verification begins by encoding these access control policies as temporal logic properties, usually in linear temporal logic (LTL) or computational tree logic (CTL). Model checkers exhaustively explore all possible state transitions and instruction sequences to ensure that unauthorized privilege escalations or memory violations cannot occur. For example, a property might assert that "at no reachable state can a user-mode process directly write to machine-mode control registers." If the model checker detects a violation, it generates counterexamples that assist designers in diagnosing and resolving security gaps.

Formal equivalence checking plays a critical role in validating RISC-V core implementations versus their ISA specifications and reference models. Equivalence checking establishes that two representations—such as a register-transfer level (RTL) design and a formal ISA model—are functionally indistinguishable. Industry-standard equivalence checkers either employ binary decision diagrams (BDDs) or satisfiability modulo theories (SMT) solvers to manage the combinatorial complexity inherent in verifying complex instruction sets. The formalization of RISC-V semantics in a hardware description language format compatible with these tools is necessary for automated equivalence checks. This ensures that any optimizations or extensions introduced at the RTL level preserve the ISA's intended semantics without compromising security properties.

Extensions to the base RISC-V ISA, whether for cryptographic instructions, timing controls, or custom accelerators, introduce additional challenges for formal verification. Each extension requires augmentation of the existing formal models and property sets to capture its unique semantics and security implications. For instance, cryptographic extensions demand proofs that key material is protected both in storage and computation, ensuring no unintended leakage occurs. The property specification language must be sufficiently expressive to model side-channel resistance, such as constant-time execution, and to verify these properties across all microarchitectural states and transitions.

The RISC-V community has fostered a collaborative culture for formal verification through the development of open-source reference models and formal property suites. RISC-V Formal, an actively maintained set of assertion properties, provides a comprehensive baseline capturing compliance with standard ISA properties and extensions. This framework integrates with popular formal engines to enable continuous integration (CI) testing of RISC-V cores during development, thus embedding security verification early in the design cycle. These practices align with the concept of "correct-by-construction" design, where formal verification feedback guides iterative corrections immediately within the engineering workflow.

Workflow integration of formal verification with existing hardware design and validation processes requires careful consideration. Formal methods complement traditional simulation and emulation by covering exhaustive state spaces and ensuring the absence of corner-case vulnerabilities that typical testing might miss. However, the practical complexity of modern RISC-V designs sometimes necessitates compositional or modular verification strategies. These approaches break verification into manageable partitions, verifying components individually while maintaining assumptions about their interactions, thus improving scalability without sacrificing soundness.

Security assurance through formal methods also involves verifying the firmware and microcode that interact closely with the processor core. Microcode layers implementing privileged instructions or secure boot sequences can be formally modeled and verified to guarantee their correct enforcement of security policies. Integrating these verification targets requires combined hardware-software co-verification frameworks, leveraging theorem provers and SMT solvers that can reason across abstraction boundaries.

The formal verification of RISC-V hardware designs integrates mathematically rigorous proofs, automated tooling, and carefully crafted security properties to achieve high assurance levels in correctness and security. The rich ecosystem of industrial and open-source tools, along with collaborative frameworks like riscv-formal, affords scalable workflows that cover both base ISA compliance and complex extensions. Security-critical applications of RISC-V, particularly in environments demanding robust isolation and tamper resistance, benefit substantially from such formal assurance, setting a new standard for trustworthy open hardware architectures.

8.6. Compliance and Supply Chain Security

Ensuring secure hardware provenance within modern technology ecosystems requires a multifaceted approach that integrates trusted sourcing, rigorous compliance validation, and comprehen-

sive lifecycle management. The increasing complexity and global-
ization of supply chains have amplified vulnerabilities, making it
imperative to adopt robust standards and strategic controls to safeguard the integrity, authenticity, and security of hardware components from origin to deployment.

At the core of supply chain security lies the concept of *hardware
provenance*, which pertains to the verifiable history and origin of
a device or component, encompassing manufacturing processes,
handling, and distribution. Trusted sourcing begins with establishing a clear chain of custody that is tamper-evident and auditable,
enabling stakeholders to mitigate risks associated with counterfeit components, unauthorized modifications, or insertion of malicious elements during production or transit.

Standards such as the Open Trusted Technology Provider Standard (O-TTPS) and frameworks outlined by the National Institute
of Standards and Technology (NIST) provide foundational guidelines for securing the supply chain. O-TTPS offers a comprehensive set of best practices that manufacturers and integrators can
adopt to reduce risks of tainted and counterfeit products. These
practices emphasize transparency, traceability, and rigorous process controls, addressing critical facets such as secure design, procurement verification, and configuration management.

NIST's SP 800-161 addresses supply chain risk management for
federal information systems and organizations, introducing systematic processes for identifying, evaluating, and mitigating supply chain risks inherent in hardware acquisition. The document
highlights the importance of integrating security assessments, vulnerability management, and continuous monitoring of suppliers,
which is crucial in ensuring that components meet security requirements before deployment.

An effective strategy for compliance and supply chain security necessitates implementing cryptographic verification mechanisms,
such as digital signatures and hardware root-of-trust architec-

tures. Hardware root-of-trust elements, often implemented within Trusted Platform Modules (TPMs) or secure enclaves, provide immutable anchors securing critical measurements and identities of hardware assets. When products are equipped with these capabilities, they enable organizations to perform endpoint attestation, confirming that supplied components have not been tampered with and originate from authorized sources.

Deploying device identity and provenance credentials, in conjunction with public key infrastructure (PKI), supports a scalable trust model across distributed supply ecosystems. This combination enables the validation of hardware authenticity and integrity at multiple points, including production, transport, and receipt by end customers. Participation in trusted supplier programs that enforce rigorous auditing and certification further strengthens provenance assurance and compliance with contractual and regulatory mandates.

Beyond initial sourcing, compliance validation is extended through rigorous testing and certification processes. Conformance to standards such as ISO/IEC 27001 for information security management and IEC 62443 for industrial automation and control system security provides frameworks for evaluating the operational environment of hardware components. These standards require organizations to implement controls for access, change management, and vulnerability remediation, promoting resilience against supply chain attacks that exploit operational weaknesses.

Lifecycle management is another crucial dimension of secure hardware provenance. The security posture of hardware must be continuously maintained post-deployment, addressing firmware updates, patching, and decommissioning procedures. Secure update mechanisms anchored in cryptographic validation prevent the installation of malicious or unauthorized code, preserving the device's trusted state throughout its operational lifespan. Auditable records and logs must be kept to support forensic analysis and continuous compliance monitoring, enabling rapid response to emerging threats or anomalies.

Considerations for hardware recycling and disposal are integral to preventing the exposure of proprietary or sensitive information at the end of life. Secure erasure protocols and certified destruction processes ensure that residual data or device idiosyncrasies cannot be exploited by adversaries reintroducing devices into the supply chain. Manufacturers and operators must collaborate to enforce these procedures, often within the broader context of regulatory compliance such as the European Union's Restriction of Hazardous Substances Directive (RoHS) and Waste Electrical and Electronic Equipment Directive (WEEE).

Risk management frameworks augment these approaches by fostering a culture of vigilance and continuous improvement. By integrating threat intelligence, vulnerability scanning, and supplier risk assessments, organizations gain dynamic insights into potential vulnerabilities within their supply chains. Automated tools and blockchain-based immutable ledgers are emerging as effective enablers for enhanced transparency, facilitating real-time verification of transactions and reducing dependency on centralized trust authorities.

The confluence of standards, process controls, and cryptographic technologies forms a resilient foundation for trusted hardware supply chains. Organizations must calibrate these elements to their operational context, encompassing sector-specific requirements and geopolitical considerations. For instance, defense and critical infrastructure sectors typically mandate higher assurance levels, incorporating multi-factor verification, physical security measures, and stringent regulatory oversight in supplier selection.

Integrating secure deployment strategies complements provenance assurance efforts. Device attestation at installation validates component integrity against enrolled security policies, while continuous behavior monitoring supports anomaly detection indicative of compromise. This operational synergy reduces the probability of supply chain attacks, which often manifest through subtle modifications undetectable without continuous compliance enforcement.

Collaboration within the broader ecosystem is indispensable. Supply chain security is a shared responsibility among manufacturers, integrators, distributors, and end users. Industry consortia and government-private partnership initiatives facilitate information sharing, standard harmonization, and incident response coordination. Adopting interoperable standards and transparent communication channels elevates ecosystem-wide resilience, enabling timely adaptation to evolving threat landscapes and regulatory frameworks.

Compliance and supply chain security involve a complex interplay of trusted sourcing, adherence to international standards, cryptographic verification, continuous lifecycle governance, and ecosystem collaboration. Robust implementation of these strategies mitigates risks associated with counterfeit, tampered, or malicious hardware components, ensuring secure deployment and sustained integrity across the hardware lifecycle.

Chapter 9

Future Directions and Ecosystem Evolution

As computing continues to evolve, so too does RISC-V—its journey shaped by open innovation and a vibrant global community. This chapter peers ahead to the research frontiers, industry momentum, and governance structures that will define the next wave of RISC-V development. Join the exploration of how this architecture is adapting for cloud, edge, and domains still unimagined, and what challenges and opportunities await.

9.1. Standardization and Governance

The advancement of open hardware architectures hinges critically on robust standardization frameworks and effective governance models. Among such frameworks, the RISC-V architecture exemplifies an innovative approach to open standardization, propelled by a global community and a transparent ratification process. The role of RISC-V International, the not-for-profit organization overseeing the RISC-V instruction set architecture (ISA), demonstrates how open governance underpins the evolution and sustainability of complex technological ecosystems.

RISC-V International operates as a membership-driven consortium that coordinates the development, maintenance, and promotion of the RISC-V ISA as an open standard. Unlike proprietary architectures developed under closed corporate control, RISC-V's governance emphasizes openness and collaboration, inviting diverse stakeholders including industry leaders, academic researchers, and startups to contribute to shaping the ISA's trajectory. This inclusivity guarantees that the standard addresses a broad range of requirements, balancing performance, extensibility, and implementation feasibility.

Central to RISC-V International's process is its community-driven model for ratifying ISA extensions and updates. The ISA itself consists of a minimal base along with optional standard extensions for functionalities such as floating-point arithmetic, atomic operations, and vector processing. The extension ecosystem is dynamic, necessitating a rigorous procedure to ensure consistency, compatibility, and technical rigor. Proposals for new extensions or modifications originate from working groups or member entities and undergo comprehensive technical review, discussion, and iterative refinement in open forums. These forums enable transparent debate on architectural trade-offs, implementation impact, and long-term maintainability.

Once a proposal matures, it is subjected to a formal ratification process by the Executive Committee and Technical Committees within RISC-V International. This structured approval mechanism ensures that ratified extensions meet defined quality and interoperability standards. Such governance safeguards the ISA against fragmentation risks that can arise in loosely coordinated projects. Moreover, it facilitates a clear versioning scheme, making it simpler for hardware designers and software developers to adopt and support evolving features with confidence.

The governance structure of RISC-V International itself embodies principles critical for sustainable ecosystem growth. Its membership model categorizes participants based on their level of in-
volvement and resource commitment, spanning from academic institutions to multinational corporations. This tiered participation
mechanism balances influence in decision-making, enabling broad
representation while preserving organizational efficiency. Regular
general meetings, public working sessions, and documented decision records foster accountability and community trust.

Inclusiveness in governance is not merely a theoretical ideal but a
practical necessity in an open standard endeavor. By welcoming
contributions from diverse geographical regions, industries, and
company sizes, RISC-V International mitigates risks of centraliza-
tion that could stifle innovation or bias the ISA's future. This openness encourages experimentation with novel architectural features
and ensures that the standard remains adaptable to emerging technological trends, such as domain-specific accelerators or security
enhancements.

Furthermore, collaborative standardization underpins the
interoperability critical for software ecosystems. A well-governed
ISA standard facilitates the development of common software
toolchains, operating system support, and application-level frameworks, which in turn accelerates adoption and commercialization.
Without transparent and inclusive governance, competing
proprietary variants could emerge, imposing compatibility
challenges and fragmenting hardware and software markets.

Beyond the ISA definition itself, RISC-V International's governance extends to ancillary specifications such as privileged architecture, debug interfaces, and compliance testing. This holistic
approach consolidates the ecosystem, providing comprehensive
reference materials and certification processes that validate implementation correctness. Compliance testing suites and conformance programs, which are openly accessible to members, elevate

the baseline quality expected from RISC-V-compliant hardware, reducing risk for downstream adopters and accelerating integration cycles.

The community-led development model also promotes rapid innovation cycles. Since no single entity controls the roadmap, multiple parallel efforts exploring new architectural domains can co-exist, later merging successful concepts into the official standard through consensus. This contrasts with closed models where innovation feedback loops may become bottlenecked by internal decision hierarchies. The iterative review and ratification process, while rigorous, ensures that extensions achieve maturity and broad support before becoming normative parts of the ISA.

Governance mechanisms further accommodate intellectual property (IP) considerations in open hardware development. The RISC-V ISA is explicitly designed to be free of royalties, with patented technologies disclosed or encumbered under terms that allow permissive implementation. The legal clarity facilitated by RISC-V International's policies encourages companies to invest in silicon and software tooling without the risk of latent IP claims. This freedom from royalty burdens expands participation and lowers barriers to entry, fostering a vibrant and diverse ecosystem.

In addition to formal committees, RISC-V International leverages working groups focused on specialized technical domains, such as the Vector, Security, and Memory Model working groups. These groups harness subject matter expertise to address sophisticated challenges intrinsic to modern computing architectures. By enabling decentralized yet coordinated development, these working groups accelerate maturation of features critical for performance and security, ultimately enhancing the ISA's competitiveness.

The success of RISC-V International's standardization and governance paradigm provides broader lessons for open technology frameworks. Firstly, it underscores the importance of transparency in decision-making processes to build a trusted consensus across stakeholders with competing interests. Secondly, it highlights how modular architectures supported by extension ratification processes enable evolutionary adaptability without sacrificing ecosystem coherence. Thirdly, it validates the premise that community-driven models can rival traditional closed approaches in delivering widely adopted, commercially viable technology standards.

As open hardware ecosystems continue to evolve, governance models will play an increasingly pivotal role in mediating technical innovation, business incentives, and collaborative synergy. Maintaining balance among these factors requires continuous refinement of governance policies to accommodate scaling membership, emerging market segments, and novel technological paradigms. Entities such as RISC-V International thus serve not only as standardization bodies but as custodians of the ecosystem's health and long-term viability.

The governance and standardization mechanisms exemplified by RISC-V International establish a robust foundation for open hardware architectures. Through community-driven processes, inclusive participation, and rigorous ratification mechanisms, RISC-V International ensures the integrity, extensibility, and sustainability of the ISA. This governance model effectively harmonizes diverse stakeholder objectives, accelerates innovation, and promotes an interoperable software and hardware ecosystem vital for the future of open computing architectures.

9.2. Emerging Research in RISC-V

RISC-V, an open standard instruction set architecture (ISA), has transcended its initial role as a minimalist academic project to become a vibrant focal point for both academic inquiry and industrial development. Recent advancements span diverse domains: from novel microarchitectural innovations tailored to performance and energy efficiency, through specialized ISA extensions for emerging computational paradigms, to the integration of domain-specific accelerators within a modular RISC-V ecosystem. This section explores these research vectors, emphasizing their implications within the broader context of computing evolution.

Contemporary efforts concentrate on refining out-of-order execution models and cache hierarchies designed specifically for RISC-V cores, targeting the balance between complexity and performance. Noteworthy are multi-issue superscalar designs that exploit the orthogonality of the base ISA with extensible instruction sets to empower dynamic instruction scheduling and speculative execution. Recent papers introduce microarchitectures employing variable-length decode and hybrid branch prediction techniques to reduce pipeline stalls and misprediction penalties. These improvements typically utilize dynamically adaptive pipeline stages that scale execution width and depth according to workload demands, optimizing power efficiency without compromising throughput.

Memory subsystem research emphasizes incorporating multi-level cache coherence protocols that align with RISC-V's open extensible memory model. Cache designs frequently leverage novel prefetching schemes based on machine learning heuristics, improving hit rates for workloads exhibiting irregular access patterns. Moreover, the heterogeneous integration of scratchpad memories alongside traditional cache hierarchies enables more deterministic latency profiles, a prerequisite for real-time embedded systems relying on RISC-V cores.

RISC-V's modular design explicitly supports custom extensions, a feature vigorously exploited by academia and industry to accelerate domain-specific workloads. Vector processing extensions, originally proposed in the RISC-V Vector Extension (RVV), undergo continual refinement. Recent research enhances vector register flexibility, predication, and masking mechanisms, enabling efficient SIMD operations critical in scientific computing and machine learning tasks.

Simultaneously, specialized instruction extensions target crypto-graphic workloads by integrating hardened accelerators for AES, SHA, and post-quantum algorithms directly within the ISA. This co-design approach improves throughput and security by reducing the attack surface intrinsic to software implementations. Firms and research groups embed these cryptographic accelerators using RISC-V's custom opcode space, preserving compatibility while achieving significant latency reductions.

Neuromorphic computing interfaces also inspire novel extensions. By incorporating low-overhead support for event-driven processing and sparse data representation, RISC-V cores accommodate spiking neural networks efficiently. Emerging instructions facilitate asynchronous data movement and temporal coding schemes, enabling RISC-V processors to interface more naturally with neuromorphic accelerators or sensor arrays.

Explorations into hybrid quantum-classical architectures increasingly position RISC-V as the control hub for near-term quantum co-processors. Research prototypes implement custom instruction extensions that provide fine-grained control primitives for quantum gate scheduling, error correction routines, and quantum state measurement. These instructions enable tight integration between classical RISC-V cores and quantum processing units (QPUs), a crucial step toward scalable quantum accelerators.

Beyond control flow, microarchitectural modifications incorporate hardware support for quantum error mitigation through low-latency feedback loops. For instance, RISC-V designs embed dedicated registers and memory-mapped interfaces accessible via atomic instructions, enabling low-latency classical error-correcting code execution that directly interfaces with quantum hardware states. This co-design paradigm aims to mitigate quantum decoherence by exploiting real-time classical processing power.

Research into approximate computing extensions also intersects with quantum applications. Emerging RISC-V architectures experiment with precision-tunable arithmetic units designed to expedite noise-resilient quantum simulations and variational quantum algorithms. These efforts demonstrate the synergy between flexible ISA extensions and the unique numerical demands of quantum computation.

Application-specific integrated circuits (ASICs) and field-programmable gate arrays (FPGAs) configured to implement RISC-V cores form a substantial research focus, especially for accelerating artificial intelligence and multimedia workloads. Heterogeneous platforms integrate RISC-V processors with domain-specific accelerators such as convolutional neural network engines, graph-processing units, and signal processing blocks.

Reconfigurability is a key enabler; recent research leverages partial dynamic reconfiguration of FPGA fabrics hosting soft RISC-V cores alongside specialized accelerators, allowing system adaptation at runtime. ISA extensions supporting hardware task migration, lightweight context switching, and secure sandboxing enable efficient multi-tenant operation in edge computing environments. These dynamic platforms integrate RISC-V cores as versatile controllers, managing the orchestration of multiple accelerator units.

Energy-efficient computing paradigms also influence design choices, with research prioritizing near-threshold voltage operation and voltage-frequency scaling techniques integrated at the microarchitectural level. RISC-V's modular nature facilitates the selective activation of functional units through fine-grained clock gating and power domains, translating high-level energy policies into hardware control signals via custom instructions or control registers.

The rapid expansion of RISC-V research inspires continual updates to compliance suites and formal verification frameworks, ensuring that microarchitectural innovations adhere to ISA contracts and maintain compatibility with a growing software ecosystem. Workgroups focused on standardizing SIMD and tensor processing extensions seek to consolidate fragmented efforts into coherent specifications that enable cross-platform software portability.

Complementing hardware developments, research-driven ecosystem expansion emphasizes open-source toolchains, simulators, and formal models built around the evolving ISA. These tools incorporate models for novel extensions such as quantum control instructions and neuromorphic event-driven operations, enabling early-stage software validation and performance simulation. Enhanced compiler backends supported by LLVM and GCC also integrate support for emergent instruction subsets, facilitating automated vectorization and accelerator offloading within familiar programming frameworks.

Security research harnesses RISC-V's open architecture to design fine-grained hardware mechanisms for provenance tracking, side-channel resistance, and confidential execution environments. Architectural enclaves inspired by trusted execution environments incorporate custom instructions for attestation, secure context switching, and cryptographic key management. In parallel, formal methods guide the verification of microarchitectural data flows, bolstering assurances against speculative execution attacks pervasive in traditional processor designs.

The extensibility of the ISA enables rapid prototyping of innovative security primitives, including isolated memory regions with hardware-enforced access policies, implemented via Control-Flow Enforcement Technology (CET)-style mechanisms adapted for RISC-V. Ongoing research explores integrating physical unclonable functions (PUFs) and post-quantum cryptography accelerators within the RISC-V fabric, blurring traditional boundaries between software security and hardware trust anchors.

Interdisciplinary approaches characterize the frontier of RISC-V research, wherein quantum, neuromorphic, cryptographic, and domain-specific computing advances converge within a unified architectural framework. This confluence facilitates heterogeneous computing systems capable of addressing increasingly complex and varied workloads in edge, cloud, and embedded environments.

The modular architecture of RISC-V fosters the seamless addition of new computational models, enabling researchers to experiment with instruction set prototypes that blur traditional boundaries between Von Neumann and unconventional computing paradigms. Such flexible extensibility positions RISC-V as a versatile substrate for experimental microarchitectures and accelerators that scale from deeply embedded IoT devices to high-performance data center processors.

In aggregate, the emerging research trends in RISC-V reflect a maturation from foundational ISA design toward sophisticated multi-domain system integration, where microarchitectural innovation, extension standardization, and ecosystem robustness move in concert to expand the potential applications and impact of this open instruction set architecture.

9.3. RISC-V in Cloud, Edge, and HPC Domains

The RISC-V instruction set architecture (ISA) has garnered significant attention as a versatile and open standard adaptable across diverse computing domains. Its open-source nature fosters innovation and permits extensive customization and optimization tailored to specific application requirements. RISC-V's adaptability is particularly pronounced in cloud computing, edge deployments, and high-performance computing (HPC) sectors, where performance, scalability, and interoperability drive adoption and advancement.

Adaptation for Cloud Computing

Within cloud computing infrastructures, processing demands involve large-scale virtualization, multi-tenancy, and elastic resource management. Traditionally dominated by established proprietary ISAs, cloud environments are now witnessing a cautious but growing integration of RISC-V-based processors due to their customizable nature and potential for cost efficiency at scale. Key adaptation strategies focus on meeting the rigorous performance and scalability requirements dictated by cloud service providers.

One principal consideration in cloud deployment is the ability to efficiently manage heterogeneous workloads, which often include containerized microservices, virtual machines, and serverless functions. RISC-V cores, with their modular extension framework, enable designs tailored for specific cloud service models. For example, lightweight cores can be employed for microservice hosting, while more capable, out-of-order cores address latency-sensitive or compute-intensive workloads.

Moreover, hardware virtualization support is indispensable within cloud ecosystems. Recent RISC-V privileged architecture extensions incorporate hypervisor features, enabling efficient context switching and isolation among virtual machines. The flexibility to implement custom extensions also facilitates security mechanisms and resource partitioning schemes optimized for cloud workloads. Such capabilities contribute to improved tenant isolation, reduced virtualization overheads, and enhanced workload consolidation.

From a scalability standpoint, RISC-V's open licensing encourages collaboration on standardized Inter-Processor Interrupts (IPIs), cache-coherence protocols, and interrupt controllers that facilitate symmetric multiprocessing (SMP) and chiplet-based multi-core designs. These extensions are fundamental to scaling beyond tens or hundreds of cores in cloud server processors. The push for chiplet architectures further benefits from RISC-V's modular ISA, allowing disparate processing units to interoperate seamlessly, which reduces development costs and accelerates time to market for cloud-scale hardware.

Interoperability with existing cloud data center ecosystems is reinforced through software stack support. Cross-vendor and open-source development initiatives have prioritized porting popular hypervisors (e.g., QEMU/KVM), container runtimes, and operating systems such as Linux and BSD variants to RISC-V. The availability of standardized APIs and runtime environments ensures that RISC-V-based cloud nodes can integrate effectively, maintaining overall system consistency and simplifying migration from other architectures.

Optimization for Edge Deployments

Edge computing environments impose unique constraints such as limited power budgets, thermal envelopes, and space, alongside the need for real-time responsiveness and local data processing to reduce latency. RISC-V's architecture offers crucial advantages in edge adaptation through its scalable design, extensible feature set, and ability to incorporate domain-specific extensions.

Optimization efforts in edge devices often prioritize energy efficiency and deterministic execution. RISC-V cores in edge scenarios frequently leverage simple in-order pipelines, tightly coupled memory hierarchies, and reduced complexity to minimize power consumption. Additionally, support for custom instructions enables embedded developers to accelerate specific algorithms, such as signal processing, sensor data filtering, or cryptographic functions directly in hardware, thereby reducing cycle counts and energy use.

Security remains a paramount concern at the edge, due to the proliferation of connected devices and the sensitivity of locally processed data. RISC-V's openness enables development and integration of transparent, formally verifiable security extensions. Examples include Physical Memory Protection (PMP), capability-based security models, and lightweight cryptographic accelerators that can be tightly integrated into processing cores without vendor lock-in.

Flexibility in peripheral integration is another significant benefit. By utilizing RISC-V's parameterizable core designs, edge SoCs can combine processing elements with specialized accelerators (e.g., AI inference engines, vision processors, or sensor hubs) on a single chip. This approach maximizes local computational throughput while avoiding high-latency cloud interactions for time-critical tasks.

Edge deployments also capitalize on heterogeneous processing. RISC-V's ability to support diverse execution units within a single SoC complements the edge's multi-domain workload nature, which may span from ultra-low-power monitoring to intermittent bursts of intensive analytics. The open ecosystem accelerates hardware-software co-design, essential for meeting stringent real-time requirements and minimizing development cycles in fast-evolving edge applications.

RISC-V for High-Performance Computing

In the HPC landscape, RISC-V presents a compelling proposition through its openness, scalability, and extensibility, pivotal for building exascale-class systems. HPC workloads demand extremely high floating-point performance, memory bandwidth, and low-latency interconnects, features traditionally provided by heavily optimized proprietary ISAs. RISC-V's progress towards fulfilling these criteria underscores its growing relevance.

Adaptations for HPC target both architectural and system-level optimizations. The IEEE 754 floating-point standard compliance across RISC-V cores provides a baseline for numerical computing required by scientific and engineering simulations. Extensions such as packed SIMD vector instructions (e.g., the RISC-V Vector

287

Extension) allow wide vector units capable of operating on hundreds of data elements concurrently, matching or exceeding performance levels seen in legacy HPC processors.

Designers leverage the modular nature of RISC-V to implement complex cache hierarchies and memory management units conducive to high parallelism and efficient use of high-bandwidth memory (HBM). Coupled with coherent multi-core clusters, these features enable scalable parallel workloads to exploit data locality and reduce memory access contention. Such hardware advancements integrate with optimized runtime and compiler toolchains that exploit RISC-V vectorization and out-of-order features.

Interconnect and communication fabric selection is crucial for HPC clusters. RISC-V's open ecosystem facilitates creation of coherent non-uniform memory access (NUMA) systems and custom interconnect protocols supporting message passing and remote direct memory access (RDMA). These developments enable efficient scaling across thousands of cores distributed over multi-node systems while maintaining stringent latency and bandwidth requirements.

Interoperability standards for HPC have seen concerted efforts within the RISC-V community to align with established programming models such as OpenMP, MPI, and CUDA-like frameworks. Compiler support, optimized math libraries, and performance profiling tools are rapidly maturing to ensure scientific codes can seamlessly migrate or be co-optimized for RISC-V-based HPC platforms without sacrificing efficiency or correctness.

The potential for customization also allows integration of domain-specific accelerators, such as tensor processing units (TPUs), neuromorphic cores, or quantum simulators, alongside general-purpose RISC-V cores. This heterogeneous computing approach is a strategic advantage for tackling a range of HPC workloads, from dense linear algebra to machine-learning-driven simulations, within a unified architectural framework.

Performance and Scalability Considerations

Performance optimization across these domains converges on common challenges: efficient pipeline implementation, minimizing memory latency, and maximizing parallelism. RISC-V's ISA simplicity contributes favorably by reducing decode complexity and enabling higher clock rates and simplified out-of-order designs. However, achieving state-of-the-art performance requires sophisticated microarchitectural techniques such as speculative execution, branch prediction, and advanced prefetching integrated with coherent cache protocols.

Scalability is realized through multi-core and many-core designs, interconnect fabric innovation, and support for chiplet-based systems. Open standards within the RISC-V community facilitate protocol standardization, enabling large-scale multi-socket systems and heterogeneous accelerators to interoperate. This scalability is essential for cloud data centers scaling out workloads, edge devices combining multiple specialized engines, and HPC systems requiring massive parallelism.

Interoperability and Ecosystem Integration

Interoperability extends beyond hardware into software and tooling ecosystems. The open nature of RISC-V has spawned a wide array of software projects, from compilers and operating systems to debugging and performance monitoring tools. Cloud and edge environments benefit from containerization and virtualization solutions ported to RISC-V, ensuring workloads developed for other ISAs can be executed with minimal modification.

In HPC, seamless integration with existing software stacks and middleware is vital for scientific adoption. Compatibility layers, optimized libraries, and standards-compliant interfaces expedite this process. Moreover, RISC-V's open ecosystem promotes transparent hardware-software co-design, allowing system architects to customize features while maintaining adherence to widely adopted software standards.

Cross-domain interoperability is further supported by RISC-V's configuration space enumeration and vendor-neutral extensions, facilitating runtime identification of CPU capabilities. This dynamic adaptability ensures that heterogeneous systems-comprising cloud nodes, edge devices, and HPC accelerators-can cohesively function within comprehensive computing infrastructures.

The combination of openness, extensibility, and growing ecosystem support positions RISC-V as a uniquely capable ISA for modern and emerging computing domains. Its ongoing evolution emphasizes balancing performance with flexibility and interoperability, thereby addressing the diverse and demanding requirements of cloud, edge, and HPC environments.

9.4. Ecosystem Maturity and Industry Adoption

The progression of the RISC-V ecosystem from its inception as an academic project to a robust commercial platform illustrates a trajectory marked by critical milestones, strategic industry engagements, and a rapidly expanding scope of applications. This evolution underscores the practical viability of RISC-V as an alternative to proprietary Instruction Set Architectures (ISAs) and highlights the collaborative development efforts that underpin its growing maturity.

Early milestones in the RISC-V ecosystem were characterized by proof-of-concept implementations primarily within research institutions and open-source communities. Initial releases of RISC-V cores such as the Rocket Chip and BOOM (Berkeley Out-of-Order Machine) validated the ISA's completeness, modularity, and performance potential. These foundational designs facilitated academic exploration and laid the groundwork for extensions and enhancements, enabling customizations tailored to diverse market needs.

Transitioning from experimental prototypes, commercial interest began to crystalize around 2017, driven by growing concerns over ISA vendor lock-in and supply chain security. This period saw the emergence of start-ups focused exclusively on RISC-V, leveraging open ISA advantages to differentiate in vertical markets. Notable among them, SiFive became instrumental in providing customizable RISC-V cores and platforms, accelerating industry adoption by offering both IP and development ecosystems suited to embedded and edge-computing applications. SiFive's early collaborations with global semiconductor foundries and design tool vendors established an infrastructure supporting rapid deployment of RISC-V-based silicon products.

Simultaneously, established semiconductor companies from the ARM-dominated landscape began investing heavily in RISC-V. For instance, Western Digital announced plans to integrate billions of RISC-V cores into its storage devices, signaling a major vote of confidence and economic scale. This commitment enabled the validation of RISC-V in mass production environments, transitioning from niche deployments to mainstream incorporation. The adoption by Western Digital was particularly impactful in demonstrating the ISA's maturity in terms of robustness, power efficiency, and tooling compatibility.

Another critical development has been the standardization and expansion of the RISC-V software ecosystem—a prerequisite for commercial acceptance. Industry consortia such as the RISC-V Foundation (now RISC-V International) played a pivotal role in coordinating roadmap strategies, fostering open standards for extensions (e.g., vector processing, bit manipulation), and encouraging industry-wide cooperation. Concomitantly, mainstream operating systems (Linux, FreeRTOS, Zephyr) added official support for

RISC-V, enabling seamless porting and deployment of software stacks. Integration with established toolchains such as GCC and LLVM further lowered barriers for development teams transitioning from legacy ISAs.

Several case studies exemplify the diverse commercial adoption across sectors:

- **Microcontroller and IoT Devices:** The low-power, modular nature of RISC-V cores has been exploited by companies such as Andes Technology and GreenWaves Technologies. GreenWaves' GAP processors, integrating RISC-V cores with AI-specific accelerators, are deployed in edge AI applications aimed at real-time sensor analytics and voice recognition. These deployments emphasize how RISC-V enables tailored low-power solutions well-suited to resource-constrained environments.

- **High-Performance Computing:** Although still nascent, the launch of initiatives like SiPearl's RISC-V-based accelerator chip for exascale supercomputing marks a pivotal expansion of RISC-V towards high-end computing domains. SiPearl's RISC-V designs prioritize scalability, vector extensions, and system-level integration, positioning RISC-V as a contender in markets historically dominated by x86 and proprietary ISAs.

- **Artificial Intelligence and Machine Learning:** The flexibility of RISC-V to incorporate custom instructions has been leveraged by startups such as Esperanto Technologies. Esperanto's multi-core RISC-V vector processors are designed specifically for machine learning workloads, achieving competitive performance/watt metrics by optimizing datapath architectures for matrix operations. This case illustrates RISC-V's adaptability to domain-specific accelerators.

292

- **Networking and Storage:** Marvell's acquisition of In-
  novium, a company developing RISC-V-based networking
  ASICs, reflects integration of RISC-V as a control processor within complex networking chips. The adaptability and
  customizable nature of RISC-V cores suit the heterogeneous
  compute requirements found in modern data centers and
  edge infrastructure.

- **Mobile and Consumer Electronics:** Huawei's development of RISC-V cores as part of their Kunpeng processor
  family demonstrates how industry leaders are diversifying
  ISA portfolios to mitigate geopolitical and supply chain risks.
  While full-scale replacement of ARM is a gradual process, the
  parallel development of RISC-V silicon indicates significant
  confidence in its future role within consumer electronics.

Collectively, these deployments attest to RISC-V's growing capacity to meet challenging design criteria across performance, power,
security, and customization. The transition from experimentation
to wide-scale production has been enabled by several ecosystem
factors:

- **Mature IP Availability:** Multiple vendors now provide
  SoC-ready RISC-V cores with proven silicon tape-outs, covering a spectrum from ultra-low power microcontrollers to
  sophisticated multi-core CPUs. This availability reduces integration risk and accelerates time-to-market.

- **Comprehensive Software Ecosystem:** Support from
  operating systems, compilers, debuggers, and simulation environments has reached parity with established ISAs in many
  application domains, mitigating traditional adoption barriers.

- **Industry Collaboration and Open Governance:** The
  governance model of RISC-V International encourages

293

transparent extension standardization and open collaboration among competitors and partners alike. This collective approach ensures continuous evolution aligned with emerging requirements.

- **Ecosystem Tooling and Verification:** Commercial and open-source verification suites, coupled with simulation platforms, have increased confidence in design quality and security compliance-prerequisites for safety-critical and regulated markets.

- **Diversification of Foundry and Packaging Support:** Strategic partnerships with leading semiconductor foundries enable wafer fabrication of RISC-V designs at advanced process nodes, ensuring competitive performance and cost.

Despite these advances, challenges remain that influence the pace and scope of adoption. Fragmentation risk due to multiple custom extensions necessitates continued standardization efforts. The integration complexity of RISC-V cores into established SoC design flows requires ongoing investment in design automation and IP interoperability. Furthermore, evolving security features within the architecture must be rigorously validated to meet the demands of sensitive applications.

The trajectory from pilot projects to production-ready RISC-V silicon demonstrates a disruptive paradigm shift in processor design and procurement. It contrasts with the historically monolithic ISA ecosystems by enabling configurable, extensible, and royalty-free architectures tailored for specific market needs. The resultant ecosystem provides manufacturers with strategic flexibility and cost-effectiveness, which are driving forces behind the sustained growth in commercial deployments.

The maturation of the RISC-V ecosystem reflects a confluence of technological innovation, industry collaboration, and strategic market positioning. The documented case studies exemplify practical realizations of the ISA's promise across a broad spectrum of applications, establishing RISC-V as a formidable and viable alternative ISA platform in contemporary semiconductor landscapes.

9.5. Interoperability and Platform Coexistence

The integration of RISC-V architectures alongside established legacy platforms requires comprehensive engineering methodologies coupled with strategic business decisions. Such integration aims to maximize system capabilities and pave the way for seamless coexistence in heterogeneous environments, addressing industry demands for flexibility, performance, and cost-effectiveness.

A primary engineering challenge lies in enabling bi-architecture systems that effectively combine RISC-V cores with legacy instruction set architectures (ISAs) such as x86, ARM, or MIPS. These hybrid platforms are critical for incremental migration approaches, where the legacy software ecosystem must remain operational while introducing RISC-V advantages incrementally. Coherent memory models, synchronized execution environments, and shared peripherals must be designed with cross-ISA compatibility in mind, often necessitating hardware-level virtualization or abstraction layers.

At the hardware-software interface, application binary interface (ABI) compatibility and efficient context switching mechanisms are pivotal. The simultaneous presence of distinct ISAs demands carefully architected runtime environments, typically involving multi-stage bootloaders and hypervisors capable of selectively dispatching workloads to RISC-V or legacy cores based on application requirements and performance profiles. Cross-ISA interrupt handling, exception management, and debugging infrastructure must also be supported to maintain system robustness and development

295

productivity.

Migration challenges are multi-dimensional, encompassing legacy software porting, debugging complexities, and testing burdens. The availability of mature compiler toolchains and development environments for RISC-V alleviates some difficulties but does not entirely remove the need for extensive software adaptation. Binary translation and emulation technologies serve as transitional tools, enabling legacy binaries to execute on RISC-V hardware with reasonable performance, but they introduce overhead and potential semantic gaps. Consequently, migration strategies often adopt a phased approach, selectively offloading non-critical or modular workloads to RISC-V cores while retaining legacy-critical code in its original environment.

From a business perspective, the coalescence of architectures must balance capital expenditure (CapEx) with operational expenditure (OpEx). Legacy systems typically entail sunk costs and entrenched vendor relationships, complicating decisions to adopt RISC-V. However, the open-source nature of RISC-V reduces licensing fees and fosters innovation, thus offering a compelling value proposition in total cost of ownership. Strategies encouraging ecosystem development, such as industry consortia, standardization efforts, and vendor partnerships, accelerate maturity and reduce integration risks.

Heterogeneous compute opportunities arise from leveraging the complementary strengths of RISC-V and legacy cores within a single platform. RISC-V's extensibility permits customized accelerators and domain-specific instructions, enabling optimized processing in areas such as machine learning, signal processing, and cryptography. Simultaneous utilization of legacy general-purpose processors ensures backward compatibility and access to legacy optimized codebases, preserving software investment while enhancing new workloads. Architectures adopting heterogeneous compute must provide robust inter-core communication mechanisms, memory coherence protocols, and workload scheduling frameworks to maximize throughput and energy efficiency.

System designers increasingly exploit advanced interconnect fabrics and cache coherence protocols to support tightly coupled heterogeneous RISC-V and legacy cores. Technologies such as CCIX (Cache Coherent Interconnect for Accelerators) and CXL (Compute Express Link) facilitate coherent communication across different ISA-based processors, minimizing latency and synchronizing memory regions. Firmware and operating system support for heterogeneous resource management enable dynamic load balancing and power-aware task allocation, crucial for embedded and high-performance computing applications.

Interoperability at the software ecosystem level mandates comprehensive support from operating systems, runtime frameworks, middleware, and development tools. For instance, operating systems must incorporate processors' diverse ISA support through modular kernel designs, enabling seamless context management and resource arbitration. Containerization and virtualization paradigms further abstract platform heterogeneity, encapsulating applications to run independently of underlying ISA specifics. This abstraction promotes portability, accelerates deployment cycles, and simplifies maintenance in multi-ISA environments.

Toolchain convergence is instrumental in bridging RISC-V and legacy architectures. Cross-compilers capable of emitting binaries for multiple ISAs, integrated development environments unified under common debugging and profiling tools, and simulation platforms supporting mixed ISA configurations collectively reduce integration friction. Moreover, organizations emphasize standardized intermediate representations (IRs) within compiler toolchains to ease retargeting and optimization across heterogeneous hardware units.

Security considerations become multifaceted in bi-architecture

297

systems. Secure boot processes, trust zones, and hardware roots of trust must operate cohesively across RISC-V and legacy cores to prevent attack vectors exploiting ISA transition points. Isolation mechanisms, such as hardware-enforced partitions or software-defined security domains, help maintain integrity during cross-ISA communication and code execution. The openness of RISC-V's specification enables tailored security extensions but necessitates rigorous verification to ensure parity with established solutions in legacy architectures.

In terms of product strategy, layered market segmentation emerges-designers can prioritize RISC-V for emerging applications while leveraging legacy platforms in entrenched markets. This segmentation encourages gradual ecosystem expansion, where RISC-V's modularity and scalability attract innovation-driven use cases and startups, while traditional enterprise and industrial applications remain anchored by legacy systems. Over time, successful integration and demonstrable benefits catalyze deeper adoption of RISC-V, progressively reshaping industry architectures.

Ultimately, the synergy between RISC-V and legacy architectures manifests in platforms that capitalize on established software assets while embracing architectural innovation. Mastery of interoperability, mindful migration tactics, and exploitation of heterogeneous compute embody a pragmatic pathway toward future-proof computing ecosystems, enabling organizations to navigate evolution without jeopardizing existing investments.

9.6. Open Challenges and Roadmap

The RISC-V ecosystem, while promising and rapidly evolving, faces a multiplicity of interrelated challenges spanning technical, business, and social dimensions. These unresolved issues demand concentrated attention to secure the architecture's long-term vitality and broad adoption. Further, existing community-driven roadmaps and speculative projections underscore both the opportunities and complexities ahead, illustrating the intricate path toward maturity.

At the core of the technical challenges lies the tension between architectural openness and the practical demands of high-performance processor design. The modular nature of RISC-V, defined through a concise base ISA with numerous optional extensions, facilitates customization yet simultaneously generates fragmentation risks. The proliferation of proprietary and custom extensions risks undermining interoperability, complicating software ecosystem development and verification efforts. There is no universally adopted standard for vendor-defined extensions, which inhibits seamless portability and slows the evolution of common tools and compilers.

Verification complexity is amplified by the lack of a fully mature, unified, and widely accepted formal specification framework. Although formal methods have been applied to certain ISA components, an end-to-end formal verification of the RISC-V specification, encompassing all standard and extended features, remains elusive. This deficiency limits confidence in the correctness and security of implementations, particularly vital as RISC-V penetrates safety-critical and security-sensitive domains.

Another enduring challenge involves the ecosystem's software infrastructure, particularly compiler support, optimized libraries, and debugging tools. While mainstream compilers such as GCC and LLVM support RISC-V, continued advancement is necessary to match the optimization levels found in established ISAs. Efficient handling of emerging extensions such as vector processing (RVV) and bit manipulation requires more comprehensive toolchain integration. Similarly, debugging, profiling, and tracing systems adapted to heterogeneous and multi-core RISC-V configurations need further enhancement to aid complex system development.

Power management and energy efficiency remain active areas. Despite RISC-V's suitability for embedded and IoT platforms, power-aware features, including dynamic voltage and frequency scaling (DVFS), fine-grained power gating, and low-leakage circuits tailored to RISC-V implementations, are still under-explored in open-source cores. Addressing thermal, power, and reliability challenges in advanced process nodes remains a technical imperative to enable RISC-V's competitiveness in mobile and high-performance segments.

Security challenges occupy a disproportionate portion of ongoing efforts. The open ISA allows for transparency but also exposes a larger attack surface, necessitating robust architectural and implementation-level countermeasures. Developing standardized security extensions that cover areas such as secure boot, trusted execution environments (TEEs), side-channel attack resistance, and intrusion detection is critical. Recent initiatives propose formalized privilege levels and hardware-isolation mechanisms, yet industry-wide consensus and adoption lag behind proprietary competitors with established security architectures.

The business landscape of RISC-V is characterized by the dichotomy between its open-source nature and the commercial ecosystems dependent on it. Monetizing open hardware designs is inherently challenging, affecting investment cycles and sustained development. Many commercial entities adopt hybrid approaches combining open ISA compliance with proprietary cores or toolchains, resulting in a complex licensing mosaic that can dissuade smaller innovators from full participation.

Fragmentation threatens to dilute the market influence of RISC-V. With multiple implementers proposing diverse cores targeting different markets-from microcontrollers to supercomputers-the lack of a dominant, feature-complete flagship product hinders broad enterprise adoption. Companies face uncertainty in standardization, making it difficult to commit to long-term product roadmaps reliant on an evolving ISA.

Supply chain integration remains an issue. Unlike established ISAs backed by large vendors with integrated semiconductor and software stacks, RISC-V must navigate partnerships across many stakeholders. This increases the complexity of ensuring consistent quality, timely silicon delivery, and extensive software support. Additionally, fabrication and packaging considerations in heterogeneous multi-die designs present barriers to rapid commercialization.

Market education and brand perception also present obstacles. Despite growing awareness, decision-makers in large enterprises and legacy vendors often adopt a wait-and-see attitude toward RISC-V readiness. Warranty, support, and quality assurance infrastructure lag due to the highly diverse nature of the RISC-V ecosystem.

The RISC-V community embodies a broad coalition of academics, start-ups, and established firms, united by the goal of democratizing processor design. However, sustaining this breadth of collaboration introduces social coordination challenges. Governance structures balancing inclusiveness with decisive technical direction are still evolving. Tensions arise between upstream collaborative goals and competitive commercial interests in downstream implementations.

Documentation quality and accessibility remain uneven, impacting newcomers' ability to effectively contribute or adopt. Although open specification documents are available, more pedagogically oriented, detailed guides and real-world design examples are needed to lower the barrier for design engineers and software developers alike. Initiatives to improve mentorship, standardization workshops, and community-driven certification programs are at nascent stages.

Furthermore, global supply chain tensions and geopolitical consid-

301

erations increasingly influence open hardware projects. Maintaining an open, neutral ecosystem resistant to fragmentation along national or industry lines requires deliberate social and political stewardship. The community must navigate export control regulations, intellectual property concerns, and varying standards compliance across jurisdictions.

The RISC-V International Technical Committee and allied research institutions have articulated multi-year roadmaps centered on key extension standardizations, ecosystem maturity, and cross-domain integration. Among the principal milestones are:

- Finalization and ratification of the RISC-V Vector (RVV) extension to establish a scalable, efficient SIMD paradigm for workloads ranging from AI/machine learning acceleration to scientific computing.

- Advancement of the Privileged Architecture (RISC-V P) to accommodate secure execution environments including hypervisor support, trusted computing bases, and secure error recovery.

- Defining interoperability guidelines for heterogeneous multicore clusters, enabling seamless integration of cores with diverse capabilities (e.g., scalar, vector, DSP).

- Development of modular formal specification frameworks to pave the way for comprehensive verification and certification, essential for avionics, automotive, and medical-grade processors.

- Expansion of standardized debug and trace infrastructures to include advanced performance monitoring and security audit features.

Speculative trends highlight an increasing convergence of RISC-V with domain-specific accelerators (DSAs). The ISA's extensibility invites embedding custom accelerator instructions tightly integrated via co-designed software stacks. Emerging collaborative efforts target establishing open standards for accelerator interconnects and memory coherence optimized for heterogeneous computing.

Additionally, future directions include the proliferation of RISC-V in edge computing and neuromorphic processors. Low-power, secure microcontroller implementations optimized for sensor fusion, federated learning, and real-time AI at the edge are receiving substantial developer interest. The community emphasizes the need to balance simplicity, power efficiency, and computational density.

Calls to action within the RISC-V community advocate for increased investment in:

- Enhanced hardware-software co-design methodologies and open benchmarking suites to objectively measure performance and energy trade-offs.

- Broader industry consortium participation to unify extension roadmaps and enforce cross-vendor compliance.

- Scaling education and training programs to build a global talent pool skilled in RISC-V architecture design, toolchain development, and secure implementation.

- Establishing mechanisms for open-source IP base cores with thoroughly vetted security and safety features to accelerate downstream innovation.

Bridging the gap between experimental architectures and widely deployed commercial solutions demands concerted efforts from both the academic and industrial sectors. The trajectory of RISC-V's evolution reflects a dynamic, decentralized innovation model coupled with growing institutional coordination. Overcoming these open challenges will define not only the technical robustness but also the socio-economic integration of RISC-V as a foundational computing architecture in the decades to come.

www.ingramcontent.com/pod-product-compliance
Lightning Source LLC
Chambersburg PA
CBHW061237220326
41599CB00028B/5451